Best wishes,

John Day

A New History of Sheffield Wednesday's Darkest Times 1973-1976

John Dyson

www.verticaleditions.com

Cover images courtesy of Sheffield Wednesday,
Steve Ellis, Sheffield Wednesday, Mick Jeffries,
Sheffield Newspapers. Cover headlines
courtesy of Sheffield Newspapers

First published in the United Kingdom in 2020
by Vertical Editions, Unit 41 Regency
Court, Sheffield, S35 9ZQ

www.verticaleditions.com

Follow us on Twitter
@VerticalEds
@OurLowestEbb1

ISBN 978-1-908847-17-1

A CIP catalogue record for this book
is available from the British Library

Printed and bound by Jellyfish
Print Solutions, Swanmore, Hants

"To my family, and the generations
of Owls that came before me."

CONTENTS

INTRODUCTION

April 29th, 1976. The spring before a long hot summer. At Sheffield Wednesday's Hillsborough stadium, 25,802 fans gathered to witness the final game of the Division Three season. Wednesday faced Southend United, and the mathematics were simple: a win or draw would keep the Owls safe from relegation, while defeat would see Southend stay up and Wednesday relegated. The game was played after the remainder of the season had been completed – as Hillsborough had been needed for an FA Cup semi-final earlier in the year. It was also, unusually, played on a Thursday evening. The blue and white side of Sheffield waited nervously.

The 1975-6 season had proven to be another difficult one for the Owls. By January 1976, the team had won only once in 15 games since manager Len Ashurst's arrival in October of the previous year. Desperate times called for desperate measures, and Ashurst's trainer came up trumps. In late January 1976, Tony Toms took the players out for a survival expedition overnight on to Broomhead Moor, with the aim of building team spirit and resilience. Even Ashurst thought the idea was "madness" given the time of year, but the Owls won the following game against Chester 2-0. In that game's matchday programme, Toms said that "what the players have been through was harder than anything they have faced before… this is one way to eradicate the worries and tensions." But whatever worries and tensions existed amongst the fanbase continued until the final day.

The Owls only slowly picked up more points over the coming weeks before a series of 1-0 home wins in April helped set up the showdown against Southend. The game itself was "less than classic" but finished 2-1 to the home team, with goals from Prendergast and Potts helping the Owls finish 20th out of 24 in the league, avoiding relegation by a single point. A season that had seen a flu epidemic strike the team, an 11-match winless streak, home attendances regularly below 10,000 and what Ashurst described as "a sick dressing room" had finally ended. The manager later described the period as the hardest six months of his life and still to this day, it remains the Owls' lowest-ever league position.

Previous years had seen similar degrees of misery for Wednesday. The manager prior to Ashurst, Steve Burtenshaw, had overseen the grand total of 14 wins from his 71 league and cup games. Since 1973, fans had witnessed eight-goal drubbings, relegation, a last-day escape, the Christmas Eve sacking of an Owls legend, outbreaks of what became known as football hooliganism at games, the sale of key players, and financial difficulties at the club along with prolonged periods without a goal or an away win. Indeed, the Owls did not win an away game between a 1-0 victory at Southampton in December 1974 and a 1-0 win at Reading in October 1976 – a total of 36 matches.

After the new year of the 1974-75 season, the Owls scored two goals. The one scored by Brian Joicey in the 90th minute of a game against Oxford in April 1975 was the first goal scored at home in over 14 hours of football. Just 7,444 were in the crowd to witness it (if everyone remained in the ground at that late stage) - a post-war low for attendance to that date (although the crowds would get even lower).

The *Sheffield Star* newspaper even launched a "Save our Owls" campaign, printing thousands of stickers, posters and badges to persuade people to support their team in the relegation battle of 1975. The Owls were relegated on April Fool's Day that season after (yet another) 1-0 defeat. Wednesday's financial situation was dire, too – the aggregate deficit since relegation from the First Division in 1970 was approaching £500,000 at the start of the 1975-6 season.

L, L, L, L, D, L, L, D, L, L, L, L, L, D, L, L, D, D, L,

D, D, D, L, D, D, L, L, L, L, D, L, D, L, L, D, D.

The Owls' away record 1974-1976

Sheffield's economy was struggling at the time, with unemployment rising above the national level by the mid-1970s and the manufacturing industry beginning its long period of decline that continued into the 1980s and beyond. Sheffield's population had begun to fall and the proportion of working-age men in the lowest social categories rose above the national average for the first time. The bright hopes of those who had built giant modern concrete council estates including Park Hill flats (opened 1961) were beginning to fade as the problems of those estates became apparent. Government surveys in 1973 showed that residents of high-rise facilities suffered more problems with their health than the rest of the population and, as early as the mid-1960s, residents of similar buildings complained that graffiti, litter and vandalism were everyday problems.

Half of residents interviewed in Sheffield's high-rise flats said that they would move if they had the chance. The global oil shock of 1974 and the increasing globalisation of trade and manufacturing dealt a major blow to British industry, and Sheffield was among the cities hardest hit. The oil shock also led to the three-day week of 1974 and indirectly to the election that followed. Edward Heath's Conservatives fought that election on the slogan: "Who Governs Britain?" and the answer from the electorate was simply: "Not you". The city and country were suffering economically and socially. Politicians struggled to provide answers and for fans of the Owls at least, their football team was in what seemed like a period of continuous decline.

Our Lowest Ebb indeed.

Previous historians of the period have described it as "the darkest hour". In his book *"Sheffield Football: A History Vol II,"* Keith Farnsworth describes a "period short on glory and long on doom" – although, in fairness, he includes Wednesday and Sheffield United in that description – and Jason Dickinson, in *"Sheffield Wednesday FC, the Official History",* said "Wednesday seemingly spiralled ever downward."

It is, of course, difficult to disagree with those points of view when confronted with the hard facts of the Owls' results and league positions. And yet... mention this period to Owls' fans who were around at the time and it doesn't take long to discern some hints of nostalgia.

A Certain Romance as a more recent Sheffielder and Owls fan might have put it.

This book is about Sheffield Wednesday at the time. It will, of course, discuss the players, managers and games that were played in this dark period. But it is more than that. It gives a voice to the fans, allowing them to reminisce about the period but also to understand how such a difficult time on the pitch is remembered fondly by many. There will be reference to games played but also the wider experience of a fan: away days, family and friendships and the memorabilia that supporting a football team attracts.

There are new insights, new interviews, rarely-seen photographs and a view of other ephemerae that has been unseen since the time. We see how gallows humour kept Owls' fans going through the difficult times and how fans stuck by the team despite results. The book is titled *"Our Lowest Ebb"*. In some ways, this may have been true for the city of Sheffield and for Sheffield Wednesday Football Club.

For the fans, this was a time when supporting the Owls took courage and a degree of bloody mindedness. To former Owls' player Jimmy Mullen, the support was "amazing at the time" and to quote one supporter: "It really was an amazing time, mainly because of the fans."

. This book will attempt to rescue the period for posterity. We will see that there were exciting players, great games, and a dedicated fanbase. The period ends with the building blocks in place for the club's renaissance in the later 1970s and 1980s. The period may well have been *"Our Lowest Ebb"* but there was light in the darkness, and reasons to remember the period with fondness.

I was born in 1975. I have been a Sheffield Wednesday fan for as long as I can remember. My Dad and my Grandad were also fans. My early years supporting the Owls were all promotions, FA Cup semi-finals and, as a young man, more promotions and trips to Wembley. I attended my first game in 1983 and am currently a season ticket holder in the Grandstand where I attend games with my two sons. I live in Solihull, West Midlands where, since

2013, I have helped organise the West Midlands Owls supporters' group. My day job is Head of History in a secondary school. Two of my main interests in life, therefore, combine in this book. I am interested in what was no doubt a difficult time to be an Owls fan.

As a social historian I am interested in the views of the fans – what it was like for those who were there. I am interested also in how that compares to the broader history of the club at the time (management, players, results) and what links there might be with the history of South Yorkshire in the period (employment, politics). This book is my attempt to tell the story of those dark and difficult years but also explain how and why those who were supporting the Owls in the decade before I started coped and continued to love the club through its darkest of times.

John Dyson, February 2020

THE CAST

The Club:
Sheffield Wednesday. Founded in 1867. Relegated from Division One in 1970.

The Chairmen:
Sir Andrew Stephen (1956-73) – also chairman of the Football Association from 1967
Matt Sheppard (1973-75)
H.E. (Bert) McGee (1975-1990)

"Club Men":
Eric Taylor ("Mr Sheffield Wednesday") general manager and much more. Retired in 1974.
Eric England – Taylor's assistant, friend and replacement after retirement
Dennis Woodhead – Commercial manager

Managers:
Derek Dooley (1971-73)
Steve Burtenshaw (1974-75)
Len Ashurst (1975-1977)

Backroom Men:
Gerry Young – Coach, caretaker manager, former Owls player
Ron Staniforth – Coach, often with reserves and youngsters
Jim McAnearney – Coach, caretaker manager, former Owls player
George McCabe - ex-referee, responsible for youth development
Tony Toms – Len Ashurst's "trainer", ex-military

Players:
A total of 43 represented the club in league and cup games in our period.

The Supporters:
Fred Stones – Supporters' Club chairman
Keith Nettleship – Supporters' Club secretary
A dwindling number of supporters at home games (the post-war low attendance record was broken several times)
A large support at many away games

THE CONTEXT

Originally "The Wednesday" football club, Sheffield Wednesday has a long, and at times glorious, history. The club was formed out of the existing Wednesday Cricket Club in September 1867 and joined the Football League in 1892 after winning the Football Alliance competition in 1890 and finishing as runners-up in the FA Cup that same season. The team moved to Hillsborough stadium in 1899 and flourished in their early years, winning the Division One title four times before 1930, and the FA Cup three times by 1935. After the Second World War the club entered a period often known as the "yo-yo" years. After promotion to Division One in 1950, they were relegated three times that decade, each time returning at the first attempt. In 1961 the club achieved its highest post-war finish, second in Division One behind an excellent Tottenham Hotspur team. The 1960s saw the club managed by, among others, Harry Catterick (1958-61) and Vic Buckingham (1961-64). Buckingham had previously managed Ajax and would go on to take charge of FC Barcelona. He is known as the man who discovered Johan Cruyff and who developed the ideas that became known as "total football." Harry Catterick was Buckingham's predecessor and went on to great success with Everton after leading the Owls to that highest post-war finish.

Behind the scenes at Hillsborough throughout the period remained Eric Taylor. Known as 'Mr Sheffield Wednesday', Taylor had acted as manager from 1942 to 1958. During the 1960s he was the club's general manager and driving force behind developments to the stadium including the building of the pioneering North Stand. The redeveloped stadium was regularly used for FA Cup semi-finals throughout the 1960s and 1970s and was a host stadium for the 1966 World Cup. The team had a period of great success in the 1960s – even beating Barcelona at Hillsborough in the Inter-City Fairs Cup in 1962 before succumbing to defeat in the second leg at the Nou Camp. The club was rocked by the involvement of some of their players in a betting scandal which was uncovered in 1964. The matter revolved around three Wednesday players (Tony Kay, Peter Swan and David Layne) who all bet against the team in a game against Ipswich in 1962. A tabloid sting operation eventually led to all three being imprisoned and banned from football for life. Kay signed for Everton before the issue came to light, Swan and Layne remained as Owls players.

The difficulties for the club that the case brought did not stop the team enjoying a degree of success in the later 1960s. Wednesday reached the FA Cup final in 1966, going 2-0 up in the match against Everton, before an impressive comeback from the Liverpool side saw the Owls lose 3-2. The team completed a lap of honour of the Wembley pitch afterwards in recognition of their role in a classic game. Owls supporters in the 1960s therefore had watched some excellent football, in a modern stadium with forward-thinking management.

This changed dramatically in the 1970s. The Owls were relegated in 1970 – finishing bottom of Division One. Under the management of Derek Dooley (appointed in January 1971), the team initially struggled in Division Two before a series of lower mid-table finishes. Attendances were dropping. Despite Dooley and the club's best efforts, a return to the happier days of the 1960s seemed a long way away by the start of our period in 1973.

1973-74

A season of two managers and a caretaker. Eight-goal defeats and ten goals in two games. From pre-season positivity, with a new kit and a new logo, to an older story of ongoing decline. A 'notorious virus' hits the club. A new chairman and manager promise change. The tale ends with a last day escape that (just) maintains the club's status. "Never Again!" promise the club.

The first season of our period began with a degree of positivity about the Owls' prospects both from within and outside of the club. Manager Derek Dooley had overseen a 10th-placed finish the previous season, had added to the squad and had undergone a successful pre-season tour of Sweden. As Daniel Gordon, in his book *'A Quarter of Wednesday'*, had it: "Optimism was high at Hillsborough."

The *Daily Mirror* saw the Owls as one of the favourites for promotion: "In what promises to be the most exciting Second Division tussle for years FA Cup winners Sunderland, relegated Crystal Palace, and West Bromwich, Aston Villa, Fulham, and Sheffield Wednesday are the most interesting prospects." The Owls were sporting a new version of their famous blue and white striped shirts (broader stripes), adorned with a new logo and seemed ready to take on the division.

If this optimism had engendered any arrogance among the fans or players, they were soon brought back down to earth. The Owls played Swindon away in their first league game of the season on what to modern eyes seems the very late date of the 25th August.

The Owls' line-up included former Sheffield United star Bernard Shaw making his debut for the club, alongside Northern Ireland international David Clements making his final appearance before sealing a move to Division One Everton. The game finished 3-1 to Swindon. The report of the match in the *"Sunday People"* newspaper ran as follows:

"SWINDON 3. SHEFFIELD WED. 1: SPINDLE-LEGGED Tom Jenkins had Swindon fans whooping with delight after this shock defeat. Swindon, lining up much the same as in their battle against relegation last season, were a revelation. And the man behind an early dangerous move? Jenkins. Commanding the midfield, piercing Wednesday's defence with a stream of passes that were gladly taken up by Moss and Treacy. Moss hit the first. Treacy nodded in the second and a Jenkins-Treacy move ended when McGovern hit the clincher. Sunley got a lucky one back for Wednesday."

However lucky David Sunley's goal may have been, the Owls did not have much good fortune in their next two games. The first home game of the season was played on September 1 against Blackpool. In front of a reasonable crowd of 15,834, the teams played out a 0-0 stalemate. Defensively, the team were solid, but struggled to add creativity in the final third. Dooley felt that the team had "created enough pressure to win, but made it difficult for ourselves by not putting the ball in the net."

"The *Green 'Un"* – a popular Saturday evening sports newspaper in Sheffield, published immediately on the final whistle and available for fans to buy on their way home from games – described defender John Holsgrove's performance as "dominant". The following Saturday saw the Owls travel to the City Ground, Nottingham and lose to a Forest team by the odd goal in three despite Holsgrove being pushed up front towards the end in search of an equaliser. That game saw the debut of Ken Knighton and a rare goal for Jimmy Mullen.

These two notable occasions aside, the draw and two defeats that the Owls had totted up saw them in 19th place after the first three games. Although the early season optimism may not have completely disappeared, the Owls needed a win. Dooley, though, still felt confident, saying: "There was no shortage of effort at Forest… I was pleased with the way Ken Knighton settled in… I think that…we have good reason to anticipate a move up the table."

The next games for Wednesday, though, were tricky ones. A midweek fixture at Hillsborough against newly-relegated West Bromwich Albion would be followed by another home fixture against Carlisle United who would go on to gain promotion that season. Dooley was expecting a difficult game against West Brom, a side he felt had "plenty of talent and skill, and I think they will present a challenge that can bring out the best in us."

His Owls team succeeded that evening, though, in front of a crowd of nearly 16,000, as goals from Sunley, Potts and Joicey sealed a 3-1 win. An unchanged team and another crowd of over 15,000 saw the Owls claim a 1-0 victory over Carlisle on the following Saturday. The goal scored by Allan Thompson ("a goalmouth scramble to which Thompson got the vital finishing touch" said the Green 'Un) was enough to move Wednesday up to 12th in the table.

The pre-season optimism that some felt may seemingly have remained at this stage. The Owls were unbeaten at home, in a reasonable position in the early-season league table but needed to improve their away form.

The perfect opportunity to do just that came just two days after the Carlisle game, with a trip to The Den to face Millwall before a long journey the following Saturday to Bristol City. Both games ended in defeat for the boys from Hillsborough. Wednesday went down 1-0 at Millwall, the hosts' goal coming just two minutes from time. Millwall's Eamon Dunphy, in his classic book "Only a Game?", described how "in terms of football we were outplayed."

Journalist Peter Ball, quoted in the same book, said "the better team lost", along with a lengthy description of the qualities of Tommy Craig. The return of John Holsgrove to the team against Bristol (replacing Jim Craig who had what was described as a stomach upset) did not improve matters as the Owls lost 2-0 and slid to 21st in the table. "Bristol showed more ideas and Wednesday could not really complain" the Green 'Un reported. The Owls at least escaped the fate of Bristol's previous opponents, Hull City, who saw goalkeeper Ray Cashley score against them from distance. Bristol's second goal was controversially allowed despite Wednesday's belief that it was offside. Allan Thompson was booked in the resulting melee and Dooley came on the pitch to calm the players. "I am not saying anything," he told journalists after the game. "If I did, I might be booked as well!"

Despite these defeats, the Owls had a good home record under Dooley (just seven losses in over 50 matches at this stage) and had two games in succession on home soil in which to make amends – a Saturday game against Crystal Palace and a midweek fixture against Millwall, offering a quick chance of revenge for the defeat at The Den.

Palace were without a league win at this stage, though started the game with their £155,000 defensive duo of Barry and Jeffries. Whatever defensive abilities they had were sorely tested by the Owls who romped to a 4-0 win with a Mick Prendergast hat-trick and a further goal from Sunley. The Millwall game saw more prowess from the Owls' forward line as goals from Potts, Prendergast (again) and an own goal secured a 3-2 win. Millwall's Eamon Dunphy, perhaps showing his frustration at being left out of the squad for that game, described the London team's performance as "a shambles… terrible… diabolical." The *Star* trumpeted the Wednesday team's success, however, shouting "Owls Glory" as its headline the following evening.

Positivity from these results was soon turned on its head, though, as the Owls fell to two straight defeats. At Sunderland, the hosts went 3-0 ahead before a late long-range goal from Coyle got the Owls on the board, before a home defeat to Portsmouth despite Wednesday leading 1-0 at half time through Brian Joicey. The Pompey defeat was the Owls' first defeat in the league at Hillsborough for almost a year, and was described by Derek Dooley as "a big disappointment".

Around those games, Wednesday eventually progressed in the League Cup after THREE games against Bournemouth. The first finished 0-0, the second 2-2 after extra time. Only in the third did Wednesday eventually prevail, again after extra time, with goals from Prudham and Prendergast.

Back in the league, though, Wednesday needed a boost and received it on the road at Cardiff, when Ken Knighton scored a last-minute winner for the Owls. Unfortunately for Wednesday fans, though, the victory was to be the last time they would win in the league until January 19. The Cardiff game was played on October 20. Wednesday were soon preoccupied by other matters, as over a dozen players – and manager Dooley himself – fell victim to a mystery virus, known as "Virus X". Wednesday appealed to the Football League to postpone their home game against Notts County, but their request was denied. "The matter's ended," said Eric Taylor. "There's no point in protesting." But the matter made the national press. The *Daily Mirror's* report read:

"Wednesday Must Play, Say League: Sheffield Wednesday must play today's home match with Notts County despite having seven first team players hit with a stomach virus. Wednesday, whose manager Derek Dooley has also been hit by the bug, approached the Football League on Thursday for their ground to be closed for seven to 10 days. But yesterday League secretary Alan Hardaker said: "There is not sufficient evidence to justify closing the ground and the club has a sufficient number of players available for selection."

A patched-up Owls team, including youngsters Danny Cameron and Eddie Prudham and featuring a returning Willie Henderson (broken nose), put up a battling show to draw 0-0. "Just the Tonic!" read the *Green 'Un.* "Virus-hit Owls put on best show of the season". The *Daily Mirror* returned to Hillsborough in the days after the game describing in mock-up match report style how the dressing rooms were fumigated. "A two-man Public Health squad…abandoned orthodox patterns like 4-2-4 or 4-3-3 and relied on their usual spray gun tactics.

In an unfamiliar strip of dark blue overalls and jackets, breather masks with yellow snouts and see through goggles they simply destroyed the opposition." The article went on to quote a Wednesday spokesman who drily commented: "We hope that we never have a return match". The humour was maintained by the Owls' scoreboard operator who, on the day of the game against Notts County, advertised the next game as "The Owls virus A.F.C. Bournemouth". The replacement of versus with virus was wryly described in the *Sheffield Star* as a "sick joke".

All joking apart for the Owls, the games came thick and fast in this period. Defeats at Villa (1-0 on November 3), at home to Orient (2-1, Joicey, November 10) and away at Luton (2-1, Joicey, November 17) combined with a humiliating 8-2 loss (Knighton and Prendergast with the Owls goals) away to Division One QPR in the League Cup on the sixth of the month led to rising discontent among some fans. The Owls struggled against a resurgent Villa side and their manager, Vic Crowe, said Villa *"could have scored five goals and not been flattered."*

By the time of Wednesday's next game, at home to Oxford on November 24, a group of fans began to call for change. An article in The *Star* was headlined 'Boycott Wednesday Call by Angry Fans". Those fans printed hundreds (maybe thousands) of leaflets at their own expense, the contents of which are reproduced on the following page.

The leaflet was signed by J. Fletcher, M. Fletcher and J. Nadsworth, with no further details or address. The independent shareholders association, led by Andrew Flear, had long been campaigning for change at Hillsborough, but claimed to have no connection with this action. Regardless of the truth of the matter, the atmosphere at Hillsborough was becoming more and more toxic.

"True supporters of Sheffield Wednesday will realise that the situation at the club has now reached crisis point. Even if we beat lowly Oxford United this afternoon the best we can hope for is a mediocre position in the League and yet another season of struggle in Division Two. If Oxford should win, the appalling and unthinkable possibilities of relegation to Division Three would have to be seriously considered. So much for the annual ritual of pledges and promises from Sir Andrew Stephen and his Board of Directors. Since the team was relegated in 1969-70, they have failed to even get in the top six of the Second Division, let alone sustain any kind of promotion challenge. No wonder the few promising young players on the books are reported to be unsettled. Who can blame them?

Believe it or not, Sheffield Wednesday have won NOTHING since 1935 – not one League Championship win, not one FA Cup win, and not even a chance in the League Cup, or of course, in Europe. Managers come and go (six in the last 12 years) but the slump continues with the inevitable sackings. Who appoints the managers and coaches? The Board of course. Elected and re-elected, year in, year out, by shareholders who obviously consider that the Board is composed of knowledgeable, ambitious, and far-sighted men in whose hands the successful future of Sheffield Wednesday is completely assured. Do you believe this? We do not, and neither it seems, do two-thirds of Sheffield Wednesday's supporters. Look at the facts. Gates are down to 12,000 or less, yet we all know that a successful Wednesday team would draw at least 36,000 fans per match – remember that over 45,000 came along (after a shocking season) to see the fateful relegation clincher with Manchester City.

As regular supporters who have stood and suffered at Leppings Lane for over 12 years we believe that it is essential for the survival of Sheffield Wednesday that the present Board of Directors be kicked out of office, lock, stock and barrel, by any legitimate means possible. Heaven only knows, they've had chances enough to show what they can do. In fact, could anyone do much worse? Most of you who have come this afternoon are supporters, not shareholders. You have no power to vote either for or against the Board but there are two obvious ways in which you can show your feelings: "Write to the local press, boycott matches – a difficult thing for diehard fans to do, but as long as there are even 10,000 fans in the ground the Board will imagine that they enjoy our confidence and the fall into obscurity and financial insolvency will continue.

"FOR YEARS THEY HAVE FAILED THE CLUB, THE FANS AND THE CITY. NOW THEY MUST GO BEFORE IT IS TOO LATE!"

The *Star* interviewed a series of fans in advance of the game with comments such as: "I agree with getting rid of people on the Board" ... "There's been something wrong at Hillsborough for years" ... and "If Wednesday don't buck up by Christmas, they'll go down this year." The team were struggling for form as well as health. Dooley and the club did not want to use the virus as an excuse but, with frustration mounting, an improvement in results was needed.

Whether affected by the protest or not, the attendance for the Oxford game was a disappointing 7,998 – the lowest league gate of the season. The Owls also lost the game (1-0) despite Dooley's belief that the Owls "have begun to turn the corner after the difficulties created by the virus which has dogged us for weeks." The games didn't get much easier for the Owls as they faced top-of-the-table Middlesbrough in their next game but beforehand, Dooley took his squad to Blackpool for three days, giving them "a chance to live, talk, eat and sleep football together for a spell".

A much-improved crowd of 11,992 saw the Owls take the lead twice (Prendergast and Joicey) but be pinned back both times, finishing only with a 2-2 draw. Dooley saw this as a creditable result, admitting:" We can see some light at the end of the tunnel." Dooley may well have been aiming some of his comments at the boardroom for, as we see elsewhere in the book, this period was one of great change at the top of the Hillsborough hierarchy. The Owls' next game was to prove pivotal to the history of our period.

*****

Key Game: Sheffield Wednesday 0-3 Fulham, December 15th, 1973

Derek Dooley felt somewhat buoyed by the result against Middlesbrough in the previous game and, despite three players again being sent home with the "bug" – as he called it in his programme notes – was able to name a solid looking team for the home fixture with Fulham.

1 Springett
2 Rodrigues

3 Shaw
4 Thompson
5 Eustace
6 Craig (T.)
7 Henderson
8 Knighton
9 Joicey
10 Prendergast
11 Potts
Sub Sunley

Fulham named an unchanged team, though had problems of their own, as some supporters were angry about the recent sale of star players Steve Earle and Paul Went to Leicester City and Portsmouth for a total of £250,000. Owls supporters' anger about the situation of the club and team manifested itself in another very low crowd, of only 7,925 – slightly below the crowd for the Oxford game. One group of fans unveiled an ironic "Boo!" flag on the North Stand before the start of play – with a dry sense of humour about the club's predicament.

The game itself gave plenty of opportunities for those Owls' fans to boo. Conway put Fulham ahead after 18 minutes, Barrett scored a second after 40 minutes, and the game was over with Busby's third five minutes into the second half. The *Green 'Un's* report that evening describes the events:

"The match as a spectacle was a massive non-event but Fulham's three goals without reply may prove eventful for Wednesday. The game was instantly forgettable, but its significance is massive as it made Wednesday's fight against relegation even harder. Fulham did not look a particularly good team, but they won quite comfortably. Wednesday achieved little of note – one cynic remarked that the club is now on a three-day week and Saturday is not one of those days. Ken Knighton tried to get things moving in midfield and Mick Prendergast chased but generally Wednesday had little to offer. Football is unpredictable. How could Wednesday threaten Middlesbrough and then play so abysmally on Saturday?

That's one for Derek Dooley to solve. Star player: Ken Knighton – some midfield drive."

Dooley attempted to address the issue by keeping the players back after the game, before finally emerging from the dressing room at 5:34pm – over an hour and a half after the end of the game. "I wasn't satisfied with the display," he told reporters. "The pitch was bad, but Fulham played on it, and it was the same for them. The less I say about it the better. Last Saturday we were not great, but played better than for some time. We went back to square one today." Dooley may have seen the proverbial writing on the wall if he had heard new chairman Matt Sheppard's remarks also after the game. "It was a very poor performance", he said. "You have to make decisions in light of the facts before you." Another unnamed director was quoted as saying: "I was speechless for half an hour after the match. I was too full for words."

Dooley did understand the situation he was facing. As we shall see elsewhere, he accepted that he now lacked friends and allies on the board and, with the team struggling, he conceded in an interview with the Sheffield Telegraph that "there's no smoke without fire." He went on to say: "There have been changes at boardroom level, and there has been a change of chairman. I don't know what might happen." When asked by The Star whether he thought his job was in a precarious position, Dooley replied: "I thought that when I took the job. It's one of the hazards, but you don't have to look at that."

Dooley still felt confident in his ability to improve matters, telling journalist Michael Morgan: "I need time – but time is a commodity you don't have in football. It's a cruel game. Nobody knows that more than me. I've got confidence in myself and the coaches at Hillsborough, our position is by no means irretrievable. I'd like the directors to think that way. Nobody has said anything to me at this stage, but I don't know what they are thinking. We've got problems out on the pitch, and we've got to solve them. It's up to us."

The Fulham performance was evidently a very poor one. As

supporter David Harpham remembered it to me recently: "I sat in the North Stand for this car crash of a game. Possibly the worst ever performance I've seen by a Wednesday team. We were lucky to get nil. Like most fans, I left well before the end of the match." Dooley knew or suspected that he was living on borrowed time. The changes at boardroom level were likely to lead to a change in manager at some stage. This match proved the turning point, after it there was no going back for Dooley.

The result against Fulham left the Owls in 20th place, a relegation position, and their next game was a 0-0 draw at struggling Crystal Palace. The *Green 'Un reported: "Wednesday gained a valuable point... they fought hard... and showed the necessary application."* The People were not impressed by the spectacle, with their headline reading: "Yes Mal, it was Shocking!" – referring to Palace's manager Malcolm Allison. The article added: "The suffering spectators must have wished that they had given into their wives and gone Christmas shopping instead!" *The People* did accept that the Owls were the better team, especially in the second half – where Potts and Prendergast both hit shots over the bar, and David Sunley hit the post. The *Green 'Un* added a description of a "glorious shot from Potts which produced an equally fine save from Hammond." The *Green 'Un* had Allan Thompson as man of the match, The *People* chose Eric Potts. Either way, it seems that the Owls put in a determined performance, much improved from the display against Fulham a week earlier.

The game, though, was Dooley's last as manager. The circumstances surrounding his dismissal are covered elsewhere in the book but two days after the Palace game, on Christmas Eve, he was sacked.

Dooley's replacement in the short term was Gerry Young who was thrown straight into action as the Owls faced three games in quick succession. The first two games, both at home, ended in creditable 1-1 draws before an uneventful 0-0 draw away at Blackpool on New Year's Day, 1974. Some relief from the league was then offered in the shape of an FA Cup third round tie against First Division side Coventry City, which finished in another 0-0 draw. The headline in the *Green 'Un* read "Fighting Owls Worry City" and the *Coventry Evening Telegraph* also highlighted Wednesday's fighting performance, on a quagmire of a pitch: *"Today City were unable to make their superior skill and technique count and Sheffield, despite their Second Division problems, battled long and furiously to stretch the Sky Blues to the limit. But neither side overcame the strength-sapping conditions, and at times, the players must have felt they were ploughing through a paddy field."*

The replay was scheduled for only three days later at Highfield Road and given the limitations of the three-day-week, kick off was 1:30pm. This did not stop Owls' fans attending and the London Owls sent a blow-by-blow account of their day at the game to the *Green 'Un* (despite only just making the game, after delays on the train leaving Euston!) The game ended in a 3-1 defeat with the greater quality of the Division One team showing.

"Coventry Into Fourth Round as Hutchison Takes Revenge" screamed the headline in the Birmingham press of a game "played in clinging mud, high winds and lashing rain".

"Wednesday were adequate going forward," the report added, "but their defence, with midfield players Peter Eustace and Ken Knighton at centre half and left back respectively, made many mistakes: Added to this was an eccentric display of goalkeeping from Peter Springett."

Not a great day at the office for the Owls, who returned to league action with a tricky looking trip to Carlisle. Roy Coyle and Jimmy Mullen put the Owls 2-1 ahead – at which stage it seems the Green 'Un had already printed its headline of "Top Gear Owls Rock Carlisle!" Unfortunately for Wednesday (and the Green 'Un's editors), Carlisle scored a late equaliser and the game finished 2-2. The Owls then returned to Hillsborough for what would be Gerry Young's final match as caretaker, against Swindon.

A late winner by Eric Potts, bundled in from close range, sealed a 2-1 victory after David Sunley's earlier goal. This game was the 14th since the Owls last tasted victory, three months previously. Relief seemed the overwhelming feeling around the club, tempered with a dose of realism. As one correspondent with the Green 'Un (Mr M.A. Riley of Loxley) put it: "The Owls are out of the race already.... Do something or go directors, before the only cheering at Hillsborough is that of ghosts cheering long-past glories".

Ten days after the long-overdue Swindon victory, Wednesday announced their new manager: Steve Burtenshaw. That period had generated much conjecture about his identity; some members of the Sheffield press put two and two together and made five about Brian Clough's supposed unhappiness in Brighton and suggested he would be the man for the job. Some fans were also keen on Clough. *The Star's* letters page filled with comments such as "Send for Cloughie" and "The Wednesday board should offer the outspoken but talented Brian Clough a contract he could not refuse." Urban myth suggests that he was interviewed for the post, or at least visited Hillsborough, but as the chairman's wife found him "uncouth" he was not offered the job. I have found no evidence to confirm or deny this!

Clough himself later relayed the tale of being approached by a journalist about the Owls job. Clough thought of himself as "the best man in the business", and when asked by a Wednesday official to apply for the job (rather than simply being offered the post), felt better of it. "Had they gone about the affair the right way, I would probably have gone but the deal never really got off the ground," he was quoted as saying in a 1976 Football Post article. Others looked to Ron Atkinson, or Don Megson. Megson was beginning his managerial career with Bristol Rovers at the time but had been a great servant to Wednesday as player, leaving in 1969 after playing in 386 games.

He tells the tale of being "tapped-up" for the Owls job in his autobiography but felt that the unofficial approaches were people "pulling his leg". Megson says that he "kicked himself ever since" for not applying. Atkinson was also at the start of his managerial career and an outsider for the job, though this is not the only time his name was linked with the position in our period. Burtenshaw's appointment was greeted in the *Star* with the headline: "*It's Burtenshaw For Owls to End Guessing Game.*" His first game in charge, away at Fulham's Craven Cottage, would prove to be a baptism of fire.

Burtenshaw had ordered new tracksuits for the players for the trip to London; smart, blue tracksuit tops with white piping, designed to impress upon them that this was a new start under a new regime. The first half of the game was an even affair – Danny Cameron's equalising goal for the Owls coming on the stroke of half-time after Viv Busby had put Fulham ahead early in the half. The second half was Fulham's, though, as Busby completed his hat-trick in a 4-1 win.

Cameron's strike was to be his only league goal in English football and despite Burtenshaw's reign starting with defeat, the consensus was that the Owls had not been entirely outplayed - more that they were unlucky to come up against a player in sparkling form.

The Owls had a slightly longer wait than usual to make amends as continuing problems with power supplies meant that the club arranged for their first ever Sunday game to be played, with Bristol City the visitors to S6. The government's move to preserve electricity in the face of strikes and the rapid increase in oil prices saw the introduction of the "three-day week" with football clubs banned from using floodlights.

Eric Taylor was convinced that the resulting early kick-offs on Saturdays were costing the club spectators and money. The Sunday game was an experiment to see if attendances picked up.

Given the Sunday trading laws at the time, the Owls were not strictly speaking allowed to charge for admission, instead charging the ticket price for a team-sheet. Ironically, the team listed on there was incorrect! The attendance was a promising 15,595 - amongst the highest of the season to date. The Owls won the game convincingly (3-1) with goals from Joicey, Henderson and Bernard Shaw. Interviewed in the *Sheffield Star* the following week John Holsgrove admitted: "I am more confident that I was a few weeks ago. I think we are in with a fighting chance."

Peter Springett added that there was "no chance" that the Owls would go down. Springett's comments came after he was left out of the team in favour of new loan signing Bobby Ferguson (from West Ham). The Hammers had paid a world-record fee for a goalkeeper when they signed Ferguson for £65,000 from Kilmarnock in 1967 and he remained the Hammers' first-choice goalkeeper for many years, winning the team's player of the year award in 1972. Despite his background, the move caused consternation among some fans as it had been expected that Alan Paterson – a 20-year-old Northern Irish keeper who was already at the club – would make his debut. Ferguson though made a solid debut, the Green 'Un reporting "impressive kicking and a fine save."

The Owls could look forward to their next game with a degree of confidence, as they travelled to Bolton the following Saturday. The game only went ahead after three pitch inspections and after only a minute, the Owls were possibly wishing referee Roger Kirkpatrick made a different decision as Bolton took an early lead. Things then went from bad to worse when the hosts scored three more goals in a six-minute spell and although Wednesday pulled two back through Joicey and an own goal, the damage had been done.

A tricky midweek trip to Fratton Park saw Wednesday make the long trip back north with a point from a 1-1 draw, before a home game against Sunderland saw a bumper crowd of 17,816 at Hillsborough. Sunderland, though, netted a 13th-minute winner and another defeat, at Hull City, left the Owls stuck in the relegation places with just ten league games remaining.

Very few fans would then have predicted the results of Wednesday's next two games, away at Notts County and at home to Cardiff City. Amazingly, the Owls scored ten goals across the two fixtures – beating County 5-1 and Cardiff 5-0. After goals from Prendergast (2), Joicey (2) and Potts, the Green 'Un reported how "Wednesday shook off their relegation blues with their best performance of the season." The Cardiff game saw the Owls make a more sedate start – with goals by Potts and Craig seeing them 2-0 up at the break – before further goals from Joicey (2) and Thompson ensured that Wednesday scored five goals for a second game. There was a pleasing amount of method about Wednesday's build-up and Cardiff were rarely able to break the grip that the Owls had on the game," said Wednesday correspondent Ian Vickers in the *Green 'Un*.

Peter Springett had returned in goal for these games after Bobby Ferguson's loan spell expired and made his 150th appearance for the club against Cardiff. Joicey made his 100th appearance in the same game. They, and the fans, were able to celebrate the team moving up the table to the relative heights of 17[th.]

Wednesday continued their good recent form with victory away at promotion-chasing Leyton Orient, with a first-half goal by Tommy Craig proving the winner. Craig had asked for a transfer away from Wednesday late in Derek Dooley's reign and there had been rumours of a player plus cash swap for Bobby Ferguson. The player was keen to develop his international credentials with Scotland, something he managed in 1976, long after leaving Hillsborough, gaining one full cap. "That's why I want to get away," he said.

"As I see it, it is going to take at least four years before Wednesday get back in the First Division." Burtenshaw persuaded Craig to stick it out a little longer at Hillsborough and his winner at Orient kept Wednesday 17th, and seemingly maintained their confidence levels going into the final matches of the season. "In training we've worked and worked," remembered Joicey, "and I think all this work is starting to pay off."

April Fool's Day saw Aston Villa visit Hillsborough, and it was the Owls who were made to look foolish on this occasion. A season-high crowd up to that point of 22,094 saw Wednesday go behind 2-1 at half-time, before capitulating and losing 4-2. One fan wrote to The *Star,* lamenting how "in the first half they had taken Villa to pieces with sharp, short, accurate football played on the floor (before)… they reverted most noticeably to the pre-Burtenshaw days of that hopeful high ball down the middle that only needed a leg-up to conquer Everest." The mood of the fans was not improved after the next game which saw the Owls travel to Oxford, only to return empty-handed with a 1-0 defeat. That game was Wednesday's eighth against Oxford – they had won none of them.

Back-to-back defeats had sucked Wednesday back into relegation trouble, and three games in four days would define their season. The Owls travelled to Preston on Good Friday, faced Luton at home the following day and then hosted Preston again on Easter Monday. These were vital games as Preston, managed by World Cup winner Bobby Charlton, were involved in the relegation shake-up with the Owls and Luton were challenging for promotion.

All three teams needed results but Wednesday's 0-0 draw at Deepdale didn't really help either side. Wednesday also suffered a further blow when Mick Prendergast was stretchered from the field with a broken leg. Things looked more promising against Luton when goals from Joicey and Potts put the Owls ahead, before Luton hit back to draw 2-2 in front of a 16,492 crowd.

Wednesday were still above water, but two draws were not ideal. Fortunately for the 17,332 who converged on Hillsborough for the Easter Monday game against Preston, Craig's 17th-minute goal was enough to give the Owls the points – and indeed, the margin of victory could have been greater were it not for the heroics of John Brown in the Preston goal.

Wednesday were now 18th in the table, two places above the drop-zone, and still not safe from the threat of relegation. Indeed, results elsewhere over the Easter weekend meant that Wednesday were still only two points ahead of their nearest rivals, Oxford and Crystal Palace – both of whom also had games in hand over Wednesday. The Owls' next game? Away at Middlesbrough, who had already won the league and were in celebratory mood as they prepared to receive the trophy on the day of the game.

Wednesday's team was remodelled to cater for Prendergast's absence; Danny Cameron came into midfield and Eddie Prudham returned in a forward role. The match was played in a carnival atmosphere. A pipe band played before the game, and Football League chairman Len Shipman handed the Division Two trophy to Boro manager Jack Charlton ahead of kick-off.

The carnival atmosphere remained when the game kicked off and with Graeme Souness dominating, the Teessiders were 3-0 to the good by half-time. The second half was worse for the Owls as they completely capitulated and lost, 8-0. Souness finished with a hat-trick as Wednesday suffered their second eight-goal defeat of a very difficult season.

"A nightmare for Wednesday at Middlesbrough this afternoon when their hopes of avoiding relegation took a severe jolt as Middlesbrough crashed goal after goal past them at Ayresome Park," wrote Ian Vickers in the Green 'Un. *"Middlesbrough, presented with the Division Two trophy before the start, continued the celebrations when play began. Wednesday were up against it right from the start, conceding an early goal and from then on it was an uphill struggle against confident opposition. Middlesbrough gave the Wednesday defence a harassing time, while up front, the Owls didn't make much impression. Prudham toiled hard up front, but "toiled" is the word as the afternoon belonged comprehensively to Middlesbrough, and these goals could prove crucial if relegation is decided on goal average."*

Steve Burtenshaw did not mince his words afterwards. "They want their backsides kicking," he said of his players. "There are no excuses. The Sheffield public are tired of excuses… they want something to cheer." The *Star's* headline on the Monday following simply read: "Black Weekend: Burtenshaw Raps Team's Lack of Application." Fans letters in the following week's *Green 'Un* were certainly angry about the result. Their headlines included: "Do the Players Really Care?", "Just Pray for Survival" and "Pay Them for their Efforts".

One letter, from Mr Hodkin of S14, read in full: "I feel that I must write in protest as one of the Sheffield Wednesday supporters at Middlesbrough on Saturday who hung their heads in shame when leaving Ayresome Park. We as a party stayed until the final whistle blew. The fans who could not stay to watch anymore when Wednesday were already five down were jeered out of the ground by the Boro fans.

"I wonder if the Wednesday players realise, or care, what the thousand or more fans who support them at every away game felt at the most disgusting display of football by Sheffield Wednesday that I have ever seen."

National newspapers were scathing about the Owls' performance. The *Daily Mirror* commented on "Wednesday's humiliation", the *Sunday Mirror* describing the Owls as "a disgrace to professional football" and the *News of the World* added that "it became just a question of how high the score would mount." Fans who were at the game told me how many Owls supporters left with the score at four, five, six or seven. Ian Fox though stuck it out, almost to his cost. "It was my first ever away game", he told me. "Most people left at half time, we stayed and missed our coach. I ended up sat on my Grandad's knee on another coach that picked us up! Not a great day!"

Others remember being embarrassed at school or work afterwards. In a common theme for the time, others seemed to take it in good humour, with David Bonser telling me that: "I came out at 7-0. Lots did. Got on bus and it was eight. 'We'll support you evermore' was our chant for quite a bit, followed by: 'We had joy we had fun, we saw Wednesday beat eight none', to the tune of the Terry Jacks song – Seasons in the Sun!" Ian Allaway told me that he left at half-time, or rather he was "thrown out by a copper!" He has, though, kept his ticket for the game. A souvenir of a desperate day.

All seemed lost at full-time. Some Owls fans were convinced that results elsewhere had also gone against their team and that relegation beckoned. But as the other results that day filtered through, it became clear that the Owls had a final chance – Palace had also lost, and Wednesday were out of the relegation places as it stood. Two places and two points behind them were Preston, who had a considerably lower goal average and so could not catch the Owls. Palace were one place behind Wednesday; two points adrift, but with another game to play.

Wednesday knew though that, whatever else happened, they would be safe if they won their final game. Once this situation became obvious to those Owls fans who witnessed the humiliation at Boro, then a smile returned to some of their faces. As Daniel Gordon recounts in his book: "There they were, loyal Wednesdayites, grown men hugging each other and exclaiming; 'We can do it! We can still do it!'"

Chairman Matt Sheppard spoke to the team on their coach back: "Well lads, that was bloody awful, but try to forget it for next week." The Owls had one final chance. A last game show-down, where victory would ensure survival, the following Satur-day, at home to Bolton Wanderers.

* * * * *

Key Game: Sheffield Wednesday 1-0 Bolton, April 27th,1974

The Owls' fans and players knew that they must put the humilia-tion of the Middlesbrough result behind them in their "do or die" game against Bolton. A win against the Trotters would guarantee survival. Anything else risked relegation to Division Three for the first time in the club's history. Steve Burtenshaw was without the key trio of Prendergast, Rodrigues and Thompson – all injured, all watching from the directors' box. Owls skipper Ken Knighton returned to the side after missing four games with injury. Peter Rodrigues failed his fitness test that morning, but Henderson and Sunley were passed fit to play their part, so the Owls lined up:

1 Springett
2 Cameron
3 Shaw
4 Mullen
5 Holsgrove
6 Knighton
7 Potts
8 Sunley
9 Joicey
10 Craig (T.)
11 Henderson
Sub: Eustace

Although Bolton had little to play for sitting 11th in the table with no chance of relegation or promotion, they put out a strong team - including John Byrom who was the Division's third top-scorer with 18 at the time. A crowd of 23,264 came along to support the Owls - the highest crowd of the season which followed rising crowds at other home matches over the previous weeks. Bolton were managed by Jimmy Armfield and had only lost two of their previous 20 games. The game itself was a very tight affair, settled by a goal from captain Ken Knighton inside the last few minutes. Wednesday were safe.

"So, it all ended happily after all," read the report in The *Star.* *"It might not have been a classic, but at least Wednesday avoided the drop into Division Three. They won the match they had to win in a tension-racked 90 minutes, which in fairy-book fashion provided the dramatic finale when Ken Knighton scored the most important goal of his career with just four minutes to go. Wednesday have had a nightmare season and there is no escaping the fact: so it was a moment to savour when Knighton lashed the ball home from about six yards following a left-wing centre by Craig. His immediate triumphant salute to the Kop told of the relief his goal had brought; that he should be chaired off at the end by the fans was a demonstration of their gratitude for his achievement. It would be unfair and illogical to be critical of Wednesday's overall performance. The importance of the occasion produced an anxiety which quickly spread through every single genuine Wednesdayite in the season's top crowd."*

Shortly before Knighton's winning goal, Tommy Craig had missed a very serviceable opportunity. He ran on to a typically excellent Henderson pass, took the ball in front of goal but shot across the face. It is testament to Craig's resilience that only two minutes later he provided the cross for the winning goal. Knighton described his goal after the game: "The ball fell to my feet and I dropped my shoulder – like all good players do – and scored!" Burtenshaw paid credit to his captain: "The wholehearted endeavour he has shown since I've been here has been a great help. It was fitting that he should score the goal." Both Knighton and Burtenshaw praised the fans and two supporters invaded the pitch immediately after Knighton's goal, before thousands more joined them on the final whistle. Knighton was carried from the pitch by jubilant Owls.

"Owls are Safe!" was the simple headline in the *Green 'Un* that afternoon, and the Kop was described as "a mass of blue and white as the crowd cheered Wednesday home." Of course, these scenes were a celebration of not dropping into Division Three. The celebrations were not those that many Owls would have hoped for at the start of the season. It would not take long for the investigations into the season to begin.

The 1973-74 campaign had proved a long and difficult one for the Owls. What began with dreams of promotion ended with a last-day escape from relegation. A well-loved manager had been sacked, to be replaced by one who aimed to play fluent and attacking football. The boardroom had altered dramatically with a new chairman and other directors. The fans had shown their displeasure at times, and key players had left (Dave Clements) or expressed their desire to leave (Tommy Craig). The team had also faced its share of injury problems, perhaps the most serious being Mick Prendergast's broken leg. The team gained 35 points from 12 wins, 11 draws and 19 defeats. They finished in 19th position, one place, and one point above the relegation places. It could not be seen, therefore, as a successful season.

In the aftermath of the final game, the chairman, manager and captain of the club all spoke out about the need to improve. Matt Sheppard, chairman, promised: "It's my intention that this club will never again come this close to the Third Division. We have had one problem – to stay in Division Two. All other matters have had to be put to one side. Now the board will be taking a long, hard look at the future. The objective will be Division One as soon as possible." Manager Burtenshaw added: "We've got money and we are prepared to spend. We owe it to the club and to the players. I intend strengthening the squad but will not be getting new faces just for the sake of it. This club has had more than its share of bad luck this season." Ken Knighton said of Burtenshaw: "I think this chap deserves a lot of credit. With Steve and Gerry Young we are looking forward, with confidence to next season." Young was Steve Burtenshaw's assistant and described himself around this time as "totally a Wednesday man."

The Owls had amassed 14 points at Christmas, gaining another 21 afterwards. There was a period where the team played the fluent, attacking and successful football that Burtenshaw was looking for. The new chairman had begun to understand what was needed to turn the club around. Maybe, just maybe, the Owls had reached their *"Lowest Ebb"*, and could look forward to 1974-75 with optimism. Of course, we know what happened – but it doesn't take too much imagination to understand why there may have been optimism at this stage. It couldn't get any worse. Could it?

AN INTERVIEW WITH
EDDIE PRUDHAM

Eddie Prudham was a muscular forward player who appeared both on the wing and in the centre forward positions for the Owls. Born in Gateshead, he signed for the Owls as a youngster in 1967. He made his first team debut in 1971, going on to play 21 games and scoring three goals for the club. Prudham had a successful loan spell with Partick Thistle in 1974 before signing for Carlisle United, who were in Division One at that time. His later career saw spells with Hartlepool, Workington, Stockport and Bournemouth, before a lengthy career in the prison service. Eddie now lives on the Isle of Wight and it was from there that he spoke to me in 2019. We chatted for a while about my reasons for writing the book, and Sheffield Wednesday more generally before discussing Eddie's career.

How was it that a lad from the North East signed for the Owls?
Well, as a boy, I trained twice a week with Newcastle – Tuesday and Thursday nights. I was a Sunderland fan though! The sessions with Newcastle, I'd have been 11 or 12-years-old. They were really busy sessions and I began to feel that they wouldn't notice if I didn't turn up, you know.

So how then did you turn up at Sheffield Wednesday?
Well, Wednesday were a big club at the time, they had scouts in the North East. One of them must have seen me play for the boys' club. Anyhow, one day Alan Brown knocked on my Mam's door asking if I'd come down to Hillsborough.

The manager Alan Brown?
Aye, that's right – I was only 13 or so, and you can imagine that made me feel really wanted. After that Lawrie McMenemy looked after me and the other lads – he'd drive me and a couple of other

lads down and back from the North East for training. I remember him breaking down on the A1 once though! In the holidays, the club would put lads who came from a distance away up in the Hunters House hotel. We'd get taxied to and from training. It all felt like the club really wanted us.

It sounds like you really enjoyed being at the club?
I did yes, let me tell you one story for the book! In 1965 I think; Hillsborough had held the FA Cup semi-final between Manchester United and Leeds United. Well, I don't know if you know much about those teams, but they were often at each other's throats. Anyhow, during the game there was a fracas between various members of the teams, and to cut a long story short, Denis Law ended up with the shirt ripped off his back by Jack Charlton, I think. Anyhow, on the Monday morning I was walking past the club's laundry room and there, on the floor by the washing machine, was what was left of this red shirt. I asked the cleaner if I could have it, and she agreed with no problem as she was about to throw it out. I got it home to my Mam who managed to reattach the collar to the shirt – she'd been a tailor's seamstress, so she knew what she was doing. I then kept the shirt for the next 40-odd years!

Tell me how you moved up to the senior ranks at Hillsborough?
It was Jack Marshall, I think, who signed me up on senior terms at Wednesday. The training was tough – really tough – especially under Danny Williams. He used to line us up on the halfway line; make us run towards the Kop, get to the top and back – twice, then run around the pitch and back to the halfway line. He'd do it with a stopwatch, you'd get a short recovery time, and then all over again. It was two hours of training, but he worked us hard!

It took a couple of years for me to make my debut though, and it was Derek Dooley who gave me that – in a 4-0 defeat to Cardiff in January 1971. I had to wait until the following season for my next games, and my first goal – away at Aston Villa in the last game of the season. We lost again!

You played many more games the following season (1973-74) - was that related to the virus?

I don't really remember the virus, but I do know that Derek was very good at giving young players a chance. I played a good number of games then, both starting and as substitute. I also scored my first goal at Hillsborough in a League Cup game against Bournemouth. So yes, there might well have been a virus that caused Derek to bring more youngsters through. We had a good reserve and youth team at the time. I know some supporters stuck to watching the reserves at that time – and stopped watching the first team!

Did things change for you when Derek Dooley left?

Not immediately, as I played in the next game and scored my first home league goal for the club [against Hull]. A cross from the right and I bundled it home. Derek Dooley was a smashing guy. I enjoyed working for him, and it was an awful experience sitting in the changing room that Christmas Eve when he came in and told us he has been sacked. I was only a young lad still, and Derek had given me my chance. So, it was awful, unforgivable. Derek was a gentleman and revered on the blue side of Sheffield at the time. A really sad day.

How about Steve Burtenshaw – how did you find it under him?

Steve was a good coach. He meant well. He'd come up from Arsenal or QPR I think and had a proven record. I liked him. It just didn't work at Hillsborough for him.

Why do you think that was?

Well, he was a coach not a manager I suppose. It takes a lot to build a team, and some luck sometimes. We had some good players – Tommy Craig, Willie Henderson, Peter Rodrigues – all internationals. We also had some good experienced lads and some like me coming from the youth and reserve teams. It takes something to blend all that into a team. Maybe that's where Steve went wrong. Anyhow, he soon sold me on!

Tell me about some of the players who helped you at Hills-borough.

Well, I mentioned we had some good players. I got on well as mates with Dave Sunley and Jimmy Mullen, they both came to my wedding, and I still see Dave. I used to go out a bit with Mick Prendergast and one or two others – we'd have a bet or two at the local bookies! Prendo and Joicey both helped me when I came into the team. So did Allan Thompson – he took me to Stockport with him a few years later. In many ways though it was the coaches at Hillsborough that really helped me as a young lad. I learned so much from Ron Staniforth for example, he was a massive influence. So was Bill Asprey, though he was only there a short time. Tom MacInerney as well. All of them helped. Ron Staniforth helped me build muscle – he used to take us off after training, feed us raw eggs and sherry and then have us doing weights. It worked, mind!

You moved from Hillsborough to Carlisle, I think?

I did, for £35,000. I had just had a loan spell at Partick Thistle where I'd scored five goals in as many games – including one against Celtic – Billy Bremner and all. I heard that Carlisle were in for me, and they were in Division One at the time, and I went straight from Partick to there. My debut was against Leeds United, so no easy ride! I scored a few goals for them, including one against Arsenal and ended up staying for three years. I got an injury though, so had to go out to Hartlepool and then Workington to try and rebuild myself a bit.

It was from there where Allan Thompson came in for me from Stockport. I had three of the best years of my career there – finishing top scorer for them twice. I ended up at Bournemouth for a short while, and from there moved into the Prison Service. I worked in Wakefield Prison, and all three on the Isle of Wight.

Have you any other memories of Sheffield or Sheffield Wednesday that you'd like to share?

Just to say that I've followed the Owls and their fortunes ever since. It's a great club. I rang them up in 1993 you know – because I wanted to go to the FA Cup semi-final that year against United. They remembered who I was and sorted me tickets no problem. Great club. Great people. They were struggling in the 1970s but you're right to say that there were lots of good players and some good young lads coming through.

THE MANAGERS

A tale of the original goal machine, a "Cockney" coach and a footballing stalwart. There are two short intermissions for former players to play their part. To steal a dictum from elsewhere – all managerial careers end in failure. The managers here are no different. One career though ends in the cruellest of circumstances. All oversee decline until the Owls reach "Our Lowest Ebb".

Derek Dooley: January 1971 until December 1973

The Derek Dooley story is a famous one among fans of both Sheffield football teams. It has been well-told on many occasions, not least in Dooley's very well written, thorough and thoughtful autobiography. The facts of his (cruelly shortened) playing career bear repetition, however. He scored goals at the rate of one a game in his league and cup career – 65 goals in 65 games (two in two for Lincoln, the rest for the Owls). He also scored more than 100 goals for the Owls in Yorkshire and Central League games. In the Second Division of 1951-52, Dooley's tally was a barely-believable 46 goals in 30 games. His first game for the Owls was in March 1950, his last in February 1953.

This fateful match at Preston's Deepdale ground saw him suffer a double fracture of the leg in a clash with the goalkeeper. This was followed by the discovery that his leg had become infected and gangrenous, and the rapid decision was made to amputate the leg to save Dooley's life. Dooley tells the story of how his nurse spotted the problem when she was asked to sign his "pot" and he failed to react to her playful tickling of his toes. Her actions possibly saved Dooley's life. His playing career, though, was over.

Eric Taylor, the Owls' long-serving manager at the time, suggested to Dooley that he would be better served trying to make his own way in life after the injury. As Dooley put it, if the Owls offered him employment it may seem that he was living on sympathy. Derek therefore took employment working as a telephonist then executive for a local bakery firm (owned by one of the Owls' directors, Mr R.R. Gunstone) and for one season, writing for the *Mirror* newspaper about sport. The *Sheffield Telegraph and Star* helped fundraise for Dooley and in 1955, the Owls held a well-attended testimonial game for him. Throughout this period Dooley stayed in contact with the club and helped in various ways with junior football.

In 1962 he was given the chance to return to the club full time as manager of the club's new development fund. After some thought and consideration with his family, Dooley took the job. The development fund aimed to improve the facilities at Hillsborough and any money raised could not be spent on players. Dooley made a real success of the role, with money raised contributing to the building of a new gymnasium and to the new West Stand of the 1960s. Derek Dooley therefore had a long relationship with Sheffield Wednesday and was well-regarded and popular, with successful administrative experience. He had, though, no experience in football management.

Dooley admitted in his book that he was "flabbergasted and amazed" to be offered the manager's post by the club. The Owls had flattered to deceive since relegation from Division One the previous season and as they were languishing in mid-table, it was no surprise to many that previous boss Danny Williams was sacked. Dooley's appointment was not universally popular. Wednesday's Shareholders' Association thought the Owls needed an experienced and "qualified" manager... the Owls' board confirmed that Dooley would not have taken the job if he didn't think he was capable. Dooley's wife, Sylvia, was simply concerned that her husband might get hurt. And, unfortunately, she was right to worry.

This book focuses on the seasons from 1973-76. In Dooley's time in charge before the 1973-74 season, though, he revamped the team, playing some exciting football and signing players such as Brian Joicey, Willie Henderson and John Holsgrove. Dooley also brought in the Owls' youngest-ever player in this period – blooding goalkeeper Peter Fox at only 15 years of age. He also brought back Peter Swan, who had served his ban of eight years after his involvement in a betting scandal in 1964. At the end of the 1970-71 season he appointed long-serving player Gerry Young to the coaching staff. This was a relatively exciting time for Owls' fans, epitomised by the appearance of Brazilian team Santos, featuring Pele, at Hillsborough in 1972. The 1970-71 season saw the Owls finish 15th in Division Two and the following campaign, Dooley's first full season in charge, saw an improvement to 14th. A year later Dooley had led the Owls to a tenth-placed finish, with a flirtation in early spring with the promotion spots. By the time the 1973-74 season began, many fans were confident that the Owls could battle for a return to the top-flight.

The campaign, though, proved a difficult one for the Owls, and for Dooley. He had strengthened the team over the summer with the signings of Bernard Shaw and Ken Knighton – Dooley particularly pleased by the signing of aggressive midfielder Knighton, who he had wanted since he had taken charge before paying Hull nearly £60,000 for his services.

A successful pre-season tour of Sweden, which saw the Owls finish third after winning two of their three games, further increased confidence levels around Hillsborough, but one point from the opening three games of the season soon tested that belief. Despite successive home wins, two further losses in mid-September saw the team sink to 21st in the table. Dooley, though, remained positive. "We've got to keep working hard to make up for lost ground," he said. "We have good reason to anticipate a move up the table."

The Owls though were embarking on a period that would see them win only two of the next 16 League and Cup games. After beating Cardiff in October, the Owls failed to win in the league again until January. Perhaps the greatest humiliation of this period was an 8-2 defeat in the League Cup away at QPR. The early season optimism had certainly faded by the time of that defeat in November.

Dooley's team were struggling on the pitch, at least partly due to circumstances beyond anyone's control. His squad suffered from injuries to key players, with John Sissons playing in only four of the first 24 games and the mercurial winger Willy Henderson missing 14 matches. More debilitating perhaps though was the effect of a "notorious virus" that struck the club that autumn. From early October well over a dozen senior players, along with Dooley himself, were struck down. Perhaps the most seriously affected by the bug was club captain John Holsgrove who collapsed in the Hillsborough showers after a game in October, spent a week in hospital under observation, and did not play again until mid-March. Other affected players returned more quickly but, as Dooley himself admitted, the majority returned far too soon.

Dooley and the club were loath to admit how difficult the situation had become, partly for fear of giving a psychological advantage to the opposition. The situation was not helped by the Football League who insisted that the Owls fulfilled their fixtures when the club asked for a postponement. Dooley blamed some of that decision on the fractious relationship between Eric Taylor and the secretary of the Football League, Alan Hardaker. However true that view is, the Owls fulfilled their fixtures, but needed to play youngsters to do so.

The club fumigated the dressing room and surrounding areas, kept training light and for a while told the players to stay away. By November the situation was improving but given the results on the pitch, the atmosphere among the fans had become angrier and more frustrated. Dooley appealed for calm and patience. "I am able once again to choose from a full squad," he said. "We can hope to go into 1974 in a more contented frame of mind than has been the case in the last few virus-hit weeks."

Fans, though, were staying away. Home games in November attracted crowds of well below 10,000 and some members of the 9,961 crowd for the home defeat to Orient showed their displeasure by throwing their cushions on to the pitch, and in the direction of the directors' box. Chairman Sir Andrew Stephen had started travelling to games by taxi as he feared that his car would be damaged. In December a crowd of only 7,925 witnessed a 3-0 defeat to Fulham. The Owls were 20th in the table, many in the crowd left early, and there was repeated anger at the board. It was clear that something would need to change.

By early December that change had come. Sir Andrew Stephen

had resigned as chairman of the club along with vice-chairman Keith Gardiner. Matt Sheppard took over as chairman and Bert McGee and Roy Whitehead (nominated by the Shareholders' Association – remember them?) joined the board. Sheppard was clear that he was going to improve matters, signalling his intent to "make the necessary changes to carry out the job" while Dooley felt he had lost friends, allies and people he could trust. Dooley travelled home from Crystal Palace, after securing a creditable draw, feeling more optimistic than he had for some time; in fact, the new board had met twice in quick succession to discuss his future. Two days later, on Christmas Eve, Dooley was sacked.

It seems the new board felt the need to act quickly and decisively. In doing so, they clearly lost the element of humanity that is needed in making such decisions. The decision was a surprise to all – with even the *Sheffield Star* journalists returning to work from their traditional Christmas drinks to produce a late second edition with the front-page headline: "Dooley Sacked!" Perhaps the best way of illustrating the general feeling of surprise and dismay is by the reactions of some of those who were there:

"All I got was the sack. I didn't even have time to sit down before the chairman told me. I went out shocked and waited for the players to come back from training to tell them. I made a pretty bad job of that as well and shed a few tears. It was a horrendous Christmas. My son Martyn, who was 17, was a Wednesday fanatic but he went up to his bedroom and tore down all the posters and pennants." *(Derek Dooley, speaking in 1994)*

"I was previously looking forward to Christmas Eve but now I just couldn't believe it." *(Jimmy Mullen)*

"The lads were dumbfounded." *(David Sunley)*

"The sacking was greeted with sheer horror." *(Brian Joicey)*

"It was a very black day at the club... everyone was very sad." *(Norma Lane, secretary to the manager)*

"My sacking at Christmas still hurts. The bitterness has diminished... but the memory has never stopped hurting." *(Derek Dooley, in the year 2000)*

Each player interviewed for this book still remembered the sacking of Dooley clearly and with a mixture of sadness and anger. It was a pivotal moment in the history of Sheffield Wednesday.

There are of course two sides to every story, and there is a view that in acting quickly and decisively, the club were able to ensure that there was a new manager in place with plenty of time to make a difference to the Owls' season. Dooley's team had struggled in the early part of the campaign and, with more players than usual already used in the first team, there was an argument against allowing Dooley to use more of the club's limited finances to bring in new players (something that Dooley was hoping to do soon after Christmas). There was a feeling from some that Dooley was not authoritative enough with the team. "Derek was a good manager, but for me he wasn't hard enough with the players," remembered Peter Swan afterwards. The board were also unanimous in their decision - so any remaining support that Dooley had from friends and allies on the board had disappeared or was subsumed.

In the chairman's statement, it was said that discussions were to be held with Dooley in order to find another role for him within the club – given the high regard in which he was held. I don't agree with these arguments. Dooley's sacking was a public relations disaster for the club with Christmas Eve still remembered as the date of Dooley's dismissal. When Carlos Carvalhal was also relieved of his duties "by mutual consent" on Christmas Eve 2017, reminders of Dooley's sacking were still published in the press. No suitable job was found for Dooley at the club (the only offer being one to work in the ticketing operation).

On December 13, 1973, then Prime Minister Edward Heath had announced plans for the "three-day week" to begin at midnight on the 31st of the month. The Owls brought in their own period of darkness a few days earlier. The final words on this should belong to Dooley himself:

• "Surely they could see that by choosing that moment to sack someone who had been connected with the club since 1947 and who had lost a leg playing in the famous blue and white stripes would be viewed as an insensitive action."

• "To be sacked on Christmas Eve was the most shattering experience of my life."

Dooley's career after his sacking is one that saw him become revered on both sides of the Steel City divide. Angry about his dismissal, Dooley resolved never to return to Hillsborough and spent some months working for a footwear manufacturer before, in 1974, Sheffield United asked him to return to football. Impressed by the job he had made of Wednesday's development fund, United asked him to join them as commercial manager. Thereafter his career lay with the Bramall Lane club, and he went on to become managing director and in 1999, chairman of the board, retiring in 2006.

By that time, he had made his peace with Wednesday. After declining many times, in 1992 he accepted an invitation from Wednesday's chairman to attend a match between the two Sheffield clubs at Hillsborough and was given a tremendous reception by all sides of the ground. Dooley was made an MBE for his services to sport in 2003. After his death is 2008, a section of Sheffield's inner ring-road was renamed Derek Dooley Way in further honour of his contribution to sport in the city. A statue of Dooley was unveiled outside Bramall Lane in 2010 with the inscription: "One of the Steel City's Greatest Sons." Derek Dooley certainly deserves to be remembered positively.

Dooley managed the Owls for a total of 138 games, winning 44 of them. He is rated by fans who remember the period 1973-76 as the second-best manager of that time. His final season is the first one considered by this book and was a very difficult one for Dooley with the club struggling in the Second Division. Injuries and illness decimated his team. Over the previous seasons however he had seen steady improvements and he did bring popular players to the club such as John Holsgrove, Brian Joicey, Ken Knighton, Willie Henderson and Eric Potts. His teams played good football and he achieved the last top half Division Two finish the club would see until the 1980s. And although his time as Owls manager will always be overshadowed by its ending, Dooley himself deserves to be fondly remembered as player and manager.

"Sheffield Wednesday are a great and famous club and I, as chairman, and all the members of the Board, are determined that the club will regain their rightful place among the top clubs. It was with greatest reluctance and after much deep thought that the Board unanimously decided to replace the team manager, and in accordance with tradition and good manners, it was my responsibility to inform Derek Dooley as soon as possible. It was most regretful that this coincided with Christmas Eve but... I speak for myself and all the directors without exception in stating we have a very high regard for Derek as a man and as an excellent employee...Unfortunately, our position in the Second Division is not satisfactory and the directors decided that a change was necessary. Derek has not been sacked as an employee. His contract will be honoured, and discussions will take place to see if a mutually agreed position and terms can be arranged for him."

Chairman's official statement on Derek
Dooley's removal as manager, 1973.

Gerald (Gerry) Young: December 1973 to January 1974 (Caretaker)

Gerry Young was born in Jarrow in 1936. He arrived at Hillsborough as a player in 1955, making his first team debut in 1957. Over the next five years he only made 32 first team appearances. As he eventually nailed down his first team place, Young went on to make a total of 345 league and cup appearances for the Owls between 1957 and 1971. He was a one-club man who served the Owls for over 20 years. Young was capped by England once, but suffered a thigh injury around the time he was called up for a second time and never featured again for the national team. He was famously dedicated to the Owls – to the extent that he refused the offer of missing a game on the afternoon of his wedding, travelling instead to feature for the team at Birmingham City. "There was no way I was going to miss the game," he later said.

Young appeared in the FA Cup final team of 1966, unfortunately making an error leading to Everton's winning goal. He came to accept that in the years afterwards. "If I have a regret, it can only be that having spent all my playing career at the club...

I always seem to be remembered for the slip... although these days I don't get upset when the subject crops up." He retired from playing in 1971 and was appointed to the club's coaching staff at the end of the 1970-71 season. After Derek Dooley's departure, Young was appointed as "coach in charge of dressing room and playing matters" until a new manager was appointed. As it happened, Young remained in charge for five weeks and seven matches, and lost only one; an FA Cup replay at First Division side Coventry.

The club remained 20th in the table throughout this period and Young's final game in charge was a 2-1 victory over Swindon Town; prior to that he oversaw a series of creditable draws. When new manager Steve Burtenshaw was appointed, he kept Young at the club as his assistant manager, a position that Young remained in until his dismissal, alongside Burtenshaw in 1975. He said later: "It was a sad moment when, in October 1975, I was told my services were no longer required – after half a lifetime and on my 39th birthday!" Following his dismissal Young opened a trophy and sports equipment shop alongside another former Owls' player, John Quinn, on Middlewood Road, Hillsborough.

Their business successfully traded for many years. Gerry Young was an exceptional servant to Sheffield Wednesday as a player, coach, and for this short period, as caretaker, and found watching the decline of the team hugely frustrating. "To see Wednesday in the Third Division and looking like no-hopers was painful beyond words," he said." Young's irritation in not being able to improve matters is clear. As "coach in charge" during this period he did a reasonable job, and his full career at S6 is one worthy of great respect.

Steve Burtenshaw: January 1974 until October 1975

Stephen (Steve) Burtenshaw was born in the Sussex town of Portslade-by-Sea in 1935. He had two elder brothers who were both professional footballers and spent his national service years in Germany before returning to England to begin his footballing career. He spent his entire 17-year playing career at Brighton and Hove Albion, making over 250 appearances for the Seagulls. He moved into coaching, first as player/assistant coach at Brighton. After his retirement from playing he gained a move to Arsenal as reserve team coach and later head coach. In 1973, he moved to Queens Park Rangers as head coach, a position he held for only seven months before joining the Owls.

The manager at QPR at the time, Gordon Jago, knew of Burtenshaw's ambitions to get into management, and said on his appointment to the role at QPR that it would only be temporary. Wednesday fans saw what a QPR team coached by Burtenshaw could do in an 8-2 League Cup defeat to the R's in November 1973. Burtenshaw had excellent coaching credentials, but no direct managerial experience.

Burtenshaw's appointment was something of a surprise to many Owls' followers. The club's long-serving and hugely influential general manager, Eric Taylor, had announced that he was to retire at the end of the season. Without Taylor's background influence, a common thought at the time was that a well-known "big-name" manager may well have taken the job. Taylor had a monumental influence at the club going back decades and it is difficult to fully define his role at the time. He was an organiser and administrator, and seemingly responsible for every aspect of the club away from the pitch. Transfers, infrastructure, salaries and pensions, along with the organisation of fixtures, all fell under his remit.

He took direction from the club's board, but it is telling that his secretary Isabel Brown referred to Taylor as "The Boss". Some managers had found his focus on the infrastructure of the club to be at the expense of the team and felt frustrated at their lack of influence and opportunity – most famously Harry Catterick, who went on to great success with Everton. Catterick was quoted as saying on his departure from the club: "The ambitions of Mr Taylor and I just did not mix. Mr Taylor's number one aim was the improvement of Hillsborough as a soccer stadium. My number one aim was the improvement of the team."

This was in 1961, and regardless of the rights and wrongs of the situation, Taylor remained a powerful figure at the club in the intervening years. Back to 1973. The club received over 70 applications for the manager's job and supposedly approached Ron Atkinson and Brian Clough. Atkinson was said to have turned down the job as he did not have enough relevant experience.

Other names mentioned in the press at the time included Don Megson and Colin Addison. The lure of a big club, without the supposed interference of Taylor, would seem to be one that a well-known manager may have jumped at. Burtenshaw's appointment did seem to be from the left-field for the Owls, as the 38-year-old became the club's youngest-ever manager.

Burtenshaw came with excellent references and reports from those who had worked with him. Legendary Tottenham Hotspur manager Bill Nicholson recommended him directly and Frank McLintock, who worked with Burtenshaw at QPR, said Burtenshaw "has tremendous knowledge of the game... I am sure that he will be a good man for Wednesday".

For his part, Burtenshaw admitted he was looking for 100 per cent effort from his players and that, if he got that, no-one could criticise them. The skills that Burtenshaw possessed were certainly those of an excellent and innovative coach. He has been described elsewhere as a highly-rated coach with a "big reputation" with "radical coaching methods". His new position, though, was as manager and it remained to be seen how well he would adapt to his new role.

At the time of Burtenshaw's arrival, the Owls had 16 games remaining of the 1973-4 season and were 20th in the Division Two rankings. The Owls were struggling to avoid relegation, and Burtenshaw's most pressing matter was ensuring survival. Six victories, and 16 points, was enough to do that by a solitary point and Burtenshaw's home debut as manager was another first for the Owls. Problems with power supplies relating to the three-day week saw the first ever Sunday game at Hillsborough, a 3-1 win over Bristol City in front of a promising crowd of over 15,000. The Owls also recorded impressive victories away at Notts County (5-1) and at home to Cardiff City (5-0) in successive matches in March. The two five goal displays took the Owls to what appeared to be the relative safety of 17th in the table, and reports of many of these early games contained plenty of positive praise for the Owls' displays. At face value, therefore, it seems that Burtenshaw made a successful start to his career as Owls' manager.

Yet behind all this positivity there were rumours of discontent among the players. The highs of the March victories were not repeated for the rest of the season, and the Owls suffered disappointing defeats (4-2 to Aston Villa) and humiliating ones (8-0 to Middlesbrough), before averting relegation thanks to a late goal in a 1-0 victory over Bolton in the final game of the season. Although Ken Knighton, scorer of the winning goal that day and club captain, said that the Owls' squad was "100 per cent behind the manager" others have said that Burtenshaw's methods alienated several players. In Keith Farnsworth's 'Wednesday Every Day of the Week, Dave Cusack described Burtenshaw as having "a touch of arrogance" while David Sunley admitted that "in the end he lost the respect of the players" Although the 1973-74 season had ended in celebration with a pitch invasion by jubilant fans and Ken Knighton being chaired from the pitch, it is clear in retrospect that the club's troubles were likely to mount going forward.

The 1974-75 season did indeed turn out to be one of the worst in Wednesday's history. Burtenshaw started the season with a certain degree of positivity, targeting promotion, and Brian Joicey continued the upbeat theme when he admitted he was "hopeful that next season [would] bring much better things." There were new signings (Bobby Brown, Hugh Dowd and Fred McIver) and big games against the likes of newly-relegated Manchester United, Southampton and Norwich to look forward to. Nine players were released by the club, with crowd favourite Willie Henderson moving to Hong Kong Rangers, and Burtenshaw also rearranged the backroom staff – appointing Jim McAnearney as second team coach and appointing Ron Staniforth and George McCabe to differing roles in the youth set-up.

Pre-season results were reasonably promising, including a 4-0 victory at Clyde on a three-match tour of Scotland, and although realistic Owls fans may not have been expecting a wholesale turnaround in the fortunes of the team, there were enough grounds for optimism that the club's prolonged slump since relegation from Division One in 1970 might be over. Burtenshaw seemed to agree but, by early September and just two points from four league games, it seemed that any early season optimism was likely to have been misplaced. The Owls were already bottom of the table and had been knocked out of the League Cup by Fourth Division Scunthorpe.

Late September saw the death of Eric Taylor, only two weeks after he had retired and at the age of just 62. On the pitch, the Owls also continued to struggle as they won only once in their opening 14 games. In his two-page spread in a September match-day programme, Burtenshaw said: "It is a question of plugging away at the job… there is plenty of belief we are on the right track." He soon attempted to lift the gloom by bringing in the classy 29-year-old Everton midfielder Colin Harvey. Harvey was an ex-England international who had been very successful in the top division with Everton, playing nearly 400 games. The Everton fans certainly did not appreciate his move to S6 and a banner was unveiled at Goodison Park on the day he made his Wednesday debut. It read: "£70,000 – An Insult to Colin Harvey – the White Pele."

Harvey remembers Wednesday as a club low on confidence and results did not improve after his arrival, with fans waiting until mid-October before witnessing the first home win of the season. With the Owls struggling, Burtenshaw made possibly his most successful signing by bringing in the Middlesbrough and Northern Ireland striker, Eric McMordie, on loan. The Owls had scored only nine goals in the 13 league games before his arrival and in the two months he was at Hillsborough, McMordie would score six goals and see his side move out of the bottom two places.

The dramatic 4-4 draw with Manchester United on December 7 is covered elsewhere in this book, but the Owls also scored three against York (3-0) and Notts County (3-3) in this period. McMordie returned to the North East in December 1974 with the club in 19th place but with a degree of renewed optimism. Despite the sale of star player Tommy Craig to Newcastle for £120,000, an excellent away victory at Southampton followed on December

28. Fans would surely not have believed that their team would score only two more goals in the league that season.

The year of 1975 began in relatively positive fashion for the Owls when they went 2-0 ahead in their FA Cup third round tie at Chelsea, before losing 3-2. The months that followed were desperate ones for everyone concerned with Wednesday and in many ways, the facts speak for themselves in this period. The Owls did not win a game again that season. They scored only two goals and gained only three points (from three draws) after New Year's Day in 1975. They hit the bottom of the table after a 2-0 home defeat to Portsmouth on January 18 and remained there for the rest of the season. Home crowds fell to between seven and eight thousand and relegation was confirmed on April Fool's Day after a 1-0 defeat to Nottingham Forest.

There were still five games remaining of the season. Top scorers for the season were Eric McMordie (six) and Tommy Craig (four). Both players had left the club in December. Burtenshaw was rarely quoted in the matchday programme during this period, with the anonymous "Voice of Hillsborough" section preferring general comments such as the team "concentrating on the task in hand, and working to achieve it" and telling loyal supporters that "no effort is being spared to put right the reasons for the club's continued decline." After relegation was confirmed, Burtenshaw offered his reasons for the team's failing. "One factor… is a lack of goals," he said.

"I think we've tried everything… It would be impossible for us to spend more time shooting… over the season we've made elementary mistakes … both senior and junior players have been doing it and we've not scored goals when the opportunities have been there."

Gerry Young (Burtenshaw's assistant) spoke about the need for a striker while players such as John Holsgrove and Brian Joicey later reflected that Burtenshaw was not a good fit for the club. "Very few were getting on with the manager… it was clear the club was not right for the manager," said Holsgrove, while Joicey conceded that Burtenshaw "did not know what was required for a Wednesday team."

Burtenshaw was appointed with an excellent coaching record, so if there is blame to be attached to his appointment, it must be shared with those who appointed him, and those players who did not perform to the best of their ability. That said, 1974-75 was a disastrous season for the Owls and Third Division football was their just reward. The failure of a football team is never the fault of one man alone but in the Owls' case, Burtenshaw must take his share of the responsibility. Burtenshaw's excellent coaching record and intelligent ideas did not transfer to the field of play often enough.

Given the disastrous season that preceded it, it is surprising that Burtenshaw remained in charge for the 1975-76 season. Pre-season games did not fill the fans with confidence – with two defeats in Scotland, and a heavy defeat to First Division Coventry. Burtenshaw, who admitted that relegation the previous season had left a bitter taste, did attempt to rebuild the squad, moving on players such as Peter Springett and Peter Eustace on free transfers and bringing in Neil Ramsbottom from Coventry and Andy Proudlove from non-league Buxton. Chief scout Fred Scott and physiotherapist Geoff Eggerton were both made redundant in a cost-cutting measure with the club supposedly only £5 within their agreed overdraft limit around this time.

Results, though, did not see an improvement. The first eight games saw the team gain just six points and put the Owls just one place above the relegation zone. They were also defeated (on penalties) in the League Cup by Division Four side Darlington; the club's first-ever penalty shootout loss. There was a moment of light in a 4-0 victory over Grimsby in September; but this was followed by a 1-0 defeat away at Chesterfield, in a game marred by scenes of violence and what was becoming known as "football hooliganism" off the pitch. Shortly after the Chesterfield game, the club underwent a boardroom reshuffle and Bert McGee became chairman. On October 1, 1975, Burtenshaw was sacked.

Burtenshaw remained in the game for many years after his dismissal as Owls' boss. He managed Everton and Arsenal on a caretaker basis in 1977 and 1986 respectively. He also returned to QPR as manager in 1978-79 (overseeing another relegation). He worked in various coaching and scouting positions at QPR, Arsenal and under Kevin Keegan at Manchester City before his retirement from the game in the early 2000s. He is perhaps most notorious in those years for his involvement in the so-called "bungs" scandal at Arsenal, which saw Gunners manager George Graham banned from the game for 12 months and Burtenshaw fined £7,500 and ordered to pay costs of £2,500.

Burtenshaw was manager at Hillsborough for a period that covered 71 games in league and cup. The Owls won only 14 of these games and lost 41. The club made little progress in cup competitions, losing to lower league opposition on more than one occasion. Owls' fans who remember the period place Burtenshaw as the "worst" manager of the period. With all Burtenshaw's obvious talents as a coach considered, I agree with that view. Burtenshaw oversaw one of the worst teams in Sheffield Wednesday's history, and must take his share of the blame for that. Burtenshaw seemed to lack the ability to fully bond with the players and, as more than one ex-player has commented, his man-management skills were lacking. John Holsgrove put it simply: "He could not manage people".

There is a counter argument to this negativity. Danny Cameron was more positive about Burtenshaw. Speaking with me in 2019 he said: "His enthusiasm, especially on the training ground was great but early on he fell into the trap of trying the same things that he had done with the Arsenal first team. Our squad of players were below the level he was aiming at and he probably ploughed on with the confidence in his coaching abilities without getting the improvement that his efforts deserved." Other players also spoke highly of his coaching abilities. Ken Blackburn, who played under Burtenshaw at Brighton, told me simply: "I knew him from my days at Brighton, he was a good coach!"

Neil Ramsbottom commented at the time of his signing that he was impressed with Burtenshaw while the author and journalist Alan Biggs remembers that Burtenshaw "signed the cultured Colin Harvey. Loaned Eric McMordie, who was full of flair. Together with Tommy Craig, they were fleetingly and flickeringly a fantastic attacking midfield...I recall feeling sorry for him when he was frogmarched into a room to face the media after his sacking was announced. It was akin to a public hanging. But he took it graciously and impressively." Several fans have stories of Burtenshaw's "niceness" – taking the time to talk to fans queuing for season tickets, arranging lifts for those whose coach broke down following the Owls to Swindon, presenting awards at Supporters' Club ceremonies and meeting fan representatives to discuss club matters. Burtenshaw also made some improvements to the club's youth scheme. The Middlewood Rovers team which he helped develop uncovered future first team players such as Brian Cox, Peter Shirtcliff and Mel Sterland. Burtenshaw was also hamstrung with the finances of the club, unable to prevent Tommy Craig leaving for example, and without the financial clout to bring in an adequate replacement.

It is for the results of the first team that any manager is primarily judged, however. Burtenshaw could not find a team that worked: an early version of the 'Tinkerman'. During the 1974-1975 season for instance he used six different players at right back and seven at left back, as well as four players in five different combinations in the two centre-back positions. Up front, he used 13 different striking combinations, with only one of these lasting more than three matches. It should not matter, but perhaps in 1970s Sheffield it did, that Burtenshaw was not a northerner. Dave Cusack described him as having a "Cockney attitude" and David Sunley has him as a "typical Cockney" (whatever one of those is!) Whatever the reason, Burtenshaw was not a good fit for the Owls and the decision to sack him in October 1975 was self-evidently the correct one.

Mr Burtenshaw was approached to contribute to this book. After initially agreeing to meet, I was told that, on reflection, he found thinking about his time at Hillsborough too upsetting and a little depressing. Therefore, his time as manager at Hillsborough will be fondly remembered by very few Wednesdayites, nor by Burtenshaw himself. His time in charge was perhaps the club's true *"Lowest Ebb"*.

"The directors feel that it is in Wednesday's best interests long

term for a new man to come into Hillsborough. I won't criticise Steve Burtenshaw in any way, shape or form for he did a lot of good for Wednesday. But with the lack of success we had to take action and with Gerry Young being Chief Coach he must bear some of the responsibility too. Steve took it like the man he is."

A magnanimous Bert McGee on Steve Burtenshaw's sacking. (Voice of Hillsborough, Matchday programme, October 4 1975.)

James (Jim) McAnearney: October 1975 (Caretaker)

Jim McAnearney was born in Dundee in 1935. After beginning his career in Scottish amateur football with Dundee St Stephen's he had a successful playing career at Plymouth, Watford, Bradford City and at Hillsborough, scoring 68 goals in more than 300 league games. At Hillsborough though he never completely established himself as a first team regular. He only played 40 first team games for Wednesday, between his debut, in a 1-1 Hillsborough draw with Liverpool in February 1954 and his final game, a 2-1 loss at Bristol Rovers on April 30 1959.

He was, though, on Wednesday's books as a player for almost a decade from April 1950 until January 1960. Jim's older brother Thomas (Tom) was a more regular starter at Hillsborough – making 382 appearances between 1950 and 1965 including time as team captain. Tom also returned to S6 as assistant manager in the two years leading to relegation from Division One in 1970. Youngest brother John also played youth and reserve team football for the Owls but was released without making a first-team appearance. Jim was one of the first players to gain coaching qualifications, achieving his FA coaching badge when he was only 23 years old. He moved into coaching while at Bradford, followed by a spell as caretaker manager at Valley Parade.

He then moved to Rotherham, first as coach under Tommy Docherty, then succeeding him as manager, before moving to S6 as reserve team manager under Steve Burtenshaw in May 1974. McAnearney supposedly turned down the job of managing the Iranian national team in order to take up his post at Hillsborough. After Burtenshaw and his assistant were both relieved of their duties by the Owls, Jim McAnearney was placed in charge of the team on a caretaker basis. At the time, new club chairman Bert McGee claimed to be unsure of who he would appoint next: "I want a winning kind of manager... I have not met him yet, so I cannot say who he will be." McAnearney paid tribute to the club's fans at the same time: "People can talk about the loyalty of fans at the big clubs... we owe something to those who stick by us. I hope we can get results – and in style."

He told The *Star*: "I'm a bit shocked, but confident I can do the job." Jimmy McAnearney (as the matchday programme called him) remained as caretaker manager for two games. His first was a 2-2 draw and his second a 4-1 home win. These results lifted the Owls to the relative heights of 13th in the table – the loftiest position they would occupy all season. New manager Len Ashurst kept Jim as part of his new backroom team when appointed as manager. After leaving Hillsborough, Jim later managed Frickley Athletic, Scarborough and Hallam FC, his final role in football. McAnearney continued to live in Sheffield, where he started and ran a successful machine tool hire business, before he passed away in 2017, still in his adopted city. The McAnearney brothers were great servants to football and to the Owls, and Jim certainly did not let the fans or his family down in his short-lived spell as manager.

Len Ashurst: October 1975 until October 1977
Len Ashurst had a varied and interesting career in football. In a lengthy playing career (1957-73), Ashurst played more than 400 games for Sunderland with another 40-plus at Hartlepool as player/coach along with a handful of games for England youth and England under-23s. Before making his professional debut, Ashurst was on the books of Liverpool and Wolverhampton Wanderers, and after retirement from playing he managed ten clubs in a career spanning 1971 to 1993.

He also worked for the Football Association and the Premier League. His autobiography – written by Ashurst himself, rather than being 'ghosted' by another writer - includes an introduction from the legendary Bobby Robson, suggesting the esteem that Ashurst is held in by many of the great and good in the game. On the back cover of the book, Lord Neil Kinnock describes Ashurst as "the sort of man who makes British football great." Ashurst managed over 1,000 games in his career and was inducted into the League Managers' Association Hall of Fame in 2014 in recognition of that achievement. From today's perspective, Ashurst certainly has an enviable CV.

It would seem that the Owls had pulled off something of a coup therefore when they appointed Ashurst as manager in 1975. It was, though, still early in Ashurst's managerial career. He had spent just over three years at Hartlepool, taking them from the bottom of Division Four to the top half of the table, and their league position improved in each season he spent there (although they did need to apply successfully for re-election to the league in 1971).

Moving to Gillingham was a step up to the Third Division, and he successfully steered his team to a top-half finish in 1974-75. Ashurst and his wife found life in Kent difficult, though, and admitted in his autobiography that they found it difficult to adjust from having dozens of friends to none in Gillingham. Despite taking a Gillingham side to play a Buckingham Palace team, meeting Elton John and defeating Bobby Charlton's Preston team during his time as manager, Ashurst was happy to get what he described as a "big football club opportunity" with the Owls. Ashurst left Gillingham in seventh place in Division Three and moved to Sheffield Wednesday in October 1975. He was still a young man of 36 and about to take on one of the biggest jobs of his career.

Ashurst said on arrival that he was "glad to be back among northern folk, where they call a spade a spade and expect to give a fair day's work for a fair day's pay." In language that will seem similar to more recent supporters of the Owls he went on to describe the club as a "slumbering giant that has been down in the dumps too long." Ashurst's autobiography gives an insight into the size of the task, however, describing the Owls as a club that had "slid into degradation", a task that was "formidable and onerous" and a playing staff that was "lacking in quality".

His playing squad was not lacking in number, however – when Ashurst arrived at S6, he was quoted as saying that there were almost 60 professional footballers at the club. His initial interview though suggested that "they (the players) are going to be successful" and that the team would aim to "play excitingly, because that will mean that we will be winning.".

David Cusack remembers the introduction of Ashurst to the club positively. "Lennie was very honest, very committed," he said". Club captain Colin Harvey predicted that "Ashurst will be good for the club... he has already given the players a necessary boost." Ashurst certainly seemed determined to change things at Hillsborough. Other quotes from his initial interviews saw him talking about "a new broom", things that were "missing" and his desire that "every little thing (is) right". Things would certainly change at S6. For the players, Ashurst would deliver a culture shock.

Ashurst brought his trainer Tony Toms with him to Hillsborough. Toms was an interesting character having spent time at a high level in the military (Chief of Staff in the Royal Marine Commando Physical Training Wing, to be precise) and working on television before moving into sport with Ashurst at Hartlepool and Gillingham. Toms' father had been Field Marshal Montgomery's personal bodyguard. Ashurst knew him as "Tomsie". He also knew that the fitness of the players was Toms' area of expertise. "I am concerned about every area of the club except training," explained Ashurst in his first interview with the matchday programme. "If you have an expert on your side, you don't mess around with him". It is not clear if the players were so impressed with Toms. Cusack remembers his introduction to Ashurst and Toms: "This idiot walks in on his hands and starts to do vertical press ups – it was Tony Toms." Jimmy Mullen on the other hand remembers Toms as "good as gold with the lads and brilliant for dressing room spirit." Toms described the state of the club when he arrived as "shocking" and the infamous trip to the Yorkshire Moors, organised by Toms to build team spirit, is covered elsewhere in the book.

Again, not every player was inspired by his methods – Ashurst tells the story of right back Bernard Shaw pointedly making his objections to that trip known, by completing his warm-up before the next game in a survival suit! Ashurst and Toms worked closely and effectively together. It would be unfair to describe Toms as simply responsible for fitness. He and Ashurst were a team.

Ashurst had walked out on Gillingham to take the position at Hillsborough – presumably breaking the terms of his contract with the Gills. Ashurst himself claims that he was issued a personal writ (delivered by courier) as soon as he arrived at Hillsborough. Other sources suggest that a writ was delivered to the club in 1976. Either way, the matter wasn't settled until 1977 when the Owls paid £5,000 compensation. The situation provoked some bitterness at Gillingham and, ironically enough, the Gills were to be Ashurst's fourth opponents as Owls' manager on Bonfire Night, 1975. Ashurst relates how the new manager of Gillingham instructed his players not to talk to him or face disciplinary action. It did not help the Gillingham team however, as a Brian Joicey goal saw the Owls claim their first victory of Ashurst's reign.

He was pleased with the victory, being quoted in the matchday programme as saying: "The match with Gillingham was the one I most wanted to win in (all) my years in management... I believe it will mark a turning point in Sheffield Wednesday's fortunes." Also in that programme was a plea to call the club if anyone was able to offer digs to Toms and Ashurst. Ashurst's time at S6 had started slowly but steadily therefore and it was a relief to all involved to gain that first league win at a relatively early stage of his management of the club.

Ashurst was to stay at Hillsborough until 1977 and Toms much longer – becoming an important part of Jack Charlton's successful rejuvenation of the club. I assume therefore that they both found somewhere to stay! The Gillingham game was not a turning point, however, as the team did not win another game in the league until the end of January. In that period, the team played 11 games, with seven draws and four defeats. The FA Cup saw some respite with two wins over non-league opposition before a third-round defeat away at Charlton Athletic, but this period appeared to be one of great frustration for Ashurst. After a 2-2 draw at Hillsborough vs Preston in December 1975 including a late equaliser for the away team Ashurst was furious, accusing his players of a lack of professionalism and throwing the game away, and ordering them to report for extra training the following day.

December 1975 was a difficult month for the club, with captain Colin Harvey forced into retirement due to injury and Ashurst surprising some by putting fan favourites Eric Potts, Jimmy Mullen, David Sunley and Roger Wylde on the transfer list. Ronnie Ferguson, who had scored a goal on his Second Division debut was granted a free transfer and joined Darlington. Ashurst had held talks with all the players over their futures and was determined to ensure that any deals were concluded to the benefit of the club, but Wednesday ended the year 22nd in the table having won just one of Ashurst's league games. The manager was not happy. "When I first saw this lot play, I was disgusted," he said at the time. "They had grown used to losing…. In training they were a joke… All we can do this season is hang on in Division Three… If we do that I'll be satisfied – and it hurts me to have to say it."

Ashurst was certainly aware of the extent of the task and had plans in place to move the club forward, but his time at Hillsborough would get more difficult before it got better. Wednesday were struggling financially and by mid-January 1976 the remaining members of his backroom team – Jim McAnearney and Ron Staniforth, were both made redundant for financial reasons, leaving Ashurst and Toms as the only full-time staff. The Owls were also hit by a flu outbreak in February 1976 which saw the home game against Chesterfield postponed, and Hillsborough completely closed to prevent the disease spreading further.

An away game at Shrewsbury was also postponed and Ashurst himself was laid low by the illness, with Toms left in caretaker charge. Toms went four games without defeat – " Every point you get is a golden one," he said at the time – and when Ashurst returned, the team then fell to four successive defeats, leaving them at a season-low second bottom of the table and with a huge amount to do if they were to avoid relegation.

Ashurst was determined not to let the grass grow under his feet, however, and was busy in the transfer market. Peter Feeley arrived after a protracted transfer from Gillingham, to join his old boss, and goalkeeper Barry Watling signed on an initial trial basis. Sunley left to join Hull City while Potts (supposedly) moved into painting and decorating – with his number published in the matchday programme for anyone who wanted to use his services! In reality Potts continued playing for the club through to 1977.

Although the new players did not all prove to be huge successes at Hillsborough - Watling, for example, only played one game - there were signs that Ashurst was determined to change things and bring a new attitude to the club. In a sign of the financial difficulties that the club (and by default, Ashurst) were dealing with, the new players were not given accommodation in any of Sheffield's hotels, but rather in rooms above Sheila's Café, which stood within walking distance of the ground.

In Daniel Gordon's "A Quarter of Wednesday", Brian Joicey – who left the club in the summer of 1976, remembered: "He (Ashurst) got rid of me... He got rid of a few others... But he also got rid of the losing habit." The shake-up in the team began to see some positive results as the season began to near its end. Four consecutive 1-0 home wins in March and April, along with a series of hard-fought away draws, saw the Owls keep pace with their relegation rivals. As Ashurst put it in March 1976: "All is not lost. That is what everyone has got to realise".

The final weeks of the troubled season started with more movement of players as Danny Cameron moved to Preston North End and a hero of the 1974 escape from relegation, Ken Knighton, joined the training staff with some responsibility for the reserve and junior teams. Ashurst was working tirelessly behind the scenes to improve the youth set-up at the club – something that would come to fruition in the years after he left. The manager was doing his best to rebuild a club that was, in his own words, "in the mire".

The Wednesday he joined was overstaffed, in financial difficulties, and with players who were used to losing games. The battles of 1975-76 as Ashurst put his own stamp on the club were ones that needed to be fought. To my mind, Ashurst brought the club back from the brink. This was not a painless process, however, and Ashurst may not have got every decision correct. The final battle of that season, though, still needed to be fought.

Wednesday's survival as a Third Division club depended on securing a result in the final game of the season against Southend. That game is covered elsewhere in the book but ended 2-1 to the Owls. The win doomed Southend to the drop and cost their manager Arthur Rowley his job. It also allowed Owls' fans to have a wry smile at their city rivals United, who finished rock bottom of the First Division that season under Jimmy Sirrell. Ashurst's management had helped secure the Owls' Third Division status – by a solitary point. That moment in April 1976 is the one that gives the title to this book. It was the Owls "Lowest Ebb" – the lowest league position the club have ever finished in their history.

Owls' fans who travelled away from home that season did not witness a single away victory. Home attendances regularly struggled to reach five figures and the club's finances were clearly in a dire position. And yet for many it was a moment of great positivity. Ashurst had put in place a new hard-working ethos and had proved that he could take tough decisions. The Owls had shown that they could win games and still (at times) attract a large crowd. Ashurst was now free to put his mark on the club still further and begin the rebuilding job in earnest.

Ashurst remained in charge for his only full season of 1976-77. That season was one of relative success, with the team flirting with the promotion places for a time and finishing a respectable eighth. There were still some difficult days that season, including heavy defeats at Swindon, Walsall and Preston. Ashurst was, though, building a team more in his image. He moved on more players with nine free transfers after the 1975-76 season. He successfully integrated young players such as Chris Turner into the team and as finances improved, was able to successfully bring in players such as Tommy Tynan, Paul Bradshaw and Bob Bolder.

Roger Wylde proved a formidable striker and scored over 20 goals in the league - the first Owls player to do so since David Layne, 13 years earlier. The Owls remained in with chance of promotion for most of the season and were only three points off, as late as April. A 4-0 defeat to Terry Venables' Crystal Palace effectively put an end to the team's promotion prospects, but Ashurst had seen enough to believe that only a few tweaks were needed to sustain a promotion push the following year. The fans had no reason to doubt Ashurst's assessment, either.

Unfortunately for them, and for Ashurst, the reality was rather different and Wednesday began the 1977-78 season without a win in their first ELEVEN games. Ashurst was sacked in October after defeat to Preston left the Owls bottom of the table, and the previous game had seen a banner unveiled on the North Stand (after a late Plymouth Argyle equaliser) reading: ASHURST OUT-McCREADIE IN. Eddie McCreadie was the then-Chelsea manager and after a short caretaker spell with Ken Knighton in control, Jack Charlton continued the process of rebuilding the team.

Many of Ashurst's players were part of Charlton's promotion-winning squad of 1979-80 and Ashurst himself believes that perhaps his biggest legacy was recommending Charlton to the chairman as his replacement. Ashurst appeared to show no bitterness at his departure, insisting his team had given Owls' fans a lot to be proud of and wishing the club success in the future, while Tony Toms remained at the club alongside chief scout John Harris, with both playing key roles in Jack Charlton's successful tenancy. Ken Knighton was "shattered" by Ashurst's dismissal and in his own autobiography, Ashurst remembers chairman Bert McGee telling him years later that he had "laid the foundations of the club's success in later seasons."

Overall, Ashurst was in charge for 92 league games, of which 31 had been won, with 89 points gained. His Owls teams reached the third round of the FA Cup in 1975 and the fourth round of the League Cup in 1976 – a run that included a famous "giant-killing" victory away at Wolverhampton Wanderers. He even won a trophy, with his team winning The Shipp Cup, a pre-season tournament prior to the 1976-77 season. Owls' fans who remember the period place Ashurst as the best manager of the 1973-76 period – comfortably ahead of Derek Dooley and Steve Burtenshaw. With the greatest of respect to the other two, this is an opinion I share. Len Ashurst is interviewed elsewhere in the book, giving his opinion of his time with the Owls.

Club Statement October 5th 1977: "The directors of Sheffield Wednesday announced that, as from today, Mr Len Ashurst will no longer be their manager. Until an appointment is made, Ken Knighton is in charge of team matters. The board wish to record their appreciation of Mr Ashurst's dedication and application, and it is to be regretted that success was not his reward"

As quoted in Keith Farnsworth: "Wednesday!"

Conclusions

Each of the three full-time Wednesday managers during the period 1973-76 oversaw a decline. Derek Dooley saw the team to tenth place in 1972-73. When he was dismissed on Christmas Eve that year, the team were in 20th position. Steve Burtenshaw's tenure saw the club relegated to Division Three, where he left the team in 16th place. Len Ashurst ensured survival that season (1975-76) but the team did fall to 20th place – the club's *"Lowest Ebb"*. The story of the management of the team cannot therefore be seen to be one of success, although both Dooley and Ashurst are generally well remembered by Owls' fans. The manner of Dooley's dismissal is one that still pains many and his earlier exploits as a player meant that he would always remain a hero to Owls' supporters.

Ashurst began a rebuilding process that was successfully continued by Jack Charlton later in the decade. Burtenshaw's time as manager has little to recommend it. It is possible to understand what he was trying to achieve but, given the circumstances and the players and finance at his disposal, he was unlikely to achieve it, although he did go on to have a relatively successful career elsewhere in the game. The two caretakers did little wrong in their short time in charge. My fans' survey of those who remember the time puts the full-time managers in order of "best" to "worst" as Ashurst, then Dooley, then Burtenshaw. The evidence from the time supports this view.

AN INTERVIEW WITH WILLIE HENDERSON

Willie Henderson was a talented, skilful and very direct forward player who appeared on the wing for the Owls between 1972 and 1974. Born in Bailston, Scotland, Willie had made over 500 professional appearances for Glasgow Rangers and for Scotland by the time he moved to Hillsborough. He had won a series of trophies during his time with the Glasgow club, though his time there ended on something of a sour note as he was left out of the squad for the 1972 European Cup Winners' Cup final game against Dinamo Moscow.

Willie moved to Sheffield after being released by Rangers that summer. Henderson played 56 games for the Owls, scoring five goals over the next two seasons. He later went on to play in Hong Kong, before returning to Scotland to see out his career with a brief spell at Airdrie. Willie now lives in Scotland and it was from his West Lothian home that he spoke to me in the autumn of 2019.

Tell me how it was that you moved to Hillsborough, Willie.
I'd been released by Glasgow Rangers and I was sat at home wondering what I was going to do next with my career. The phone rang – I picked it up and the voice on the other end said: "How are you, bonnie lad?" I didn't know who it was, so I had to ask. "It's Fred Scott, chief scout at Sheffield Wednesday Football Club. I tried to sign you when you were fifteen. Do you think I've a chance now?" Well, I was really pleased. I knew of Sheffield Wednesday of course, big club, and was prepared to make the move south of the border. I arranged with Fred to meet him and Derek Dooley at the Hallam Towers Hotel in Sheffield. I was excited by the thought of coming down and getting on with things.

We did need to talk about money though! Derek asked me what I wanted – so I told him. He told me that it was a lot of money, so I told him that another player – who I won't name –

had just been transferred for a huge sum of money and was not fit to lace my boots! Anyhow, we agreed the deal and I was ready to make a start. I was still only 27-years-old, and I felt I had plenty to offer.

How did you find Derek Dooley as a manager?

He was great for me. I was a direct, fast winger. I loved taking on the full back and getting the ball across. Derek let me get on with my game. He did talk tactics with the team, and plans for taking on the opposition, but he did not interfere with what I felt was my natural game. I was an orthodox winger – I hugged the touchline. He let me spend the majority of my time in the opposition half which I loved.

How did you find it when he was sacked?

I know that Sheffield Wednesday had been a huge part of Derek's life, from playing and his injury, through to management. Results hadn't been great though, and in a way it's part of football. A sad time though.

Who did you enjoy playing alongside at Hillsborough?

There were some great players there when I joined. Peter Rodrigues and David Clements, they were both internationals. Tommy Craig, he was some player, a great guy with a fantastic left foot. Peter Eustace, John Sissons, Mick Prendergast, Brian Joicey. We had some good players. Brian Joicey used to take me to task if I crossed the ball and it was further than six inches from his head! Jimmy Mullen as well, another good guy. The team had harmony. We got on well both on and off the pitch. That team and those players meant the world to me at the time.

How about particular games – any favourites?

Oh lots, I loved playing at Hillsborough particularly. There was one against Huddersfield and one against Bolton I remember. The Bolton one was early on in my first season, and I remember thinking I'd played well and reminding Derek Dooley afterwards of the other player who wasn't fit to lace my boots! I really enjoyed my football at Sheffield Wednesday. That has a psychological effect. I was enjoying the games, so I worked hard in training, and played well the next game as well. After a disappointing end to my time at Rangers I was happy in my football again, and I really appreciated that.

Did things change for you in your second season, or when Steve Burtenshaw took over?

I broke my nose that season, so missed some games. Steve Burtenshaw though was no problem. Like Derek Dooley, he allowed me to keep playing in my own style. I enjoyed playing for him. These were the days before some of the innovations of the modern game, so I was allowed again to play in my natural style. I played a good number of games for Sheffield Wednesday – and was lucky with injuries. I had a few full backs who mistook my legs for the ball, but I never got a serious one – no leg break or anything like that. For both Derek and Steve, I was lucky to play and play to my strengths.

Three questions now, Willie, that have been sent to me by fans from the era... Did you ever time yourself running one hundred metres or yards?

Good question! No, I don't think so, though I do know that I could run 40 yards in 4.8 seconds. I'd slow down a little if I had to run further than that – but that's what I would need to do on the football pitch.

Is there any truth in the stories about your eyesight?

[Laughs]. Put it this way, I played over 600 professional games, so my eyesight can't have been that bad can it!

What are your memories of Sheffield itself?

Well I lived in the city, off Ecclesall Road. I loved it there the people were always very welcoming. I was honoured one Christmas when Lulu was playing at the Fiesta Club in Sheffield. Anyhow, they asked me and her to switch on the lights in Sheffield that year. I thought that was a great honour for two people from Scotland. So yes, I loved Sheffield and playing for Sheffield Wednesday – it was a very special time in my life.

Back to the football, you left at the end of the 1973-74 season. Did you feel then that the club was going to struggle in the coming years?

No, I had no inclination of that at all. I'd signed for Hong Kong Rangers as it was an opportunity to try something new and experience a new culture in a different part of the world. The agreement was, though, that if I came back to England for any reason it was to return to Sheffield Wednesday. My contract ran for another year, but the club had let me go for the opportunity. I would have been happy to come back if needed though.

Do you have any other memories of your time at Hillsborough that you'd like to share?

Only to say that I was very lucky in my career and my time in Sheffield was part of that. I have some great memories of my career – from Sir Stanley Matthews, who was my boyhood hero, ringing me to take part in his testimonial game (forward line Di Stefano, Henderson and Puskas!) to great success with Rangers to winning titles in Hong Kong. I was very happy in Sheffield and thoroughly enjoyed my football there.

How about nowadays Willie, what keeps you busy in retirement?

Well, I act as an ambassador for Rangers on matchdays. I've done that for 17 years now, I think. I was delighted to be asked. I had great times as a player with Rangers and it was only the manager at the time I left that I had an issue with. It's kept me occupied, and I'm pleased to be back involved with the club. Then of course, there's my daughter's charity. My daughter, Michelle, died in 2012 of cervical cancer. She was only 28. She'd set up a charitable trust, The Michelle Henderson Cervical Cancer Trust, to raise awareness of the condition and in turn raise funds towards hospital equipment, medicines and support groups for women suffering from the illness. I've dedicated a lot of my time and effort since she died to help fundraise for the trust. We've raised over £350,000 and more importantly used that money to buy equipment and help save lives. We provided some equipment in Sheffield to the Jessops Hospital. I wanted to help in Sheffield as a thank you for the welcome I've always had in Sheffield, and for the good times I enjoyed there. We're trekking across the Himalayas next year, and even at 77 as I'll be then, I'm aiming to complete the whole thing!

If I think of one common denominator in my life, it's been people. The people of Sheffield were fantastic to me. And it's been none more so since the loss of my daughter. I've been approached by a few people to write about my life – I'm glad that the part about my time in Sheffield is out there. As I said, it was a special time for me.

HILLSBOROUGH STADIUM

The story of how a magnificent stadium was developed for the World Cup of 1966, and the experiences of the fans who attended games there even as the team drifted to its "Lowest Ebb". The stadium was still seen as something to be very proud of even a decade after the World Cup. "Wembley of the North"? Maybe.... Or perhaps a high-quality venue in its own right.

Before considering Hillsborough Stadium, it is worth a study of football grounds more generally. In common with much else during the period, football stadia were beginning to change in the mid-1970s. The facilities at many grounds had been developing since the late 1950s. In his book, *The Football Grounds of England and Wales,* Simon Inglis details how clubs spent £11 million on ground improvements between 1958 and 1968. Much of this development was in the First Division, and in the top league the developments continued into the 1970s. Huge new stands were built at Everton in 1971 – costing £1 million - and at Chelsea in 1974, at twice that amount.

This was a time before the out-of-town "flat pack" stadiums of more recent years. Many grounds were in tightly-packed residential areas with some, such as Leicester's Filbert Street and Luton's Kenilworth Road, accessible through turnstiles packed in between gaps in the housing around the ground. Every ground had standing areas for spectators, and it was not until 1981 that Coventry's Highfield Road became the country's first all-seater stadium.

At lower league stadia, there were far fewer developments. The rising expense of new stands (one at Chester cost over £500,000 in 1978) combined with falling attendances tended to mean that clubs managed with what they had. As gates fell, some clubs did not even feel it worth keeping all areas of their ground in a state of decent repair. Others such as Orient found it cheaper to install seating rather than improve their terracing to new safety standards. Chelsea, Brentford, Bury and York all fenced off areas of terracing, rather than meet the large costs needed.

Those new safety standards followed the Ibrox tragedy in 1971. Following the end of an Old Firm game, someone fell in a stairway and in the moments that followed, 66 people died in the crush that was caused. The government ordered an inquiry which was chaired by Lord Wheatley and led to the Safety at Sports Grounds Act of 1975, which required that grounds which held over 10,000 people must have a safety certificate issued by the local authority. Simon Inglis detailed the precision that the act required: *"The safety certificate not only specifies the ground's total capacity, but also how many each section might hold, and the number, size and situation of all the entrances and exits (including emergency and fire exits). These should be maintained and free of obstruction. The certificate also states how many crush barriers are necessary and their strength and situation."*

Terraces were to be divided into sections, home and away fans were to be segregated and it was to be no longer possible to move around the ground. The legislation was enforced over time – with Division One clubs the first to comply by 1976. Second Division clubs were to follow by 1979. These changes were expensive, and the Football Grounds Improvement Trust was created in 1975 with money from the Pools "Spot the Ball" competition to help clubs pay for the necessary work. By 1983, all 92 clubs in the English leagues had received funding from the Trust to support developments. The experience of the football fans of the mid-1970s was about to change.

Sheffield Wednesday's Hillsborough home had a capacity of 55,000 in the mid-1970s. There were three covered stands – the North, South and West Stands, and the huge uncovered Spion Kop. Under the leadership of Eric Taylor, the stadium had been thoroughly redeveloped in the 1960s. It regularly held important matches, including FA Cup semi-finals, and was used for four matches during the 1966 World Cup. The draw for the World Cup matches would see South Yorkshire play host to Switzerland, Germany, Spain and Argentina – Taylor declaring at the time that "Sheffield has come out of it quite well. We have not got the cream, but we have not got the rabbits either." Hillsborough was commonly nicknamed the "Wembley of the North" at this time and even a decade after the World Cup, was still seen by many as a world class stadium. It was well used during our period even as attendances for Wednesday games fell. The World Cup had brought a degree of pride and positivity to Sheffield and Hillsborough.

As the academic Tosh Warwick has it: "World Cup fortnight in Sheffield undoubtedly succeeded in creating positive perceptions of the "Steel City" as a result of articulating traditional, industrial northernness that brought praise from visitors to the city, the business community and Sheffielders alike."

This chapter discusses the stadium itself a decade or so after the World Cup; the perception of the fans and how they found the stadium during a time when attendances dropped dramatically. It recounts how the ground was used for other games than those played by the Owls and looks to investigate how far that positivity identified by Tosh Warwick about Sheffield and the stadium remained during the club's struggles of the 1970s.

Hillsborough Stadium was broadly the same in 1973 as it had been in 1966 for the World Cup. The South Stand was the oldest of the three covered stands, designed by the architect Archibald Leitch and opened in 1914. The stand replaced the "Olive Grove" stand that the club had moved, brick by brick, from their previous home to the new site at Hillsborough. Although the stand was the oldest in the ground, it had seen improvements for the World Cup after being converted at that stage into an all-seated area.

A total of 3,356 seats were installed, at a cost of £27,600 at that time. The South Stand was beautifully dressed with the large triangular centre piece including a famous clock and "Sheffield Wednesday, Hillsborough" written in large and impressive text. This area was obscured by a TV gantry where equipment and the people controlling it would sometimes block the view of the clock and sign. The front section of the South Stand remained as wooden "tip-up" uncovered seats during our period, the back being fully covered.

Inglis' book describes the North Stand as "the most advanced football grandstand ever built at a British football ground" at the time of its opening in 1961, after 11 months of building at a cost of £150,000. That money was raised partly by selling debenture shares which, along with a generous amount of interest (six per cent), offered the owner the right to buy a ticket for any game at the ground. All 9,882 seats were protected by the weather by the architecturally significant design; the roof was supported by huge girders which cantilevered from the back of the stand over 16 feet in beyond even the front seats. This design was very popular among supporters and the stand became known as simply the "cantilever" by many. The view from every seat was unobstructed with the steep gradient providing a feeling of being on top of the action, even in the higher reaches of the stand.

The West Stand was rebuilt for the 1966 World Cup. It was opened in 1965 and cost £110,000 to build – half of which was donated by the club's development fund. The stand was built as a two-tier structure with 4,471 seats at the top, and terraces below. These three stands were complemented by the huge Kop, which held 16,850 people and was uncovered. The Kop had an irregular shape, described as a "wild hill" by Inglis!

There were indeed some trees that grew at the back corner of the Kop giving more evidence of its wild nature. Alongside the four main areas of the ground, there was a further small area of terracing which is nowadays known as the North West Corner. Fans have referred to this area as the "cheesecake", the "Crow's Nest" and simply the "Lepp Corner". Cheesecake presumably due to its triangular shape; Lepp Corner due to its position between the North and West Stands, backing on to Leppings Lane; Crow's Nest for its viewpoint. Whatever it was called, it was a popular spot for some fans.

Hillsborough was fully floodlit as early as 1955 – with the first game to be played under lights being Derek Dooley's testimonial game. The floodlights had been installed in 1954 at a cost of around £15,000. A huge crowd of 55,000 attended that game and saw the lights, which were known as the best in the country at that stage. The floodlights remained unchanged into the mid-

1970s. The lights formed a rectangle, with one at each corner and one halfway along each of the South and North Stands.

It was only in 1977 that the club invested in a new system. The club had also invested in an electronic scoreboard in time for the World Cup. This was state of the art in the mid-1960s but by the 1970s was tired and dated. One supporter remembered how the "G" was broken. Therefore, in a game against Grimsby, the scoreboard showed "The Owls 0, Frimsby 1!"

The Penistone Road end of the ground, behind the Spion Kop, was lit up with a huge neon sign saying: "Sheffield Wednesday". Up until 1970, this was prefixed with "First Division Football at..." but this was removed following relegation from the top-flight. The other end of the ground on the entrance to the West Stand had a large sign simply stating: "Sheffield Wednesday". A large sports hall was built behind the North Stand, catering for the press at the time of the World Cup but used by the team in the mid-1970s. The hall was also available for the general public to book for football, badminton or other sporting uses.

Outside the ground notable buildings were the Ozzie Owl Club, which is covered elsewhere in the book, the commercial office (home of the development fund), and the club shop. The shop was on the south side of the stadium, towards Penistone Road and between the gates to the ground and the commercial office.

The shop shared its space with the Supporters' Club throughout our period, until the Supporters' Club moved out in 1977. The Supporters' Club office was decorated with many pennants and rosettes, gifted by Mrs Yeardley, mother of the late John Yeardley, who was a keen Owls' fan. Unfortunately, in September 1973, the office was broken into and these items stolen. Other merchandising booths were situated around the ground, which offered souvenirs including the popular Ozzie Owl range – introduced after Ozzie was launched as the club's mascot in 1967.

Hillsborough then was still an impressive stadium in the mid-70s even if in some areas it was beginning to show some wear and tear. It was, though, a stadium in need of a fanbase. The average attendance in the three seasons of this book was 14,749, then 13,292 and finally 11,038. Attendances dropped below five figures on many occasions and the averages were boosted by large crowds for some games such as those against Manchester United and Aston Villa. The match day experience then was somewhat different to what may have been expected in a full stadium. We should remember also that there was no formal segregation in those days and stewarding was very limited; so once in the ground, supporters could move almost at will. Here a selection of supporters share their memories of what it was like on match days. These experiences vary, but there are some common themes.

One fan who sat on the North Stand, Philip Baynes, told me: "My mum and I had season tickets in the North Stand. I have memories of massive empty spaces between pockets of fans, cushions thrown on the pitch after a bad performance and watching the manually operated scoreboard along the base of the south stand. From where I sat you could see the tree on the Kop, and the occasional train going over Five Arches viaduct on Herries Road! The electronic scoreboard above the Kop was pretty useless if the sun was shining!"

Another supporter, Philip Gascoyne, who sat in the same stand added: "Being short I liked going in the North Stand. You could sit at whichever end we were attacking and then move to the other at half time!" For most games the North Stand was relatively empty. A letter went around Sheffield in the close season of 1974 – purporting to be from Steve Burtenshaw. It claimed that a season ticket would entitle a fan to four seats.

Whether these were to watch the game lying down, or to go to sleep, was unclear. The letter was a hoax, but there certainly were plenty of spare seats in each of Hillsborough's stands. As fan Ian Fox put it to me, the atmosphere in there could be a little testy, "with loads of moaning from the old blokes! I sat next to my Grandad while he shook his head and tutted in disbelief."

Other fans though have a more positive memory of the experience in there. One, "Rob", told me: "Me and my dad had season tickets in the North Stand, it was known as the "cantilever" back then. There were quite a few season ticket holders around us, so we never felt lonely. But when you looked around it was very sparse."

Another supporter built on this view of the fans in the North Stand: "I had a season ticket in the middle of the North from the mid-70s to early 80s. It was the only stand with atmosphere. The Kop desperately needed a roof, the South Stand fans only good at stamping their feet and booing. We had a band of singers towards the middle/back and it was quite vociferous." The North Stand was an impressive structure and it is possible, even with the struggles of the team, to detect a sense of pride among those who sat in there.

Philip Mitchell, who sat in the South Stand, recalls the experience there. "We had shareholder tickets given to us by my Dad's boss, sat with a load of old people in the old wooden stand. My abiding memory is the cushions raining down on to the pitch to express displeasure at another woeful performance. Even though the football was the grimmest during my time following the Owls and I was there during the lowest ever home attendance, I still have fond memories of proper footballers and the feeling of sticking by a hopeless cause."

David Harpham told me how he sat there with his family: "I used to sit with my late mother there amongst the few! The view was excellent as you could have your pick of seats. You could clearly hear all the players and they could hear you... The facilities as I recall were never poor either. Functional, I suppose. You'd get the basic meat pie, crisps, KitKat, tea and Bovril. I always bought a programme, which was always my favourite bit."

The South Stand was the only stand that would be open for Central League (reserve team) games. Paul Whitaker remembers sitting in there and seeing "the woman sitting in there who typed the information that appeared on the scoreboard complete with many and varied spelling mistakes!" Another fan, Philip Bradish, told me how he "mostly sat in North Stand, only sitting in uncovered seats at the front of the South on the odd occasion, if it started raining it was race to try and find a seat on back few rows to try and stay dry!"

There was a difference in facilities between the two halves of the stand. "Behind the uncovered seats in the stand it was like a rabbit warren," Adrian Hurst remembers "toilets and a snack bar and not much more!" A further supporter remembered how hard the wooden seats were , before claiming that "funnily enough, the loudest chants came from the South Stand. (True story)." This historian cannot verify the truth of who was the loudest between the North and South stands, only repeat what I am told!

A theme of the smells of the South Stand came out from several supporters. Fans told me of the aroma of meat pies, pipe smoke, Bovril, the player's liniment cream and rubbing oil. As one supporter told me: "…The smell of pipe smoke in that stand in the 1970s was fantastic… to this day if I smell a pipe it takes me back to Owlerton." Other fans explained to me the benefits of attending games is a large stand, but with low attendances.

"You could pick your seat," Vernon Grant told me, "We used to sit with or near to the players who were not on the pitch (injured, dropped or banned). Heard all sorts from them. Used to get into the players' bar post-match. It was in the South Stand." Another fan told me how "you could move up and down always watching us attack. The tea bar was massive and there were never any queues to speak of!" Another supporter, "Richard", added to the theme of proximity to the players: "The away team dressing room could hear the crowd and hopefully be intimidated!" Not all fans were happy with what was on offer on the pitch as entertainment, as Nigel Short told me: "It was worse when it rained. You were sat down, the rain didn't just get you on your thighs of your jeans, it ran off your parka too. While you were watching the centre backs bang long balls out of defence. Depressing."

Another supporter remembered fans' views on other issues being expressed around the South Stand: "Of course the area behind the South Stand was the focal point for the supporters - probably mostly from the Kop to gather with their chants of 'Taylor Out'. E W Taylor was the focus of discontent as the team began to slip in the closing years and beginning of the 1960s/70s." The same supporter went on to remind me, though: "The South Stand in those days was really two different environments - the original South Stand was the domain of the SWFC establishment... the board and the shareholders and consequentially the quietest and least demonstrative part of the ground." People clearly had different experiences of the South Stand, even within one stand. Covered seats against uncovered; Kop end against the Leppings Lane end; centre of the stand against the fringes.

The experiences of fans who stood on the Spion Kop, on the bottom section of the West Stand, or on the North West Corner are different again. For one thing, it was cheaper. Entrance was 40p in 1974. Bob Hull remembered it as "horribly bleak". "On occasions we stood on Leppings Lane as it was more sheltered," he added. "When we were in old Division Three there never seemed to be any away support, so home fans tended to stand behind both goals." The lack of any segregation or much stewarding allowed Owls' fans to roam around the standing areas. As Paul Whitaker put it to me: "The other bizarre thing and obviously in 7,000-8,000 crowds with no fences tickets for that Lepp stand allowed you to go and stand up and move to the terrace if you wanted to.

"I used to leave my Dad and go and stand down the bottom - so absolutely no crowd control!" The coldness and grimness of the Kop was a recurring theme for some fans. "We stood under the scoreboard in all weathers, and it could get bloody cold!" recalls Mark Goodison: "I first started on the Kop and can remember the cold and wet, standing there with newspaper in your shoes and your mother's tights to keep warm!"

"We stood on the very bottom for some games and remember how you could just walk around the ground," added another. Hooliganism (perceived at least) had an impact on some people's habits as Pete Goodison describes: "My Dad made me stand on the Leppings Lane North West Corner because he said the Kop was too dangerous. However, I stood on the Kop once we were relegated... there were very few away supporters then."

Other fans picked the Leppings Lane end to stay with their friends as Michael Tompkins recalls: "During this period usually stood in Lepp triangle, though on night matches straight from Stannington College I went behind the goal on Lepp. It was the worst view in the ground, but college mates always wanted to go there – I don't know why!"

The lack of away fans was another theme of what supporters told me: "I simply don't remember there being any away fans", Paul Whitaker told me. "No real recollection of away fans from back then as didn't seem like there were ever any there other than a group of Forest fans standing in the back of the Cheese-cake with us," added Peter Gelder. Many of the recollections of those standing recall going in groups – of either family or friends: "I always stood on the Kop during this era - at the top, in front of the old scoreboard, sometimes with family, sometimes with friends, but latterly on my own, as other family members mi-grated to the South Stand seats."

Some of the younger fans remember arriving early in order to spend time with their friends: "I stood on the Kop near the front, we used to arrive at the ground at 1pm! My mum used to say 'why so early? They won't start without you!'" Steve Walmsley compared his experience to a famous (at least among Owls' sup-porters) painting: "Pete McKee's 'Early Doors' was me and my mates, stood on the Kop ages before the kick-off!" One final memory of a relatively young fan was the frustration of being charged the adult rate, despite being a teenager… "The other thing I remember that young fans were deemed to be an adult at the gate at 14! It didn't stop blokes with 'taches and full beards getting through though…!"

The experience of standing – particularly on the Kop - was very different to those who were seated in the three relatively new or redeveloped stands. The Kop had effectively remained unaltered for decades, while the rest of the stadium had been ex-tensively redeveloped over the previous 15 years or so. Standing allowed for a different match day experience, with larger groups, and tended to mean that friends or family stayed together. The lack of away fans (especially in Division Three) and the lack of segregation allowed for Owls' fans to stand at both ends of the ground and in the corners.

It is interesting that many of the memories of fans relate to how they felt, or to the senses. Football is a social experience and the supporters remembered who they attended games with and how they felt together. They also remember how attending the game made them feel physically – with memories of the sounds, smells, sights and temperatures that match-going brought them.

There remained a sense of pride in the stadium, particularly for those who sat in the North Stand which remained an architectural marvel a decade after its opening. Those who stood on the Kop or West Stand were less enamoured by the conditions. There is some sense of class differences between these recollections – or at least work and age differences. The younger fans at school, college or work, often standing; those who had a little more money being more likely to be seated.

Hillsborough had a history of hosting big games, not just those involving Sheffield Wednesday. In 1962 for example, just over 35,000 supporters saw England draw 1-1 with France at S6. The stadium had hosted a World Cup quarter final (Germany beating Uruguay 4-0) and regularly hosted FA Cup semi-finals. The Owls also had the pleasure of hosting Leeds United in 1971 after the Elland Road club were banned from holding games at home for four games following incidents of hooliganism.

In one of their games at Hillsborough, Leeds beat Newcastle United 5-1 in front of 18,623. Despite the team's fall down the leagues, the stadium remained in demand for hosting these big games during our period. In each of our three seasons, the stadium hosted an FA Cup semi-final. In 1973 it was Burnley against Newcastle (2-0 to Newcastle); in 1974 Birmingham played Fulham (1-1) and in 1976 it was Manchester United against Derby County (2-0 to United). The attendance for each game was 55,000.

Owls' supporters could apply to attend the FA Cup semi-final games. In a process that appeared somewhat bureaucratic to my 21st century eyes, Wednesday shareholders and seat season ticket holders could apply for tickets. They were to: "apply by post enclosing remittance and stamped addressed envelope so as to reach us on or before first post Saturday, 22nd March. Voucher labels marked 'F.A. Cup semi-final' are the only ones acceptable and must be affixed to the outside of the envelope containing the application, and the price of the ticket required should also be clearly indicated on the outside of the envelope. One voucher – one ticket." One supporter told me how much he enjoyed the experience: "I was there in 1976, sat in the North Stand with my Grandad who got tickets as he was a Wednesday season ticket holder. It was a good game and a fine Manchester United side. It was brilliant to see the ground full… just a pity that the Wednesday games before and after had rather smaller crowds!"

Shareholders and season ticket holders applied this way while one further group were allocated tickets – those who were Debenture Holders. They were told that they must not apply – and that tickets would simply be sent by post. Paul Whitaker discussed with me another way in which Debenture Holders received special treatment: "I recall the Debenture Holders had their own gate into the ground in the South Stand… I believe that they were allowed to take guests in for standard games - I recall some lads at school used to stand outside asking Debenture Holders to take them in - innocent times!"

I can't leave this section without including the dry humour of another fan, Andrew Thorpe: "It remains the only context in which I have ever heard or seen the word 'debenture'. I'm now in my late fifties and I still feel that the fact that I've never been a Debenture Holder somehow suggests I've failed in life!"

The semi-final games offered a reminder of the capacity and quality of Hillsborough in times where games involving the Owls often attracted very low attendances. For the Owls' fans in attendance they offered a glimpse into what Hillsborough was capable of; for the fans of those teams playing, a reminder of what they were missing while Wednesday were out of the top-flight. Opposition players also appreciated the opportunity of playing at Hillsborough. Future Owls' boss Trevor Francis, then of Birmingham City, was quoted in 1975 as saying: "It's one of my favourite grounds… I am just hoping it will prove to be a lucky ground again for me on Saturday." Unfortunately for Francis, he did not hit lucky that day. The fans who witnessed Hillsborough full to capacity probably did.

Other competitive games played at Hillsborough during the period included a series of games for Sheffield Boys in 1974 and

1975 (one of which was an 8-0 triumph over York) and a World Cup Qualifier for Northern Ireland against Bulgaria in September 1973. That game finished 0-0 and attracted a crowd of 6,292 to watch.

The Northern Ireland game is an interesting curiosity. The Owls' programme introduced it as follows: "Because of the un-happy circumstances that now exist in Belfast, the Northern Ire-land team has been forced to play their home games on away territory, and this of course, has made their task all the harder. We hope that it won't be long before peace is restored in Ul-ster and that the Northern Ireland team will be able to play their home games at Windsor Park, Belfast. In the meantime, it's up to everybody to make them really welcome when they arrive at Hillsborough."

The result, a goalless draw, was a reasonable one for the Irish team, who had lost the previous game in Bulgaria 3-0. That game saw a crowd of 50,000, two penalties given away by the Irish defence, and the sending-off of the legendary George Best. That sending off was followed by a three-match suspension from in-ternational football.

Best though also claimed to have "retired" from football dur-ing this period, although new Manchester United manager Tom-my Docherty was soon able to persuade him to return to action. Perhaps the lack of Best, who did not appear again for the na-tional team for another two years, goes some way to explaining the relatively small attendance at Hillsborough. The Northern Irish authorities were grateful for the opportunity to play in Sheffield, president Harry Cavan saying: "I would like to thank... Sheffield Wednesday for the excellent facilities and great assistance given in helping to stage this World Cup match".

Owls' chairman Andrew Stephen added: "With so many top-class players on view... the game should be a spectacular one..." While it is difficult to state how spectacular or unspectacular the resulting goalless draw was, the staging of the game at S6 does show Hillsborough's status among British stadia at the time. Au-thor Richard Crooks, in his book 'Grandad, What was Football Like in the 1970s?', certainly did not think much of the spectacle on offer, describing "a desultory game, failing to fire the imagination, or whet the appetite of the spectators." Other games staged away from Belfast were played at Hampden Park, Goodison Park, Highfield Road and Craven Cottage. Hillsborough remained among the elite of grounds.

Hillsborough also staged a series of other games during our period, including County Cup games against Sheffield United in 1974 and Doncaster Rovers in 1975; Eric Taylor's testimonial game against an England XI in 1974 and friendly games against Burnley and Morton in 1975. Taylor's testimonial attracted a good crowd of 10,939 to witness the Owls beaten 5-0 and one fan remembers Frank Worthington scoring what he described as the most amazing solo goal they had ever witnessed in person. It was the 1974 County Cup game against Sheffield United that attracted the largest crowd for any of these games, though, at 18,869.

To give it its full name, the Sheffield & Hallamshire County Cup was a cup competition involving the professional sides within the Sheffield and Hallamshire County Football Association. It ran from 1920-21 to the mid-1990s, with several gaps between tournaments. The Owls won the competition 11 times in total and during the 1970s, it provided a rare opportunity for both Sheffield sides to meet in competition. Wednesday won the 1972-73 version 4-3 on penalties at Hillsborough following a 0-0 draw, before triumphing again at Bramall Lane in 1975.

The two friendly games in 1975 provided a rare opportunity in those months for Owls fans to see the team score goals. A January game against Burnley, played on FA Cup fourth round weekend after both teams had been knocked out, saw the Owls lose 3-1 with a goal by Ronnie Ferguson in front of a crowd of 2,587. David Sunley scored twice in a 2-0 win vs Morton, played after the Owls were relegated in April, in front of 1,676. Finally, Wednesday's reserve team commonly played their Central League games at Hillsborough.

The stadium was therefore well used and well regarded. The FA were happy with its use for semi-finals, and the Northern Irish FA commented on the quality of facilities. Owls' fans took pride in the stadium – or at least those who sat in its redeveloped stands did. Those on the Kop seemed a little more tired of its facilities and atmosphere in a time of low attendances. The World Cup in 1966 was a "once in a lifetime" opportunity for Hillsborough and Sheffield to stamp their mark on the world, and the redeveloped Hillsborough certainly helped with this.

By the mid-1970s, the stadium remained impressive, and although other clubs had begun to build notable stands of their own, (Everton's triple-decker main stand being the largest in Britain in 1971 for example), Hillsborough was still highly thought of by the authorities, fans and players. If the performance of the team is separated out, then there remained obvious pride in Hillsborough and its facilities.

AN INTERVIEW WITH DAVID SUNLEY

David (Dave) Sunley was a skilful forward player who signed as an apprentice for the Owls at the age of sixteen in 1968. Born near Redcar, Sunley moved rapidly into the reserves and made his first-team debut at the age of 18 in December 1970. Although in and out of the squad during the early 1970s, Dave was a regular member of the team for much of the period covered by this book – leaving the club at the end of January 1976. He made a total of 148 appearances for the Owls, scoring 26 goals. He has lived in the Sheffield area since his time with the club and it was from his home near Dronfield that he spoke to me in the summer of 2019.

Before we move on the years covered by the book - tell me a little about your early years with the club.
I signed as an apprentice as far back as 1968, Alan Brown was the manager then. I worked mostly with Lawrie McMenemy and the other coaches. They really helped me. I was really pleased to sign for Wednesday, they were a top Division One club, with some great players – Johnny Fantham, David Ford, Don Megson, Wilf Smith. Gerry Young as well, and he of course stayed into the 1970s.

Tell me about your debut and first goal for the club.
I remember the emotions of my debut as much as the game. In fact, my memories of the game are pretty hazy. **It was against Birmingham City, I think?** Yes, it was, at their place. I remember feeling nervous, excited and running on adrenaline, I don't remember much of the game, other than we lost. **How about your first goal?** Now, I do remember that! It was an FA Cup tie at White Hart Lane against Spurs. They were a top, top team. Some great players in their team that day – Alan Mullery, Martin Peters, Alan Gilzean. It was a full-house and the game itself was a bit of a blur. Their keeper was Pat Jennings - he had hands as

big as shovels and was great goalie. Anyhow, I got one past him with a header, so I was really pleased! We lost 4-1 and I remember how difficult the game was, but I was pleased with my goal and performance. It was a great experience for a young player like I was then.

You were still in and out of the team though in the early 1970s?
Yes, I played regularly for the reserves and I was in and out of the first team as I was still developing, I suppose. Who coached you in the reserves? Ron Staniforth. He was a gentleman. He was calm, quiet, not at all vocal, took his time to explain things to you. I learned lots from him.

How did you find Derek Dooley?
Well, he again was not a shouter. He'd been larger than life as a player, a real battering ram of a striker, and I know had worked for the club on the commercial side before becoming manager. I think that's why I'd say he was both the right and wrong man for the job! He was the right man because he knew the club inside out. He was wrong though because he had to go from someone who we'd all been pally with – we'd all say "All right Derek" to him when passing - to being the manager and all that involves. Maybe he was too close to things. We'd finished mid-table under him in the couple of years before your book, and I think that was probably his limit. He knew good players, but never quite had enough about him to get us up. We weren't going to go down though either.

Do you remember the virus that hit the club during Derek Dooley's last season?
No, no I don't. I know that we were down towards the bottom of the table at that time, but no, I don't remember a virus. I know that there had been some changes at the top – with the chairman and who have you. I think they had just decided that they wanted a change. I didn't really see Derek's sacking coming, and to my mind it was the wrong time to do it at Christmas. A game or two

more wouldn't have made any difference to the season. Derek was in tears afterwards - Sheffield Wednesday had been his life. He was so hurt and disappointed.

Moving on to Steve Burtenshaw then,how did you find working with him?

Well, I wouldn't say we got on! He had tactical nous I suppose. I can't quite put my finger on it, but I never felt he was entirely straight. Like he was saying one thing to your face, and something else behind your back. He never seemed to have a settled team, or even a settled strike force. So, I was in and out of the team, and when I was playing it wasn't always with the same players. It did no good for the confidence of the players or the team. There was also a bit of a north/south thing. He'd come up from QPR or Arsenal and didn't seem to get what was needed at a northern club with plenty of northern lads playing for us. I was a bit frustrated by it all, really.

I know you refused a new contract eventually – is that what caused it?

That was 1975. The club and Steve Burtenshaw had offered me a contract on the same money as the last one. It was partly the money, though we were on a decent wage. It was more the direction of the club. We'd been relegated by that stage, and I couldn't see that there was much improvement coming. With no disrespect to anyone, the players that were coming in - permanent, on loan or whatever - weren't of the same standards as those who were leaving. Anyhow it went to a tribunal who fixed a transfer fee for me, which went down every month. I eventually left early in 1976 for £7,500 to go to Hull City.

That's interesting - there were rumours in the press in the years before that of interest from Arsenal and Aston Villa for far bigger sums.

Well, I know I was watched by various clubs. The only bid I know that the club received for me was during Derek Dooley's time. It was around £100,000 from Southampton, I think. It never got as far as me having to decide or have any talks though. I think the club turned it down. I did meet Bill Shankly outside of Anfield once, but that didn't go anywhere either!

You went on loan also?
Yes, I did, in 1975, to Nottingham Forest under Brian Clough. **That must have been interesting?** Well, I never saw him! He only turned up on match days, and on the only game I played for the first team – away at Fulham – he left the talking to others. I thought I played reasonably well in that game; it was a 0-0 draw, but we had to play with ten men for most of the game after an early sending off. I then played in the reserves for them and twisted my ankle. I stayed on the pitch, probably because I wanted to impress but it made it worse. So, I came back to Sheffield to recover.

Len Ashurst would be in charge by then. What are your memories of him?
To be honest I found him quite aggressive. He was only a short fella but quite fiery. I didn't really like his demeanour. He didn't even try and sort the contract thing and as I said, I left for Hull shortly afterwards. His management and coaching were less focused on the tactics than Steve Burtenshaw had been. He wanted his teams to be physical, to get stuck in. Nothing wrong with that as such, I think the fans expect the players to do that. It seemed to be at the expense of other things though. He brought Tony Toms with him – ex-military guy – and it was all work on fitness. **Were you still at the club for the infamous team building trip on to the Moors?** No, luckily enough I left for Hull that week (laughs!) I know that it was cold, though, talking to some of the other lads afterwards!

Where would you say you were happiest after leaving Wednesday?
I played at a few clubs, Lincoln, Stockport, a few in the non-league. I think I was at my happiest though after moving to Hull. They were in danger of relegation when I joined them. I don't want to blow my own trumpet, or say I saved them by myself,

but I scored six or seven goals in the last 13 or 14 games of that season and helped keep them up. I enjoyed that.

You were with the Owls for most the time covered by the book. Can you explain why the team struggled during the period?

It was a mixture of things. We lost some quality players during this time. Derek Dooley knew a good player – so you had players like Dave Clements, Tommy Craig, Peter Eustace, Willie Henderson, Peter Rodrigues and others. They all moved on for one reason or another. Again, I mean no disrespect, but the players who came in – under whichever manager - didn't seem to be of the same quality. Then of course you have the changing of managers and coaches. It's difficult to keep continuity when you have new people coming in with different ideas and methods.

Thanks Dave. Have you anything else you'd like to add?

Well, I hope I haven't been too negative with any of that. I enjoyed my time at Hillsborough. I came back after leaving for Hull to watch the Southend game. I couldn't believe that the club I'd joined as a top Division One club could be so close to Division Four. I was glad to see things improve for the club, certainly when Jack Charlton took over.

1974-75

The worst season in Sheffield Wednesday's long history. Relegation. A goal drought. Key players leave. The lowest crowds in post-war history. To provide some light relief from the misery the season also features possibly the most exciting game of the decade and a loan star who briefly provides some hope. Relegation is confirmed on April Fool's Day, after which the team finally score a goal. Could things get any worse?

After the difficulties of the previous season there was some optimism about the Owls' chances in the new season. A successful pre-season tour of Scotland had seen the team return with two wins and a draw (4-0 vs Clyde, 1-0 vs Kilmarnock, 1-1 vs Dundee). Although winger Willie Henderson had left, there were new signings in Hugh Dowd and Bobby Brown on permanent deals and Fred McIver initially on loan. The back-room team also saw some reorganisation. As Steve Burtenshaw put it in his first programme notes of the season: "Last year after my arrival our target was to stay in the Second Division. That achieved, our next goal is to climb up the table: in effect to improve the overall strength and position of the club. This is something that will be achieved by the use of skill, judgement and effort in many directions; and it will be a long-term rather than a short-term achievement." Burtenshaw's statement shows the desire for improvements tempered with realism about the work needed to achieve his aims.

This realism about the work needed was soon brought into sharp relief with early season results. The Owls started their campaign with back to back away games – Oldham Athletic in the league, followed by Scunthorpe United in the League Cup. The results were back to back defeats. Despite taking a 1-0 half-time lead at Oldham, through a twice-taken Tommy Craig penalty, the Owls succumbed to a 2-1 defeat at full time. Wednesday then fell to a 1-0 defeat at Scunthorpe described in the *Green 'Un* as "a sickener" as "the match was there for Wednesday's taking." The Owls therefore went in to their first home game in need of an early-season tonic.

That match was against Bristol Rovers, managed at this time by ex-Owls legend Don Megson. Ably assisted by other former Owls, Alan Warboys, Gordon Fearnley and Colin Dobson, Megson had guided the Bristol outfit to promotion the previous season. A crowd of 14,343 turned out to watch the game. Rovers took a first half lead, and it was only in the 86th minute that Peter Eustace scrambled in the equaliser. "The result brought a wry smile to the face of Don Megson," commented that evening's *Green 'Un*. The team ended their August fixtures with a trip to Norwich where, despite Craig giving the Owls a half-time lead, they were held to a 1-1 draw. August ended with the Owls on two points from three games and in a disappointing 17th place in the table.

The Owls next game was a home fixture against Cardiff. The Bluebirds ended the season with relegation but came away from Hillsborough with a 2-1 victory. All the goals were in the first half, and the Owls' goal came when Cardiff's Albert Larmour headed into his own goal under pressure from Eddie Prudham. This defeat, in front of a crowd of only 9,850, left the Owls bottom of the table but Steve Burtenshaw acted quickly, bringing in ex-England international Colin Harvey from Everton. Harvey made his debut in the next game, away at Bolton, and Bobby Brown scored the winner in what the *Sheffield Star* called a "merited victory". "I was impressed by the manager, and his ideas for the future," Harvey said. "I decided that if it meant first team football, which is what I wanted, then Wednesday were a good club to join. I thought last week went fairly well for me. I settled in reasonably well, and they are a grand bunch of lads."

The Owls' next game was trip to Bristol Rovers; a rapid chance for Bristol's manager to face his former team again. Don Megson may have thought he had a good opportunity to catch the Owls off guard, as trouble in Bristol traffic meant that the Wednesday players had to get off the team coach early and walk to the ground. Any sense that the Owls were shaken by this was soon put to one side though as an early goal by Peter Rodrigues put Wednesday into the lead. The goal was from an unlikely source –one of only two that Rodrigues scored in Owls' colours. It was also spectacular, described in the following match programme as a "30-yard stunner". Unfortunately for the Owls that was as good as it got in the game, with Bristol equalising before half-time and the game finishing 1-1.

The points gained in the two away games helped the Owls move away from the relegation zone of the early-season table and look forward to two home games. The anonymous "Voice of Hillsborough" section of the programme for the first of those games (against Nottingham Forest) read: "We are always assured a great reception from you (the fans). Let's hope the Hillsborough Hoodoo vanishes today." A 15,295 crowd watched an exciting game, but one that continued whatever "hoodoo" there was at Hillsborough as Wednesday lost 3-2, despite goals from Craig and Joicey.

In his programme notes for the next game, against West Brom, Steve Burtenshaw bemoaned a lack of consistency from his play-ers. "I don't want the players getting any sort of phobia about playing here at Hillsborough," he wrote. "If we are going to make things happen it has got to be here in our own backyard." Wednesday drew 0-0 with West Brom in front of 12,333 sup-porters, and the game was notable for the rare event of Tommy Craig missing a penalty - the ball hitting the inside of the post and bouncing away to safety.

Wednesday then travelled to Orient and lost 1-0, in a game that turned on a sending off and another penalty. Ken Knighton was sent off for the use of "industrial language" and famously kicked the dressing room door off its hinges in frustration afterwards. The penalty came late in the game, and Orient's Mickey Bullock scored it – hitting the inside of the post and going in – somewhat ironically given Tommy Craig's miss in the previous game. These games saw the Owls finish September in 21st position in the table, struggling to score goals and yet to win at home.

The next game was a home fixture against Sunderland who would finish the season in fourth place, just missing out on promotion. This was a midweek game played in very stormy conditions during a strike on Sheffield's buses. Gerry Young wrote the programme notes for the game – saying: "It is disappointing... that we have yet to give our faithful fans their first Hillsborough success, but I am not talking about the home hoodoo". Again, hoodoo or not, the Owls struggled. A goal in each half saw Sunderland come away with a 2-0 victory in front of 11,490 fans.

The *Star's* headline read: "Unlucky Owls Slump to Another Defeat in Lively Game". Wednesday's misfortune related to an early Eric Potts effort which hit the post but, unfortunate or not, this was the Owls' third game without a goal, leaving them stuck in the relegation positions. They faced another home test next with Bristol City visiting Hillsborough the following Saturday. Steve Burtenshaw commented in the programme that "Nothing breeds success like success, and once the players pick up a win bonus here at Hillsborough it could just be the thing to put them on the right road." Unfortunately for Wednesday, the Bristol City game did not see the Owls players pick up that win bonus – though John Holsgrove did put the team ahead just after half-time. The game, witnessed by 10,088, ended in a 1-1 draw. Steve Burtenshaw was quoted afterwards as saying: "After Wednesday night (the Sunderland game) I thought we were going to put a show on, but it was not to be."

Around this time, Burtenshaw was heavily rumoured to be in line for the recently vacated manager's position at QPR. Neither Burtenshaw nor chairman Matt Sheppard commented in an article in The *Star* on October 10, but nine days later the manager insisted: "Chairman, at no time have I put myself forward for the manager's job at QPR." Wednesday, though, accepted that QPR had made an official approach, which was met with a "firm, but polite, rebuff from our board." A sum of £30,000 was mentioned in the press as suitable compensation – the Owls suggesting that this figure was actually too high. Among all this speculation, the Owls played two away games. The first was at Oxford United, where they lost 1-0, making it nine games played against the U's – and no victories for the Owls. The second game was a return fixture with Bob Stokoe's Sunderland team. This game finished 3-0 to Sunderland – all the goals coming in the first half. As Burtenshaw put it afterwards: "Sunderland are an exceptionally good side, by far the best we've played".

Wednesday then returned to home soil to face Hull City and before the game, forward Eric McMordie had been signed on loan from Middlesbrough. By this stage, the anonymous 'Voice of Hillsborough' addressed fans from the matchday programme, rather than the manager or others, and commented rather icily that the sum of compensation mentioned in the press "implies that the manager is on a salary far removed from the one which he is paid. Right now, he has got the job of earning it." McMordie helped Burtenshaw take some steps towards earning his salary in the game against Hull, scoring the equaliser before Colin Harvey scored the winner to finally break Wednesday's home hoodoo, in front of 11,498.

Back to back 3-1 defeats, away at Aston Villa and Blackpool, left Wednesday rock bottom of the table moving into November before York City's first-ever Division Two visit to Hillsborough saw them comprehensively beaten 3-0. Ronnie Ferguson scored on his debut (at the age of 17) to give Wednesday a half-time lead, with further strikes from McMordie and Potts after the break. McMordie's goal was a well-balanced and powerful volley from just inside the area, and Wednesday's performance was the best of the season at that stage. Colin Harvey and Tommy Craig pulled the strings in midfield, Potts caused havoc on the wing and the two strikers - McMordie and Ferguson - remembered where the goal was.

That excellent display was soon to be followed by another entertaining game at Notts County. McMordie's initial loan was due to end before this game, but he, the Owls and Middlesbrough agreed to extend it for another month – leaving boss Burtenshaw delighted. McMordie celebrated by opening the scoring, before a rapid Ian Scanlon hat-trick (within two and a half minutes or so) saw County go 3-1 ahead. Potts then scored with a 30-yard shot, before McMordie equalised. An exciting 3-3 draw. These games certainly provided plenty of action and entertainment for those watching. "It is a considerable source of pride for the club that despite our lowly Second Division position we are riding high in the table for entertainment," wrote 'The Voice of Hillsborough.'

The results couldn't help Wednesday out of the relegation positions, though, with Burtenshaw hoping a run of home games could give his side some much-needed impetus. Simply, the Owls needed results as well as entertaining performances. Their next game provided just that, as a second-half goal from McMordie was enough to win at home against Fulham in front of 12,373 fans. That result, presumably, led Burtenshaw to proclaim that his side's next game, away at fellow strugglers Portsmouth, was "important...but not vital" and from Wednesday's point of view, it was probably just as well as they went down to a disappointing 1-0 defeat. The defeat left the Owls in the relegation places in the lead up to the biggest game of the season up to that point– Manchester United at home.

* * * * *

Key Game: Sheffield Wednesday 4-4 Manchester United, December 7th,1974

Manchester United had been relegated from Division One the previous season but were determined that they would not spend long in the second tier. In fact, they ended the season as champions. Their supporters meanwhile were gaining a reputation for travelling in numbers and for various instances of "football hooliganism". The Owls' matchday programme suggested that "when Manchester United and their hordes come to Hillsborough…. it will be the biggest crowd of the season, so Wednesday fans, come yourself and bring a pal." The match did indeed see the biggest crowd of the season, with 35,067 packing into Hillsborough for what was an incredible game.

Steve Burtenshaw was quoted in the press before the game giving due respect to the United team. "They are a very, very good side," he said. "They have hardness and skill and combine them both very effectively." The *Star's* football writer Ian Vickers extended on Burtenshaw's comments with the lines: "Sheffield Wednesday are all set for their match of the year against Manchester United at Hillsborough tomorrow and the policy will be ATTACK." Burtenshaw did give some fuel to this view by saying: "We have got to go out with our heads up high and play as well as we are capable. Our strike force is looking better, and we have tightened up at the back."

Ken Knighton had just completed his suspension after the sending-off at Orient but was felt not ready for an immediate return to action. Burtenshaw therefore named the following line up:

1 Springett
2 Rodrigues
3 Shaw
4 Thompson
5 Dowd
6 McMordie
7 Potts
8 Harvey
9 Ferguson
10 Craig
11 Sunley
Sub: Wylde

This was a team with attacking intent, along with some real quality in the midfield. It is unclear though if Burtenshaw, the team, or the supporters foresaw what was to happen during the game. The *Star's* report of the match vividly described the events:

"Hillsboro's Memorable Super Show. You had to be there to realise just what an amazing match it was and that 4-4 scoreline in the Sheffield Wednesday – Manchester United spectacular gives some clue as to the excitement. The third best crowd in the League on Saturday and predictably Wednesday's largest of the season witnessed a great spectacle. At one stage it seemed that the game might be halted when fans spilled on to the pitch. Fortunately, that didn't happen and credit referee Ken Baker and all the players for showing such good sense. It's a pity that the

louts in the crowd didn't follow their example. After Macari had hit the Wednesday post, Houston gave United an early lead when his free-kick went in – a bad goal from Wednesday's point of view. Soon afterwards came the Holton incident when the big centre-half broke his leg after a completely fair confrontation with McMordie. Tommy Docherty's claim that United would not have let four in if Holton was there is arguable, particularly as the strong Greenhoff had a good match at the back. Wednesday then took a three-goal lead and normally that would have been it, but you sensed that in such a seething arena of noise, anything could happen. It did. United's second goal should never have been scored. Wednesday should have cleared McCalliog's free kick, but the equaliser, from Pearson was excellent. Yet again the balance altered when Craig put a free kick on the usual six pence and Sunley's head did the rest. Still it wasn't over and the dangerous Macari somehow found the corner of the net to make it 4-4. Then Wednesday had to endure some tricky moments from the elusive Morgan but at the end it was United, not Wednesday who were playing for time. A match to remember. We called it Wednesday's Match of the Year.... And it was."

The match itself was a thrilling spectacle full of drama and excitement, but the match report above touches also on some of the problems of hooliganism that occurred. The fans' experience of this is covered elsewhere in the book. Suffice to say here that 60 fans were injured and more than 100 arrested in the worst scenes of violence and disorder seen at Hillsborough during our period. At one stage injured fans spilled on to the pitch side after fighting on the Kop, and mounted police were needed to restore order. There was much discussion after the game of an FA inquiry into the matter.

Owls' secretary Eric England said: "Our conscience is clear, we tried to cover every contingency," while Red Devils boss Docherty added: "I saw a lot of blue and white involved as well. We can't be held responsible at away matches as well... it's a Sheffield Wednesday problem." In some ways of course this took away from the excitement of the game, and the quality of the performances on both sides. The four goals scored by the Owls - Shaw, Harvey and Sunley (2) the scorers - were all well-crafted strikes that would not have looked out of place in a team competing at a much higher level.

Burtenshaw felt the 4-4 result was fair, and again paid credit to a "youngish, skilful, fit and well organised" United team. Docherty was equally positive about the Owls: "Wednesday played exceptionally well... they don't belong in the bottom half of the table." Owls coach Gerry Young was quoted as being disappointed at how the team lost the lead, but happy with the quality of their passing, and Docherty returned to the game in his programme notes for the return match at Old Trafford: "The Hillsborough match was quite remarkable ."

David Sunley told me in 2019 that he thought the Owls had risen to the occasion, the huge crowd helping spur them on. He felt though that the early injury to United defender Jim Holton had given a boost to Wednesday. "My first goal was a bit lucky," he told me, "it was a tap-in from a corner..., that never would have reached me if Holton was on the field." He continued to describe his second goal: "That one came from a cross from Tommy Craig from a free-kick. It was a great cross, I got a good header on it, and it flew past Stepney in the United goal." He told me about what the players saw of the trouble in the crowd: "I saw some supporters on the edge of the pitch, pulled out of the crowd I suppose. I also saw the police horses on the Kop. From the pitch though it didn't affect me... it seemed like the police had it under control, and I was focused on the game."

A postscript to the match came on January 24, 1975, when the FA announced that they would take no action against the Owls with regards to the violence on the day. Eric England welcomed the decision: "It is pleasing to know the FA have taken that decision... As I said at the time, we felt absolutely sure that we, in co-operation with the police, had taken every precaution, and I think that point has been proved."

Burtenshaw hoped that the game would mark a turning point in the Owls' season. "It will do us the world of good and I don't see any reason to be despondent with a point, "he said, hoping that the drama of the United game would lead to increased attendances. "I feel some of the Sheffield people we brought in will want to come again." Burtenshaw and the Owls would soon find out, as their next match was at home against Oldham Athletic the following Saturday.

As it happened there was a minor boost to the attendance for the Oldham game as 13,338 turned out to watch a game notable for being Eric McMordie's final game of his loan spell (he was made captain for the occasion). It also turned out to be Tommy Craig's final game for the club. McMordie was developing his business interests in Middlesbrough, in preparation for his retirement from the game, and could not be persuaded to stay at Hillsborough any longer, while Craig gained his long-held wish of a transfer to Division One with Newcastle in the days that followed.

Their send-off was a relatively flat affair, with Wednesday losing the first-half lead given to them by Bobby Brown and then missing a penalty on their way to a 1-1 draw. Brown then scored his second goal in as many games in Wednesday's next outing, at fellow strugglers Millwall, but the Lions won 2-1. The *Green 'Un* described the result as a "Sorry Christmas Start by the Owls" before suggesting that Wednesday were ready to splash the cash on new blood after the shock of losing Craig to Newcastle.

There was, though, no new blood in the team by the time Wednesday faced a tricky fixture at home to Bolton Wanderers on Boxing Day. "There will not be much time for festivities", announced the "Voice of Hillsborough" in the programme, "for the manager, his staff, and players... will be out for points". Unfortunately, though, none were forthcoming as Wednesday lost 2-0 in front of a crowd of just over 17,000. Despite Wednesday signing off 1974 with victory – Eric Potts scoring the winner on the south coast in a 1-0 win at Southampton – the Owls finished the year second from bottom. Even the club programme made no attempt to sugar-coat the club's plight, admitting: "Most Wednesdayites will probably be glad to see the back of 1974."

The Owls could hardly have begun 1975 in better fashion, as they enjoyed the relative glamour of a trip to London to face

Division One side Chelsea in the FA Cup. Wednesday rose to the occasion and went 2-0 up at Stamford Bridge, before a second-half collapse saw them lose 3-2. A familiar face then returned to haunt Wednesday when they lost 2-0 at Old Trafford, with former Owls striker Jim McCalliog netting twice for Manchester United in a comfortable victory.

Mick Prendergast made his return to the Wednesday side after his broken leg the previous Easter, and he and Fred McIver both wore a Wednesday number 10 shirt in the first half. Referee Ray Toseland initially didn't notice, and the mix-up was only sorted at half-time when McIver changed into the missing number 11 shirt!

Defeat by the same 2-0 scoreline at home to Portsmouth sent Wednesday bottom of the table; a position they would not move from for the rest of the season. This prompted The *Star's* 'Save our Owls' campaign, with the aim of encouraging support for the Owls and introduced by the newspaper's then-sports editor, Peter Howard.

"SAVE OUR OWLS... It's a short slogan with a simple message. Tonight, The Star launches a campaign. Its objective is important. We want YOU to help Wednesday stave off relegation. Wednes-day are in dire straits: a look at the Second Division table is all that is needed to confirm that. They are suffering financially, as chair-man Matt Sheppard explained on Friday. And there's no doubt that if the club nosedives into the Third Division for the first time in its long and illustrious history, it will not just be Wednesday that suffers. The whole of Sheffield will suffer... The city needs United and Wednesday doing well in the First Division...In short, the thought of Wednesday in the Third Division is almost too much to stomach. We would feel the same if United were in this critical position. What can be done to right the situation for Wednesday, to give them breathing space for real improvement? The team, even if the board and manager can infuse some new blood before transfer deadline, needs encouragement. THE PLAYERS NEED IT NOW. We would like to see at least 20,000 at the Blackpool match,

more if possible... We are concerned for the future of Wednes-
day, and I think most fair-minded people in the city are as well.
Wednesday need help – YOUR help, and they need it now."

The first fixture following the start of the campaign was a Friday
night trip to York City. Fans' experiences of the game are covered
elsewhere in the book – suffice to say here that huge numbers
of Wednesday fans travelled to the game. A total of 24 coaches
from S.U.T. (Sheffield United Tours) took over 1,000 fans, another 1,600 travelled by train and more by their own means. "Road
and rail routes to York... were a sea of blue and white scarves,"
reported The *Star.*

Boss Burtenshaw had taken the team away to the FA's training
facility in Lilleshall before the game. Unfortunately, the weather
curtailed much of his plans, with a blizzard leaving several inches
of snow on the pitches. New signing Jimmy Quinn, who had initially arrived on trial at the club after his release by Celtic, made
his debut at left-back, with Ronnie Ferguson and Brian Joicey the
chosen strike-force. The first half of the game itself saw a steady
if uninspiring performance from the team to leave the match
goalless at the break; the second half saw another Owls' collapse,
conceding three goals to lose 0-3.

The *Star* ramped up their 'Save our Owls' campaign in the days
leading up to Wednesday's next game, eight days later at home
to Blackpool, and the club had agreed a deal where buying ten
tickets in advance would gain two additional tickets for free. They
produced thousands of car stickers, badges and posters (some
of which we see elsewhere in the book). The paper published
exhortations for pubs, clubs, offices and works to organise trips
to the game.

"No side will relish coming to Hillsborough if they are confronted with a cauldron of noise by a mass of Wednesdayites,"
read the paper's lead article. "Where there's life, there's hope,"
said Fred Stones, chairman of the Supporters' Club. The *Star*
themselves arranged for 100 of their staff to attend the game.

That hard work had a limited effect. A crowd of 14,342 attended the game – well short of the 20,000 target set by The

Star, but still an increase on recent fixtures. Those who were in attendance saw the debut of a new signing, Phil Henson from Manchester City, while John Holsgrove also returned to the team for the first time since November as Wednesday battled to a 0-0 draw. "True there were no goals," reported Wednesday's match-day programme, "but the endeavour and spirit of Steve Burtenshaw's reshaped Wednesday side certainly bridged the significant gap between the two clubs."

Henson described the fans as "tremendous" after the game but having been knocked out of the FA Cup, the Owls had a two-week break in the league before returning to action with another home game – this time against Notts County. In the interim, the Owls were in County Cup action, defeating Doncaster Rovers at Belle Vue, with Henson scoring one of the goals.

The *Star* continued their campaign, with Burtenshaw saying before the match: "We are not lying down and accepting the current situation... We realise that we have to do our part. I think it's bloody marvellous that the club has this support from the local newspaper." Just under 15,000 watched as a second-half goal gave County a 1-0 win, meaning the 'Save our Owls' campaign had so far spanned three games and just one point gained for Wednesday, with no goals scored.

Defeats at Fulham (2-1) and West Brom (4-0) prolonged that run, although the latter game was at least notable for the debut of David Herbert, who played alongside Roger Wylde up front as Burtenshaw hunted for a way of ensuring that his team scored goals. The *Green 'Un* reviewed the game simply: "Owls Crushed".

The *Star* had quietly dropped its 'Save our Owls' campaign by this stage but even before that point, there was plenty of dissent on its letters page. One contributor, J.L. Dobing of Middlewood, wrote: "The campaign... is ridiculous. You are asking the equivalent of drinking sour beer at the local and allowing my wife to buy stale and inferior food, to keep the respective businessmen trading." Another, N.J. Poppleton of Chapeltown, suggested that "this campaign will give a great relief to the Owls' board who for the past decade should bear full responsibility for the club's pathetic plight." Other letters questioned why Wednesday were getting seemingly special treatment from the paper. "This all-out boost for the Owls gives one the feeling that Sheffield United are non-existent," one read. The *Star's* decision to run the campaign was later held against it as a supposed example of a non-existent 'bias' towards Wednesday, over their city rivals United.

Whether descriptions of sour beer and stale food were fair or not, the Owls were certainly struggling to score goals with Burtenshaw admitting that a few goals in their next outing against Orient "would certainly do wonders for the forwards". This game was on March 15th and marked the start of the final ten games of the season but did not mark a return to goalscoring form for Wednesday as they lost 1-0, in front of 8,492. The Owls were almost beyond saving, with even the "Voice of Hillsborough" suggesting that "Wednesday must continue to fight purposefully against relegation until the job of escaping is complete – or the task of avoiding the drop becomes mathematically impossible."

The bookies certainly felt that relegation, if not a certainty, was an odds-on bet and one was offering a bet of 1/8 in favour of the Owls being relegated. That was before Wednesday's next game; a difficult trip to Ninian Park to face Cardiff. The Owls reached 0-0 at half-time but rather than slip to a customary defeat in the second half, defended steadfastly and returned from South Wales with a point from a goalless draw at full time.

The Cardiff draw at least showed that Wednesday had the ability to grind out results, ahead of a run of three games in 72 hours. Wednesday, if they were to avoid the drop, would need to pick up points over the Easter weekend; instead, they lost all three by a 1-0 scoreline. The third, to Nottingham Forest, mathematically sealed the relegation that had been all-but inevitable for months.

The home games against Millwall and Southampton were watched by disappointing crowds of 8,171 and 8,505, with the *Green 'Un* reporting the Millwall defeat as "the now familiar Wednesday story... good approach work wasted because of poor finishing". Up front for Wednesday that day were David Sunley and Roger Wylde; Burtenshaw reshuffled his pack for the

Southampton game, bringing in Ronnie Ferguson and Mick Prendergast (neither of whom had featured in the team for several weeks previously).

Burtenshaw altered the team again for the Nottingham Forest game, bringing Danny Cameron into midfield for his first appearance of the season. The resulting defeat was the nail in the coffin of Wednesday's relegation, and April Fool's Day 1975 saw the Owls facing up to the reality of Division Three football for the first time in their existence.

The club though still had five fixtures of the Division Two campaign to fulfil and a post-war low crowd (at that stage) of just 7,483 turned out at Hillsborough for the midweek visit of Norwich City, which saw Wednesday lose 1-0 after Ferguson was guilty of what the *Daily Mail* described as "the miss of the season" when he "failed to hit an empty net from only one yard". Wednesday's miserable run continued with a 1-0 defeat at Bristol City – their sixth defeat by that scoreline in their previous seven games – and Wednesday had by now gone eight games without scoring a goal, a run stretching back to December 14 the previous year. Next up at Hillsborough? A clash against their bogey side, Oxford United.

*****

Key Game: Sheffield Wednesday 1-1 Oxford United, April 19th, 1975

Six of the seven previous games between Wednesday and Oxford had seen The U's win 1-0, and the odd one out was a goalless draw between the two sides in April 1972. The crowd of 7,444 set another post-war attendance low.

1 Fox
2 Cameron
3 Quinn
4 Mullen
5 Dowd
6 Shaw

Our Lowest Ebb?

7 Potts
8 Harvey
9 Sunley
10 Henson
11 Joicey
Sub Wylde

The game started poorly for the Owls with future Wednesday favourite Andy McCulloch scoring after just eight minutes. At this stage the Owls were actually down to ten men, with Hugh Dowd receiving treatment for an ankle injury. He was unable to return to the action, so Wylde was called into the fray after just nine minutes. The *Green 'Un's* report takes up the story:

Superb Saves Thwart Owls: After only five minutes Wednesday were dealt a blow when Dowd went down in pain in his own area. He has recently been out with an ankle injury and it looked as though he had gone over on his ankle trying to stop an Oxford raid. He went off the pitch for treatment and Wednesday played with ten men. After eight minutes Wednesday were rocked when Oxford took the lead. McGrogan's corner on the left was neatly headed on by Derek Clarke and though Colin Clarke, in a fine position, saw his shot blocked, McCULLOCH scored from close range. A minute later Wednesday brought on substitute Wylde for Dowd, Shaw pulled back into the middle of defence with Wylde going into midfield. Wednesday then did get the ball into the net, but the referee's whistle had gone for a foul on Potts just outside the box. Potts took the free kick, but Oxford cleared.
A neat move taking in Shaw, Potts and Cameron ended when Cameron was held back by Derek Clarke when overlapping down the right flank.
The free kick for Potts was headed away by Colin Clarke and when it came to Quinn, his shot from the edge of the box was deflected away. Sunley then burst through only to see Milkins block his shot. Milkins then had to fist away with Joicey challenging him. Wylde crossed from the left and Henson by the far post, saw a header and then its subsequent shot somehow saved by

114

Milkins. In the final seconds of the half a header by Joicey, follow-ing a corner by Potts on the left, was kicked off the line.

The Owls had dominated the rest of the half following Oxford's goal, but a mixture of bad luck, great goalkeeping and a lack of confident finishing had prevented them from scoring. Long-suffering Owls may have been forgiven for thinking that the team would never score! Their side, though, began the second half in a similarly determined vein. The *Green 'Un* again takes up the story:

Wednesday were quick to attack and a 25-yard low drive by Quinn was easily saved. Potts, collecting the ball inside his own half from a throw by Fox, weaved his way into the Oxford dan-ger zone and Sunley shot over. Oxford replied with a fine run by Derek Clarke and he gave Wednesday problems before shooting wide from inside the box.
Wylde then fed Quinn whose cross from the left evaded Sunley and then Joicey's shot was off target. Potts and Henson combined down the left and after Sunley had tried to find a way through, the ball came to Potts, whose shot was saved second attempt by Milkins. Quinn, prominent this half with runs down the left, saw Milkins cut out his low cross.

The report ends there, with production deadlines presumably meaning that there was a need to ensure that the copy was with the printers in time to ensure that the *Green 'Un* was avail-able quickly after the game. An opening sentence was included, though: *"A close-range goal by Brian Joicey in injury time against Oxford this afternoon ended Sheffield Wednesday's goal famine and earned them a 1-1 draw, before 7,444 fans, Hillsborough's lowest crowd since the war."*

The goal is described in more detail by Owls' historian, Jason Dickinson, in his book *'100 Years at Hillsborough'*. "As the game entered the five minutes of injury-time added by referee Ken Walmsley, Wednesday attacked, and Jimmy Mullen swung in a high cross from the left wing. This wasn't properly dealt with by Milkins, allowing David Sunley to steer the goal towards the net with his head. As the ball headed for the net Brian Joicey made sure it was over the line."

The Owls had finally scored! It was their first goal in 14 hours and 10 minutes of football, and their first at Hillsborough in 14 hours and 25 minutes. The match was played in front of a low crowd – some of whom had drifted for the exits before the game reached its conclusion – but for those who remained – it was something of an "I was there" moment. The *Green 'Un's* front page headline commented somewhat drily: "Blades Storm Back to Win Key Game and (Wait for It) Owls Score!" It was the end of a dreadful sequence, but Wednesday still had two games to play before they could put the season to bed.

The first of those was a home match against Aston Villa, who were chasing promotion and needed the points themselves. Villa fans swelled the crowd to 23,605 and left Hillsborough by far the happier of the two sets of fans, as their side hammered Wednesday 4-0. The result effectively sealed promotion for Villa. Their supporters invaded the pitch at full-time in celebratory mood, only adding to the misery of the Wednesday fanbase and their already relegated team. Then, it was the turn of Wednesday to take impressive numbers of supporters on the road as 22 coaches of fans made the trip to Hull City for the final game of a miserable season, making up roughly half the crowd of 7,652 that day.

One man who didn't travel to East Yorkshire, however, was manager Burtenshaw, who was reportedly away watching another game in preparation for the following season. In his absence, it was a familiar story for Wednesday as they slipped to another 1-0 defeat and perhaps the most excitement during the game came from the replacement of the ball after only five minutes after the players complained it was too soft. Wednesday's team stayed on the pitch at the end of the game and applauded the fans; Matt Sheppard later named that support as his brightest moment of the season.

Possibly the worst season in the club's history was finally over. Wednesday had amassed a measly 21 points from 42 games, and finished 12 points from safety. They lost 26 games, drew 11 and won just five; scoring just 29 goals in the process. The Owls failed to score in 22 of their 42 games. Their top scorers were Eric Mc-Mordie (six goals) and Tommy Craig (four). Both men had left the club by the end of 1974. Wednesday were knocked out of both cups at the first time of asking, and were now facing the prospect of Division Three football for the first time in the club's history. With the gallows humour of fans at the time, some Owls supporters suggested that the club should have run a "month of the goal" competition. Crowds had reached a record low, and the club's finances were seemingly spiralling out of control. Things surely could not get any worse for Wednesday. Could they?

Chairman Matt Sheppard was interviewed by *The Star* in the weeks following relegation. "I, along with my colleagues on the board, am bitterly disappointed that Sheffield Wednesday have been relegated despite all the efforts made by everyone concerned," he said. "However, we are equally determined that every effort will be made to climb back at the earliest opportunity; if at all possible, next year."

When The Star asked exactly what went wrong, Sheppard admitted: "The team failed to score anything like sufficient goals. This failure to score, often when playing attractive and determined football early in most matches, put a good deal of additional stress and strain on the players causing their play to become ineffective. The results often bore little resemblance to the pattern of play. The set-up at Hillsborough is being geared for the sustained effort which will be required to bring lasting success to Hillsborough as soon as possible and this must begin with a rapid return to the Second Division."

Not everyone was as confident. Owls' historian Daniel Gordon states: "There was no buzz around Hillsborough; the team was depressed and so were its followers. Recovery would clearly not come in the foreseeable future." That future was in Division Three, where the team still had further to fall. Much would need to be done before that return to the Second Division was achieved. Much would change before Sheffield Wednesday reached its *"Lowest Ebb"*.

AN INTERVIEW WITH DANNY CAMERON

Daniel (Danny) Cameron was a Scottish full back and midfielder. Born in Dundee, he moved to the Owls as a youngster. He made his debut during the virus-hit months of 1973 and went on to play 38 times for the club, scoring one goal. Cameron moved to play over a hundred games for Preston, also spending time with his native Dundee. He moved to South Africa in the 1980s and it was from there that we discussed his career.

Thanks for helping Danny. My first question is - what memories do you have of coming into the team as a youngster?
My first appearance, albeit unofficial, for the first team came on a pre-season trip to Sweden in 1973. That came about as I was included in the travelling squad after Dave Clements refused to travel. I made my debut away to West Brom. The events leading up to that were definitely star aligned. The game was on a Wednesday evening and the rest of the professional players had been given the day off. Remember, no cell phones. I had arranged to meet a couple of others at the ground to go for a game of snooker or the like. In any event it was pure coincidence that I was sitting in the home dressing room when Derek Dooley came through and, on seeing me, told me to go home and get suited up as I was needed to travel with the first team as Rodders (Peter Rodrigues) had succumbed to the virus as well. My recollection of the game was that I held my own up against the superfast Willie Johnson. However, we were to lose the game. Subsequently more players contracted the bug and despite appeals, the league insisted that we complete our upcoming fixtures.

You soon made your home debut as well I believe?
Yes, Saturday came quickly, and we were at home to Notts County in front of the Yorkshire TV cameras. The game finished 0-0

and my recollection is of a proud DD (Derek Dooley) despite the prevailing circumstances.

You did well enough to stay in the team, I think?
Well, yes, I then played five games in a row including the 8-2 League Cup loss away to QPR [2-3 at half time]. It is no exaggeration to say that on chances created the game could have ended 12-12 but Phil Parkes was inspired and Springo [Peter Springett], who was captain for the night, just couldn't keep them out. DD had taken me aside to tell me to not be nervous given that it was my first game against Division One opposition and that I was to forget any mistakes and get on with the game; even my more experienced teammates would make some mistakes. Well, I needed those words as I scored an amazing own goal after just three minutes, heading home a Stan Bowles cross! I still have a photo of that goal. After the game we sat eating sandwiches at our hotel, shaking our heads in disbelief at the scoreline.

How did you find Derek Dooley as a manager?
I am fairly sure that we had opened the Middlewood training ground by this time, but we still changed at Hillsborough and obviously DD couldn't actively take part in training, leaving that up to Ron Staniforth, Gerry Young and George McCabe. I can't say that he didn't have the dressing room but there were quite a few very experienced players that he had to deal with at that time.

What are your memories of his sacking?
My thinking regarding the sacking on Christmas Eve was that it highlighted the total insensitivity and ruthlessness of the board of directors. Reflecting on DD I only have good things to say about him; starting from that afternoon in Germany when he took the youth team to a tournament. Some of us wanted to go for a walk and on asking his permission he said, as he tossed it to us, that we could, if we took along his tin leg as he was tired! I've said before that his appointment was EW Taylor's way to protect the season ticket sales at the time and that part worked. Derek was too nice a man for the job in hand and I am sad to say that my

last two memories of him was his optimism on the return journey from Crystal Palace after we had gained a credible draw – obviously buoying his spirits for the fight ahead – and then when he told us players, through his tears, that he'd been sacked that Christmas Eve. Unbelievable.

Did things change after Derek Dooley had left?
Well, if you look at the subsequent run of games from then on, we went the whole of January with only one loss, away to Coventry in the FA Cup replay. That to me didn't smack of a relegation-doomed team. In fact, that was our only defeat from the Palace game until Steve Burtenshaw's first game, which was away at Fulham. That result of 4-1 looks bad but I don't think that there was that much between the teams. Probably only Viv Busby being the difference as he bagged a hat trick on the day.

Am I right in thinking that game saw your only goal for Wednesday?
Yes, you are! My counter as I recall was in fact the equaliser coming close to half time. We had a corner from our left which they cleared towards the halfway line. I gathered the ball and driving forward I tried to play a one-two with Tommy Craig. He let the ball run across his path and smashed a left foot shot goalward. I continued forward past the outcoming defenders and arrived in the box at the same time as the ball rebounding from the crossbar onto the goalkeeper's back, leaving me a tap in. I turned back as you do to get the embraces of my teammates for the goal... only to see everyone mobbing TC!

You were in and out of the team then for the remainder of the season?
I played the following week but when Peter Rodrigues was fit again, I went back to the reserves. SB's first six games brought in three points and I think dropped our league position dramatically. The next game up was away to Notts County and I had trained with the reserves all week. Friday comes and I get told to train with the first team. We practised a shadow play type

exercise whereby I, as a midfield player in the eleven, followed Gerry Young, the only opposition player, and closed him down whenever the ball was turned over to him. The plan as it turned out was to include me in the first team midfield to mark Notts County's Scottish international Don Masson. I hadn't played in midfield since Sunday League football as an under 15. Anyway, the plan worked, and we won 5-1. I had a stormer and played in six consecutive games in a row in midfield, with three wins, two losses and a draw. That series of games went a long way to giving us a chance of survival.

You must have had high hopes for the following season?

My memories of the following season after our miraculous escape are somewhat bitty. I was included as 12th man for the opening game away to Oldham but from then on seemingly relegated from SB's plans for the season. So much so that when we signed Phil Henson in Feb 1975, I entered the home dressing room and was immediately confronted with the sight of Phil wearing my number 30 training kit. I was told that SB wanted to see me. He told me that he'd agreed to let me go out on loan to Colchester for the next month, so off I went as it meant first team football. I had five good performances for them, but Jim Smith told me that they couldn't pay the 10 grand transfer fee and be able to look after me as well. So, it was back to Hillsborough and the reserves.

You did return to the first team though?

Yes, a couple of weeks later at the end of the Easter weekend I'm included to play at Forest for the injured Colin Harvey. My first appearance of the season was to be historic. I play in midfield and whilst clearing a corner I was adjudged to have fouled Barry Butlin. The referee gave a penalty which they scored to beat us 1-0. That was the sixth-last league game of the season and as a result of that penalty, it was then mathematically impossible for us to stay up. Obviously, relegation was inevitable but to be forever associated with the final nail, so to speak, was upsetting to me as I was still a relatively young man.

How did you find the drop to Division Three?
The season had started quite poorly results-wise, but I was holding down the right back slot until I suffered a knee ligament injury in training in the week following a 1-1 draw at Palace – a game that was featured on Match of the Day. Shortly thereafter SB was sacked and in came Len Ashurst, accompanied by his fitness guru Tony Toms. When I was fully fit again, I naturally expected to be involved with the first team, but Len just didn't give me a smell, despite playing almost everyone in the league team at some point. Also, he had brought in Richard Walden whilst I was out injured, and the writing appeared to be on the wall for me at Wednesday.

I went to see Len and the upshot of that meeting was that I could go for free if a club came in for me. My name was circulated and shortly thereafter Preston approached me; Harry Catterick was the manager and Nobby Stiles was his first team coach. I jumped at the opportunity. I played a couple of games against Wednesday during that period – including what was to be a kind of bittersweet game at Deepdale which finished 2-1 to Preston. I cleared the ball off the line twice in the last few minutes and Wednesday took the decision to let Len go the following day after that result.

In seems as if you still had a bit of a soft spot for the Owls then?
[Laughs] Yes! Some of my fondest memories are of coming of age in the Sheffield of the early 1970s. It was vibrant and we were able to make friends as young pros with many of the rank and file Kopites. We'd play for the Northern Intermediates on the Saturday morning and then join the local Wednesday fans in the Ozzie Owl club in the lead up to kick-off. We were able to mix with the fans in the pubs and clubs of Sheffield with great ease and, as young adults, our feet were kept firmly on the ground through those liaisons. When I broke into the senior squad, I felt that everyone had my back if I was honest and gave everything in every game. Circumstances and opinions shape your career and I never thought that I would ever leave Wednesday once I settled

there. I am safe in the knowledge that I for one gave everything I could for the cause in every appearance that I made in a Wednesday shirt.

History has indicated that the club was broken from the late 1960s and the downward slide was in some ways inevitable. My seven years there are filled with some fantastic memories and some sad unbelievable happenings. Sheffield will always be close to my heart and I hope one day that you see your beloved club back in the top echelon of English football.

THE PLAYERS

A tale of swashbuckling strikers, tricky wingers, international class players, never-say-die defenders and a real loan ranger. It makes you wonder how the team struggled so badly, given the qualities of these players identified by the fans as their favourites of the era.

The research for this book took place in 2019. In an online survey of fans who remembered the Owls' teams of 1973-76, I asked the following question: *"Please name your three favourite SWFC players 1973-76. Please comment as to why underneath."* This provoked a series of interesting responses from the supporters. This chapter provides a countdown of those fan favourites in reverse order of the votes they received. It is not intended as a scientific survey of who the "best" players were during the period; more a recognition that many players are remembered fondly and an attempt to explain why.

Across the three seasons covered by this book, 43 players appeared for the Owls in league and cup games (see appendix for the full list). Two players represented the club on only one occasion (Dave Clements and Barry Watling). Clements had played regularly in previous seasons; Watling saw out his only appearance in January 1976. At the other end of the spectrum two players appeared over 100 times across the three seasons (Bernard Shaw and Eric Potts).

Three players scored more than 10 goals in total across the time period (Potts with 20, Brian Joicey with 17 and Mick Prendergast top of the list with 24). The next few pages will attempt to do justice to some of the crowd favourites. I will attempt to explain why certain players are remembered so positively among a team that was struggling so badly.

Number Ten: Ken Knighton
Ken Knighton was signed by Derek Dooley in the summer of

1973 from Hull City for the interesting sum of £57,777. He was a tough and uncompromising player whose playing career with the Owls coincided with the time frame of this book. Between 1973 and 1976, when he moved to the coaching staff, Knighton played 84 games and scored four goals. The most vital of those goals was the 86th-minute winner against Bolton on the last day of the 1973-74 season which saved the Owls from relegation. Knighton was club captain at that time and was carried off the pitch by delighted Owls' fans after the game. He was dedicated to the cause and famously kicked off the visitors' dressing room door in frustration at being sent off away at Orient in 1974. He was sent off after only 29 minutes for using industrial language at one of his own players – the referee assumed that the language was aimed at him!

Some fans saw this as evidence of Knighton's determination to help the team. In my survey he is remembered as "an Iron Man figure… a rock", and as a player who "always gave 100 per cent". Knighton played over 400 games in his career. He went into coaching and management, including spells as manager at Sunderland and at Orient (who did not charge him for the broken door!) His time at Hillsborough was not successful in terms of the team but he played with determination and courage and therefore deserves to be well remembered by Owls fans. Knighton did not want to be fully interviewed for this project but did pass on his best wishes for its success and hopes that the book becomes a best seller.

Number Nine: David Sunley

David (Dave) Sunley signed for the Owls as an apprentice in 1968, after writing to then manager Alan Brown asking for a trial. He made rapid progress through the youth and reserve teams and made his debut in the first team at the age of 18 in 1970. In our period, Sunley played 67 times, and scored nine goals. Two of those goals were in a 4-4 draw against Manchester United in 1974 – helping earn him a place in Hillsborough folklore as part of one of the most exciting games of the era. In the survey Sunley is remembered as a player who "could really jump – dribble too", and as someone who had "real skill, not an out an out striker, but a very talented forward player." Sunley was in and out of the team in 1974-75 as Steve Burtenshaw hunted for a goalscoring partnership that worked.

Partly out of frustration with this, Sunley refused to sign a new contract in 1975 and after a short loan spell at Brian Clough's Nottingham Forest, he signed for Hull City in early 1976. Sunley was a talented player, who scored some memorable goals for the club. The fans remember him as talented, if somewhat unfulfilled. Dave himself talks through his Hillsborough career with me elsewhere in the book.

Number Eight: Willie Henderson

Willie Henderson joined the Owls from Glasgow Rangers in July 1972. He had a hugely successful career at Rangers, playing 478 games for the Ibrox team and scoring 36 goals. He won two Scottish League championships, the Scottish Cup four times and the League Cup twice. He was also part of the Rangers team that got to the finals of the 1960–61 and 1966–67 Cup Winners' Cup competitions – playing in the final in 1967 against Bayern Munich. He also played 29 times for Scotland, scoring another five goals.

Henderson was nicknamed "Wee Willie" as he stood just 5ft 4ins tall. He was also famous for his short-sightedness, wearing contact lenses to play football. Legend has it that, late on in a crucial Old Firm match, he inquired of the sidelines: "How long to go, how long to go?" Jock Stein then replied: "Go and ask the other dugout, you bloody fool – this is the Celtic bench!"

Henderson signed for the Owls after a fall-out with the then-Rangers manager Willie Waddell meant he missed the 1972 Cup Winners' Cup Final in Barcelona. Derek Dooley was very happy to sign him for the Owls and he went on to play 56 times for the Owls – although only 22 of those games were in the timeframe covered by this book.

He is remembered clearly by those who completed my survey: "An old-fashioned winger who could dribble and cross a ball and get the crowd going", "very tricky with some great skill", "magician on the wing", and "cult hero", are just some of the many comments about him. It is obvious that Henderson had talent and the ability to excite a crowd.

He left the club in 1974 to ply his trade in Hong Kong and, for the relatively short time he was with the Owls, and given the teams that he played in, it is evident why he is so well-remembered by the fans of the time. Henderson is interviewed elsewhere in the book where he explains how his years at Hillsborough were a "special time" for him.

Number Seven: Peter Rodrigues

Peter Rodrigues was already hugely experienced when he joined the Owls in October 1970. He had played internationally for Wales, earning the first of his 40 caps in 1965, and had played in the FA Cup final for Leicester City in 1969. Rodrigues played regularly for the Owls, making 174 appearances and scoring two goals before his departure at the end of the 1974-75 season. One of those goals was a stunning 30-yard effort at Bristol Rovers in 1974 that may have earned his place in this top ten on its own. Rodrigues' qualities are recognised by the fans in my survey: "International full back whose ability shone above the rest in defence...", said one. "Had a great name, and moustache!" added another.

Jimmy Mullen picked Rodrigues in his fantasy ex-Owls team at the time of his testimonial, explaining that "His pace and tackling make Peter an obvious choice for me." Rodrigues moved on to Southampton after leaving the Owls, winning the FA Cup with them in 1976, before being forced into retirement with a persistent knee injury the following season. Lots was expected of Rodrigues on his arrival at Hillsborough: "Wednesday have paid a big fee," said the club's programme on his arrival. "At 26 and with 22 full international caps [he] should bring the stability and experience needed".

Rodrigues himself said: "I consider myself a First Division player and I want the rest of our team to adopt this attitude of mind each time we play." He suffered from playing in a team in obvious decline, but his class and quality still shone through at times and it is obvious therefore why he remains a favourite of some of the fans from the time.

Number Six: Jimmy Mullen

Jimmy Mullen was dedicated to the Owls' cause throughout the 1970s. He made his debut on Boxing Day 1970 as an 18-year-old – seeing the team lose a 4-1 lead to draw 4-4 against Hull City. He was in and out of the team for the early part of the decade, before playing 41 games in the 1975-76 season. He maintained his place in the team for the next few seasons and captained the promotion-winning team of 1979-80. Mullen was not a flashy performer, describing himself as "a bread and butter player", adding he was "not one of those players who can do fantastic things on the ball." Fans in my survey remember him similarly: "Always solid," said one, "just did his job," added another.

His teammates also appreciated his qualities. Brian Joicey said Mullen "never let Sheffield Wednesday down," while Ken Knighton remembered "a terrific lad who works very hard at his game". Eddie Prudham told me in 2019 that Mullen "was a great guy and a solid player." Mullen played 262 games for the Owls in total, in a professional career where he appeared a total of 431 times. He moved on to Rotherham and later Cardiff, achieving promotions with each, before switching to coaching and management. Jimmy Mullen was unlikely to come top of any poll of fans' favourite players of the 1970s, but his dedication, hard work and effort deserve the recognition he is given here.

Number Five: Eric McMordie

"Eric" McMordie (real name Alexander) signed for the Owls on loan in October 1974. He was a talented striker, friends with George Best, and went on to win 30 caps for Northern Ireland. He initially came to England for trials at Manchester United at the same time as Best, both 15-year-olds deciding to return home to Belfast on their first day in Lancashire. "I felt bad about it for a long time as we were treated so well. We were just too young." McMordie remembered in 2015. While Best was persuaded to return McMordie remained in Northern Ireland, working on building sites, before returning to football with local team Dundela. Just over two years later he came back to England a little older and wiser, and signed for Middlesbrough aged 18. He joined the Owls on loan from there a decade later after being unsettled on Teesside for a while. After his first Wednesday game produced a goal and a win, he admitted: "Considering I have been out of top-class football for a year, I didn't play too badly."

He certainly didn't play badly for the Owls – scoring six goals in his nine games before returning to Middlesbrough in December. McMordie declined to move permanently to Hillsborough, citing personal and business interests in the North-East. The Owls fans who completed my survey remember McMordie very simply. One asked how a short-term loan could end the season as top-scorer, while another described him as the "best loan ever". That last statement may be debatable, given the amount of loan players the Owls have used in recent years, but it is easy to see how a goal-scoring loanee is remembered fondly from a season of goal drought.

Number Four: Tommy Craig

Thomas (Tommy) Brooks Craig was born in Glasgow in 1950, and his footballing talents first came to attention with the Lourdes School team and Glasgow Boys. He gained schoolboy international honours before joining Aberdeen's ground staff at 15. Tommy turned professional with Aberdeen on his 17th birthday in November 1967, before his transfer to the Owls in May 1969. Tommy chose the Owls over Aston Villa – a fact which pleases this West Midlands-based Owl no end! Tommy and his transfers set a variety of records during his career. His initial transfer to Hillsborough was for a British record fee for a teenager of £100,000.

He was also the first-ever Scotsman to join an English club for a fee reaching six figures. The fee was also Sheffield Wednesday's record outlay. His eventual transfer from the Owls to Newcastle United in December 1974, saw Wednesday receive a club record £120,000 for his services.

He made 233 appearances for the Owls across seven seasons and scored 40 goals. In the time period covered by this book, he played 63 games and scored nine goals. Craig left Hillsborough and continued to have a successful career in the game. He played another 124 times for Newcastle, before moving on to Aston Villa, Swansea City, Carlisle United and finally back to Scotland with Hibernian. He also gained one full cap for Scotland in 1976 and played a total of 571 professional games, scoring 89 goals. After retirement he worked in coaching and management including spells as assistant manager at Celtic, first team coach at Newcastle and in the manager's chair at Charleroi and most recently, St Mirren. Former Scottish international and ex-Celtic assistant manager, John Collins, described Craig as the best coach he ever worked with.

Tommy should not be remembered simply for the records, however. He was a favourite of many at Hillsborough, known for his cultured left foot and expertise at penalty taking. One fan in my survey described him simply as the most talented by far while another saw him as "stylish… one of our few relatively big-name players in that period". "A class apart in midfield and scored his fair share of goals," was the view of another supporter. "I don't know how we held on to him for so long in such a poor side but so glad we did!"

A fellow fan describes Craig as their all-time Wednesday favourite, and he is included in the book 'Sheffield Wednesday – Illustrating the Greats', pictured as one of the Owls' finest ever players. Jason Dickinson, Wednesday's official historian, described Craig as possessing "an outstanding left foot, tremendous shooting ability and did not look out of place in the top-flight". Jimmy Mullen described him as "one of the best left footers in the game – with a terrific shot" while his manager at Aberdeen, Eddie Turnbull, said later that Craig's "talents were obvious… it was a crying shame to lose him."

Craig was Wednesday's regular penalty taker during his time at Hillsborough and although one fan admitted he couldn't remember him ever missing one, he did in fact miss a handful – although on one occasion, against Preston in March 1972, he was able to right the wrong of hitting the post from the spot by later crashing home the winning penalty in the 75th minute.

Craig admitted at the time that he "liked the responsibility of being on the spot" and that he had the penalty-taking job in every team that he had played for. In more recent times, in discussing his time at Hillsborough, Craig admitted he had found it difficult to find his feet and revealed the problems of establishing himself in a team that was struggling.

He described Derek Dooley very favourably as someone who "went out of his way to make me feel wanted, constantly showing faith in my ability to succeed." He also tells the story of how he ensured that he was near to Pele at the end of the famous friendly with Santos in 1972, in order to swap shirts with the Brazilian.

Overall, Craig remembers his time at S6 with fondness: "I shall always have a special affinity with Hillsborough," he said. "Plenty of good memories." But when interviewed in the later 1970s, during his time with Aston Villa, Craig was less positive about his stay at Hillsborough. "A lot was expected of me during my stay there and, if truthful, I never fulfilled that promise," he said. "I honestly can't say that I have any general good memories of the place."

Those frustrations, though, seem to have faded over time, as later in life he was much more positive about the Owls. Craig was a very talented and classy player.

It is unfortunate for Owls fans that he never played in a successful Wednesday team, as his talents deserved to be seen at the highest level. When he left the club in December 1974, most fans understood that he had earned the right to be playing at a higher level.

One fan from my survey explains the feeling clearly: "Tommy Craig is my all time Wednesday favourite. Even though he never played in a successful side, he was a brilliant player with a beautiful left foot. He served the club loyally.... Luckily for him he found success later in his career at Newcastle United."

Craig left the Owls before the club truly reached its "Lowest Ebb." He had a prodigious talent and some affinity for the club, and so is held in high esteem by Owls' fans of the era for his quality and efforts in difficult times.

Number Three: Eric Potts

Eric Stanley Potts was born in Liverpool in 1950. Part of his school-days were spent at the Anfield Comprehensive School, within a stone's throw of the home of Liverpool FC. He began his foot-balling career as an amateur with Blackpool, though never played in the first team for the Tangerines. He moved into non-league football with New Brighton and Oswestry Town, and the Owls signed him from Oswestry for £4,000 in December 1969 on the recommendation of scout Bill Evans. Potts made his debut in October 1970 and was in and out of the team over the following seasons until gaining a regular place in the side in 1973.

Potts was a mainstay of the team for the seasons covered by this book – enjoying a consecutive run of 94 appearances that ended in February 1976. He was the only ever-present player in the disastrous 1974-75 season and ended that season as the club's Player of the Season, a feat he repeated in 1976. He appeared a total of 182 times for the Owls, scoring 25 goals between 1970 and his departure in 1977. In the three seasons focused on by this book, Potts made 137 appearances and scored 20 goals.

Potts left Hillsborough in a £14,000 deal with Brighton and Hove Albion. He played only one season for the Seagulls, often appearing as a substitute (four of his five goals were from the bench) before moving for £37,000 to Preston the following summer. He moved on two years later to Burnley (for £20,000) and in 1982 to his final league club, Bury. He played non-league football with Witton Albion and Clitheroe before retirement. His career, with five clubs, had seen him play over 350 league games, scoring 42 goals – the last of which came in his very last game.

Both of his sons have played football. Eldest son Colin was initially with Preston but played all his first team football in non-league. His youngest son Michael started his career as a schoolboy with Manchester United before moving on to Blackburn Rovers, where he was a member of the team that reached the semi-final of the FA Youth Cup in the 2008/09 season.

Although Michael never played first-team football for Black-burn, he did make 13 appearances and score three goals for York City in their return to league football in 2012-13. Potts is remembered well by the fans who completed my survey. "Eric Potts – great winger, exciting to watch", said one supporter. Another commented that Potts was a "tricky little player on his day" and another described him as "a bright light in a very dull team." Brighton were certainly happy to have signed him in 1977 and a *Shoot* Magazine article at the time commented that "Potts' will-o'-the-wisp skill has electrified many crowds and will quickly win over the Brighton supporters.

An exciting individualist, his darting runs and 90-minute wholeheartedness will undoubtedly set the terraces buzzing at his new club just as he did many times in the seven years he was with Wednesday." Potts remembered his time with the Owls fondly. "I've had some good years with [*The Owls*] and got on well with the directors and supporters… you can't play for them for seven years and not have them in your heart. The supporters made me… they pushed and pushed by letters to the press and in other ways to get me into the side."

Potts also said that looking back the high spot of his career was playing against the legendary Pele when with Sheffield Wednesday. His former team mates also appreciated his talents. "A 90 minute live-wire winger," was how Jimmy Mullen described him, "Eric was quick and skilful and the type of player to win a game." Potts was certainly popular among fans and was regularly featured among the pictures in the matchday programmes of the period.

His style of play was energetic and busy. He was determined and as one fan has it: "Little Eric often provided the few moments of excitement in a dreadful season (*1974-75*)." Eric Potts made a good career from football and served the Owls well. His career at Hillsborough peaked with the seasons that saw the team at its *"Lowest Ebb"* – but he provided some excitement in those difficult times and was deservedly a fan favourite. Eric is now living in retirement in Lancashire, where he encourages one of his grandsons who is in Preston North End's academy.

Although he did not want to be fully interviewed for the book, he wished the project every success and remembers his time at Hillsborough fondly.

Number Two: Brian Joicey

Brian Joicey was one of the Owls' key strikers for the period of this book. Born in Winlaton, County Durham in 1945, he joined the Owls from Coventry City for £55,000 in August 1971 in a double deal with Dave Clements. Joicey had spent time in non-league football and did not make his professional debut (with Coventry) until he was 23. He had previously scored at Wembley in the FA Amateur Cup Final for North Shields and impressed Derek Dooley with his performances for Coventry's reserve team. On joining the club, Joicey said: "Sheffield Wednesday belong in the First Division and I will strive to help them get there."

He quickly became a crowd favourite at Hillsborough, scoring 16 goals in 1971-72 and a further 20 in 1972-73. These early goals included hat-tricks against Crystal Palace in an FA Cup re-play in 1973 and in the league against Leyton Orient in 1971. Dooley described him as "strong, big-hearted and fearless" while Joicey himself described his own style thus: "As a professional footballer, you cannot afford to be soft. I know I have a deter-mined streak, but I also believe I have skill too."

Joicey remained at Hillsborough until 1976 and was not as successful in later seasons, though he was the club's top scorer with 12 goals in 1973-74. His final two seasons were plagued by injury and saw him score only five more times; al-though one of those goals famously ended the club's lengthy goal drought in 1975 when he scored a late equaliser against Oxford United.

At the end of the 1975-76 season Joicey was granted a free transfer to Barnsley where he regained fitness and form – scoring 43 goals in 93 appearances. Famously, Mick McCarthy cleaned Joicey's boots as a young player at Oakwell!

After collapsing on the pitch in a game in 1978, Joicey was diagnosed as having suffered a minor stroke and retired from the game. He had scored exactly 100 goals in professional football, netting them in all four divisions, the FA Cup and in European football. A 1979 testimonial at Barnsley was well attended by both Owls and Barnsley supporters, and the descriptions of Joicey in the brochure for that testimonial give some idea of how well regarded he was. He had "a priceless blend of skill and courage", provided: "many moments of delight" and "never provided anything less than value for money." Later life saw him open a car dealership and work for Honda in Sheffield before retirement in 2010. Brian remains a regular visitor to Hillsborough with one or more of his four "Sheffield Wednesday-daft" grandsons.

The story of Joicey's stroke diagnosis is somewhat harrowing, and worthy of recapping in his own words:

"I got a kick in the kidneys before half time and I went in to see the physio. I went to the toilet and was passing blood so that was a bit of a shock. I was sent to the chemist when I got back and just told to take some tablets and to be in training on Tuesday. I've got no bad feelings about Barnsley but nowadays you'd be sent straight to hospital. On the Monday I woke up I could barely stand up; I rang the club and was told to get across. I got in the car but couldn't drive, my mate took me over, but I was sent to hospital. Ten days later I was shopping with my daughter and wife, who was pregnant with my son at the time. My wife asked me what I thought about this toy pram and I opened my mouth but couldn't speak. It was on the Moor in Sheffield, I just collapsed. The funny thing is there was a sign there which I collapsed outside, it said 'The Gateway to Health' I went to hospital, I didn't know what was happening, I heard 'stroke' mentioned. I was lucky. I could nod my head, but I couldn't speak. I couldn't even say 'yes' or 'no'. I could just nod my head."

Jimmy Mullen described Joicey as a player who "always gave everything and went for every chance, even at the risk of personal injury." Joicey played football with a smile on his face and with determination and grit. A feature in the matchday programme in 1975 revealed his professional ambition was to finish above Malcolm Macdonald in the goalscoring charts and his "biggest drag" in soccer was simply "not scoring". Joicey must have felt that drag through the difficult months of 1974-75 when neither he nor the Owls could score goals. Joicey broke a lengthy goal drought with a scrappy goal against Oxford in April 1975 but always remained confident in his ability. "I knew I wasn't the best but... I knew exactly what I had," he said. "Which is why I gave everything in every match – that's why I think the people of Wednesday and Barnsley liked me a little bit."

Similarly to Eric Potts, action photographs of Brian Joicey were featured regularly in the match programmes of the period. The images show him giving his all for the team and give a glimpse of his goalscoring talent. Joicey struggled for form and with injury during the period covered by this book. In those three seasons, Joicey made 79 appearances and scored 17 goals. He was clearly popular with players and fans. An adopted Wednesday-ite, he is still well-regarded by Owls fans and certainly made the most of his talent in very difficult times for the club. Brian Joicey now lives in retirement near Sheffield and although not fully interviewed for the book, did send his best wishes and commented how pleased he is to still be remembered by Owls fans.

Number One: Mick Prendergast

Michael John (Mick) Prendergast was born in the South Yorkshire mining village of Denaby Main in 1950. He signed for the Owls in 1966 on youth terms and made his league debut in 1969 – scoring in a 3-2 win over Newcastle. He went on to score 59 goals for the Owls in 207 appearances. Prendergast was named the supporters' player of the season for the Owls in 1974 and scored crucial goals during the three seasons that this book concentrates upon. One of those goals was scored in the 2-1 win over Southend that ensured survival in Division Three in 1976. In the three seasons focused on by this book Prendergast made 77 appearances and scored 24 goals.

Prendergast played in youth teams in the Don and Dearne Valley League and for Yorkshire Boys before joining the Wednesday youth system. He turned professional on his 17th birthday in 1967 and finished the top scorer in the club's reserve team in 1968-69. His most prolific campaign for the Owls was the first following relegation into Division Two, as he scored 16 goals in the 1970-71 campaign. Much of his career was interrupted by injury. He suffered a broken leg at Preston towards the end of the 1973-74

A poster and stickers advertising the Sheffield Star's "Save our Owls" campaign of early 1975. *Micheal Roe*

OWLS MANAGER IN THE MOOD FOR SHOWDOWN TALK

a defender of real

BY IAN VICKERS

SHEFFIELD Wednesday manager Steve Burtenshaw is to seek talks with new chairman Bert McGee following the linking of Cambridge manager Ron Atkinson with the Hillsborough job.

'I must get away' insists Owls star

By PETER COOPER

TOMMY CRAIG, Sheffield Wednesday's first and only £100,000 player, has underlined his determination to leave Hillsborough.

The 22-year-old Scot, signed from Aberdeen in 1969 asked for a transfer late last year but was still awaiting an answer when Wednesday fired their manager Derek Dooley on Christmas Eve.

Craig has since had talks with new manager Steve Burtenshaw, who asked Craig to delay a decision until the end of March—after the deadline for unrestricted transfers this season.

But Craig could now be in line for a move to West Ham, in part exchange for

'keeper Bobby Ferguson whose month's loan to Wednesday expires after Saturday's game at Hull.

Scotland Under-23 international Craig said last night: "I know deep down I need a change of club.

"I came down here from Aberdeen with high hopes of playing in the First Division and representing Scotland.

"Neither aim has materialised. The club has done nothing but struggle and we're relegated to the Second Division in my first season here.

"This in turn has affected my form—my obviously harmed my chances of playing for Scotland.

"I now have no chance of helping Scotland in West Germany, which has been my burning ambition, and can only hope for the next World Cup.

"That's why I want to get away. As I see it, it is going to take at least four years before Wednesday get back in the First

TOMMY CRAIG ... "Wasted ... Hillsborough."

A ray of sunshine at last for the Owls

DAVID Herbert is already making a habit of proving so effective just when all is lost, writes Ian Vickers.

The young Wednesday forward, who last month took a large share of the credit for an own goal by a Brighton defender which gave the Owls a point, was in the right place at the right time (just) to give his side their first Division Three win, 1-0 over Wrexham.

His header came with only 11 minutes to go to provide Wednesday with a happy ending to a strange sort of match.

The first half was not one to remember but the match came to life after half-time when both sides went close several times.

Perhaps the turning point came shortly before Wednesday scored when Ramsbottom, whose performance could not be faulted

out a shot from Thomas at point-blank range.

This was at a time when it looked as though a goal must come sooner or later. It did and for once Wednesday struck.

Yet they will not want to remember their first half display which could have so easily left them one down. Just before the interval Lyons shot from inside the box yet Ramsbottom kept out the effort with his feet.

Wednesday substitute Ken Knighton, on for Bobby Brown, added bite to the side – emphasised with one great tackle which not only dispossessed his Wrexham opponent but set Wednesday attacking.

Anyway we shall se shouts of "Char from one fan aft seem a bit prematu

All's well that e however and the wir providing Wednesda result at Swindon o day, bring them m the next home mate the Wrexham gate w cidentally, was the best in Division.

Newspaper cuttings covering the Owls during our period.

Sheffield Newspapers

THOMPSON IS THE MAN TO LEAD OWLS REVIVAL SAYS ASHURST

BY IAN VICKERS

SHEFFIELD Wednesday captain Allan Thompson, who has just signed a new contract and is now off the transfer list, was paid the highest compliment by manager Len Ashurst following Saturday's home draw with Rotherham.

Ashurst said: "If we are going to get out of the Third and into Division Two, he is going to be the lad to take us there."

Thompson's form on Saturday justified the confidence placed in him. He read the game well and was the pick of the defence.

Thompson, who has captained the side since Ashurst's arrival, said: "I feel as though I'm respected by the manager. He's given me 100 per cent and I'm giving him that. I think he'll do

I enjoy being captain and I just go out on the pitch and try to get through to the lads what the manager wants.

These past few months have been remarkable for Thompson, 24 last month.

At the end of last season he thought his career at Hillsborough was over and in May was in dispute with the club over pay.

During his career he's put in numerous transfer requests but they seem a thing of the past now.

It's clear that the two Liverpudlians, Ashurst and Thompson, have a mutual admiration society!

SOMETHING TO SHOUT ABOUT

'A DISGRACE OF SHEFFIEL

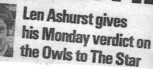

Len Ashurst gives his Monday verdict on the Owls to The Star

'The Owl' Focus on

Mick Prendergast

Full name: MICHAEL JOHN PRENDERGAST.

Birthplace: Denaby Main.

Date of birth: 24th November, 1950.

Height: 5 ft. 9½ in.

Weight: 11 st. 10 lb.

Married: No.

Car: MGB-GT.

Favourite player: Geoff Salmons.

Favourite other team: Denaby United.

Most difficult opponent: Chris Nichol.

Most memorable match: Crystal Palace (Cup replay).

Biggest disappointment: Preston North End— broke leg.

Biggest thrill: Début.

Nicest country visited: Italy.

Favourite food: Chips, beans.

Favourite TV shows: Tom & Jerry; Road Runner.

Favourite singers: Frank Sinatra; Carpenters; Beatles.

Favourite actor/actress: James Cagney; Katherine Ross.

Miscellaneous likes: Golf; racing; eating.

Miscellaneous dislikes: Travelling; injuries.

Best friend: I have many.

Biggest influence on career: Parents.

Biggest drag in soccer: Bad referees.

Personal ambition: To be happy.

Professional ambition: To help Wednesday back into First Division.

If you were not a footballer what would you like to be: Gravedigger.

Which person would you most like to meet: Lester Piggot; ex-President Nixon.

Above: A feature in the programme with Mick Prendergast - a lover of chips and beans, with many best friends and an ambition to become a gravedigger! *Sheffield Wednesday.* Below: Len Ashurst has his say in The Star, December 1975. *Sheffield Newspapers*

THE OLD ORDER CHANGES — SO NOW WE'LL DO IT MY WAY

I HAVE now had over two months to get "bedded in" at Hillsborough and I think it is an opportune time to put into print my thoughts on the situation at the club.

It was obvious with a club that had slipped from grace like we have over the years that the set up was not right and the quality of player was not in the club in enough numbers.

There is no reason for a new manager to make radical changes in the set-up and

LEN

ASHURST SAYS:

United. But at my club we have been losing for years and it was obvious that a sound appraisal of the staff was very necessary.

When I had chosen the players, for various reasons, to leave the club, the circular which went out to all league clubs was the first step in the building process which is so necessary.

The biggest factor which is stopping a lot of the players from doing their stuff is that they are used to losing.

ACCEPTANCE

If you check up on some players they have not won more than half a dozen times in the last 18 months. There is an acceptance of

defeat in the dressing room with certain players because that's what they are used to, and so, for this reason alone, a change of club for some and new faces in the team for those who I think can do a job will help to eradicate this particular cancer.

It's not easy to effect change overnight, and certainly Tony Toms and I coming to the club have not set the team alight with results, but from our point of view we are effecting change in the attitude of the individual in the team.

The morgue-like pre-match dressing room has now gone and in its place we have a professional, bubbling atmosphere with eleven lads ready to put

everything into the 90 minutes.

They understand how to compete and having done it, they are beginning to like the feel of it. Supporters will see the biggest change in this respect in Allan Thompson and Brian Joicey.

EXAMPLE

In Thompson's case you all know what a different man he is from the attitude angle and he would be the first to admit it. A number of other players are sharper and more aggressive than in previous months because they have quickly caught on to what we are looking for.

These are the two best examples but you too can pick your own men out. At

apprentice level changes have been made. They now change with the senior players, they mix with them within the club and as often as possible they train with the seniors so as to get the feel of what is required of them.

I am trying to establish a pattern of the way I want everyone to play throughout the club and top of the list is that they have to be competitive and hard to beat.

Then, if you have the quality you are in with a shout. At the moment we are starting to compete well but having put out a circular which carried a lot of names, it's obvious I am not happy with the quality.

We have too many players

on par with each other in ability and football sense as well as having a few who are past their best days. This all has to change before we see a rise in our fortunes.

I have not mentioned finance. Already many minor cuts have been made in the general running of the club because our financial situation is serious and to put the team on its feet I will need a few new faces.

My board realise the problem on the park and will stretch themselves to the limit to help me do the right thing. There will be no big money signings at the moment but we will have new blood and when the time is right in the future, we will "cast our bread on the water and reap our rewards."

Above: Happier times at Hillsborough as Brazilian superstar Pele signs autographs after his appearance in a friendly game between Santos and the Owls in February 1972. Featured in the picture, from left to right: Tony Pritchett (journalist); Derek Dooley (manager); Jimmy Mullen, Pele, Allan Thompson, Tommy Craig (players) and Eric Taylor (general manager). *Sheffield Newspapers*

Tommy Craig rises to head the ball in front of the home fans standing on the north-west corner. *Sheffield Newspapers*

Eric Potts leaves the field at Hillsborough after taking part in a kickabout during a club open day in 1976. *Mark Ford*

H.E. (Bert) McGee showing his determination to rectify the club's financial situation with the 1976 share issue. *SWFC*

Key men at the beginning of our period, Eric Taylor and Derek Dooley, pose outside Hillsborough. *Sheffield Newspapers*

Friends for life. A recent picture of Eddie Prudham and his former Wednesday teammate, David Sunley. *Eddie Prudham*

A Happy Xmas & A Sporting New Year

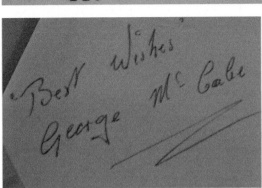

Above and top: "A thoroughly nice man" - A Christmas card sent to
all youth team players by George McCabe.   *The Herbert Family*
Right: Home and away tickets in the mid-1970s.   *Vernon Grant*
Below: Hillsborough from above, 1974.   *Sheffield Wednesday*

Hillsborough

the home of SHEFFIELD WEDNESDAY

"Soccerpix" advert. A free poster was produced by the Sheffield Star to affix player pictures that could be collected by purchasing copies of the paper and collecting the vouchers inside. And, amazingly, some have survived to this day! *Sheffield Newspapers*

Mick Prendergast's testimonial brochure. *SWFC*

The Owls Shop

All that's best in Soccer Souvenirs, plus great new lines

Left: An extensive price list for the Wednesday club shop, 1974-75, showing a wide range of souvenirs. Silk scarves were all the rage! *Sheffield Wednesday*

Combs	0·10	Blazer Badges (Blue & Black)	0·35
Lapel Badges	0·25	Patches (Round)	0·32
Pennants, Maxi	0·55	Patches (Finger)	0·32
Pennants, Medium ...	0·30	Patches (Round)	0·35
Ties	1·65	Duffle Bags (post 15p) ...	1·10
Autograph Books	0·25	Shoulder Bags (post 22½p) ...	2·10
Scarves, Silk, B/W/Yellow	**0·60**	Metal Badges, SWFC (Various)	0·25
Scarves, Silk Blue/White & W/B	0·60	Metal Badges, Assorted Clubs	0·25
Scarves, Silk, Assorted Clubs	0·60	Key Chains	0·50
Scarves, Woollen, College B/W	1·20	Licence Holders	0·15
Scarves, Woollen, Bar, B/W	1.00	T-Shirts, 26"	1·10
Scarves, Woollen, Bar, Yellow, B/W	1·00	T-Shirts, 28", 30", 32", 34"	1·20
New Owls Scarves ...	**2·10**	T-Shirts, Men's Large ...	1·25
New White Silk Scarves ...	**0·60**	Cigarette Lighters	1·70
Yellow, Blue & White Silk		Biros	0·05
Scarf	**0·60**	Fibre Tips	0·10
Bob Caps	0·70	Pencils	0·04
Post Cards (Hillsborough) ...	0·05	Address books	0·15
Tankards (Blue & Gold)		Wallets	0.07
(post 20p)	1·50	Key fobs	0·10
Beakers (post 17p) ...	0·40	**Owls Mascot**	**2·50**
Individual Photos ...	0·02½	**Small Owls (Gonks)** ...	**0·70**
Car Stickers (Round) ...	0·10	Teddy Bears (Blue & White)	1·50
Rings	0·35	Teddy Bears (Blue & White)	2·80
Necklaces (Gold & Silver) ...	0·65	Postage and packing 10p extra,	
Bracelets (Gold & Silver) ...	0·50	unless otherwise stated	

The Owls Shop, Sheffield Wednesday F.C. Ltd., Hillsborough, Sheffield S6 1SW

Above: A Wednesday Supporters' Club tankard and pin badge. *Adrian Hurst/John Dyson*

Half-time entertainment at Hillsborough in Autumn 1974 as the (recently opened) Radio Hallam take on the Supporters' Club in a football game - using a huge plastic ball! *Adrian Hurst*

A collection of Owls memorabilia including a mid-70s cushion from the North Stand. These are now very rare given the propensity of Owls fans to throw them onto the pitch in frustration. *Mick Jeffries*

campaign that kept him out of all but five games of the following season.

Prendergast grew frustrated with the club's situation and placed a transfer request in the dying days of Steve Burtenshaw's reign in September of 1975. That was rejected and despite further injuries he was top scorer again in the 1975-76 season. He gained the dubious honour of being the first man to score for the Owls in the third tier in a 2-1 defeat at Southend in the first game of that season, before yet more injuries reduced the number of games he was able to play over the next two campaigns.

Prendergast featured regularly in the club programme during his time with the club with action shots of him scoring or in other action poses being common. The pictures clearly demonstrate his determined attitude and proverbial desire to run through walls for the team. Len Ashurst described his "wholehearted approach" and Keith Farnsworth, then sports editor of the *Morning Telegraph*) doubted "if there have been many more plucky performers."

In 1977 his ten years as a professional with the Owls were recognised by a testimonial game against top-flight Leicester City. Ron Springett and Peter Swan returned to the Owls line-up for that game which finished 3-2 to Leicester, in front of 3,179 fans. The testimonial also included a disco at Tiffany's nightclub, with a notice that casual dress could be worn, and a social evening at the Timbertop pub on Shirecliffe Road, as well as a sponsored greyhound meeting at Owlerton Stadium. Prendergast's time in Sheffield was coming to an end, though, and his final appearance for the club was in March 1978 against Chester.

"Prendo" then signed for Barnsley for £14,000 before moving on to Halifax Town on loan and ending his playing days in the non-league with Mexborough Town and Denaby United. Prendergast only made a total of 16 further league appearances after leaving the Owls and his professional career ended at the age of only 29. His injuries meant that he was advised to retire completely from playing in the early 1980s, and a second testimonial was arranged by Denaby United around this time. In 1986 Prendergast underwent a hip replacement operation as a result of the injuries sustained during his playing career. His body had certainly paid the price for his all-action and determined style of play.

Later in life Prendergast suffered with illnesses and unfortunately died in 2010 aged just 59. He died in Mexborough and his funeral service was held in Denaby. A Sheffield Wednesday scarf, along with a piece of coal, were placed on his coffin for its final journey – to represent his values. Over 300 mourners attended the service, and the St Alban's Roman Catholic Church in Denaby was so packed that some of the mourners had to stay outside.

Prendergast is remembered with great fondness by fans, players and others. On the announcement of his death in 2010 the discussion of Prendergast and his contribution to the club and team extended to seven pages on the Owlstalk fan forum. All the comments were positive. Brian Joicey – who played alongside Prendergast from 1971 to 1976 – described Mick as a "fantastic player and a fantastic guy" while Jimmy Mullen remembered him as "brave, strong and quick, could shoot with both feet and was always likely to score." Mullen also named Prendergast in his "ex-Owls team" of favourite players he had appeared alongside. One fan in my 2019 survey described him as "one of our own who sweated blood for the club up front, scored some great goals and was a true Wednesday legend".

His friend Peter Pettit, who read the eulogy at his funeral, said: "Mick Prendergast lived the dream of being a professional footballer. He was a special person, who was well-liked, and a shining beacon to us all. He was one of Denaby and Conisbrough's most famous sons and we will miss him greatly." Pettit also revealed Prendergast had turned down a move to Chelsea because of his love for Sheffield Wednesday and South Yorkshire. Prendergast certainly did enjoy playing for the Owls. "In my ten years at Hillsborough I have many wonderful memories of the times when performance has enjoyed that bit of extra edge," he said in his testimonial year, "because nobody can fail to respond to the support afforded by a Wednesday following." He also had a dry sense of humour as seen in his responses to a questionnaire in the club programme in 1974. Favourite Food? Chips and beans. Job if you weren't a footballer? Gravedigger!

As a player, Prendergast was whole-hearted, determined and prepared to put in all he could for the team. The last word on his time at the Owls should therefore go to him: "It is going to improve performances, and help us win a few matches, then I am happy to do it."

Prendergast was talking about the overnight survival session organised by Tony Toms. His comments could easily be applied to his time in an Owls shirt overall, though. It is not possible to answer the question "what if…", but it is difficult to imagine the Owls going through their long barren spell in front of goal in 1974-75 if "Prendo" had been fit and firing on all cylinders. His goal against Southend in 1976 helped save the club from the abyss and his performances and goals provided some enter-tainment and enjoyment as the club moved towards its *"Lowest Ebb"*.

Prendergast was clearly one of the favourite players of those who remember the Owls teams of the mid-1970s. It is obvious to me why this is, given his South Yorkshire roots, his style of play, dedicated approach and goalscoring prowess. As The *Star's* Ian Vickers had it: "He's a popular player with the fans and no won-der. It is to do with that kind of attitude, his style and the fact that he's a striker." Prendergast himself may have suffered from his injury record and for playing for the Owls at such a difficult time for the club. His popularity was earned the hard way and was certainly well deserved.

Mick Prendergast: 1950-2010. Rest in Peace.

Conclusions

The Sheffield Wednesday teams of the period were in decline year on year. Many fans, though, remember some of the players with a feeling of nostalgia. The players discussed here vary in terms of their position on the pitch and style of play. There are common-alities between many of them, though, which I believe help ex-plain their popularity. Players who are determined and who give everything for the team are always popular among fans. Mick Prendergast, Brian Joicey, Jimmy Mullen and Ken Knighton all fit that group. Players who excite the fans and show some skill and flamboyance are also often popular: Willie Henderson and Eric Potts fit that category.

Fans also recognise when players enjoy playing for the team. Many of the players here and others clearly enjoyed their time at Hillsborough. Roy Coyle illustrated this point in a recent interview: "I loved every minute of my time there. It was living the dream. If you love the game, you want to be a professional footballer." Players who have true class and ability are a third grouping: Tommy Craig and Peter Rodrigues fitting that box. Finally, goalscorers will always be popular: like Prendergast, Joicey, McMordie and to an extent Potts, Sunley, Craig and Henderson.

Finally, those players who provided some of the magical moments during the era will remain popular: Knighton's goal against Bolton; Prendergast and Potts' against Southend, Sunley's two against Manchester United and Joicey's goal after the long drought against Oxford all provide memories that will live long in the minds of those who were there. Fans are often called supporters. The players here gave the fans things to support during the difficult times: goals, excitement, flamboyance, determination, ability and class. The players discussed here deserve to be remembered positively for their efforts.

FINANCES AND
THE BOARD

A tale of hard times and hard decisions. A changing of the old guard for the new. Money matters, and the Owls did not have much. Fans rally round and bingo really does make a difference. Save our Owls went the cry! A period of austerity follows but even at "Our Lowest Ebb" there is light at the end of the tunnel.

Introduction

Sheffield Wednesday faced considerable financial difficulties during our period. In each of the three seasons the club reported a deficit in their accounts – totalling £240,038 across the time frame. The club had three chairmen during this time: Sir Andrew Stephen, Matthew Sheppard and H.E. (Bert) McGee. There were also two club secretaries/general managers – Eric Taylor and Eric England. This chapter considers the finances, along with the efforts to improve them and personalities of those involved.

1973-74

This was a particularly difficult season for the club, both on the field and financially. The club's accounts for the season show an overall deficiency of £102,724 for the year while income in all areas (season tickets, match tickets, transfer fees and miscellaneous) fell compared to the previous season. Expenditure rose. The club's assets as reported in the accounts also fell and the club reported a secured overdraft of £135,488. The total deficiency would have been nearer to £150,000 but for a donation from the club's development fund of £47,205. These figures were the worst of the 1970s to that date, although each year following relegation had seen the Owls run at a deficit. It is clear, even from a cursory look at these figures, that something would need to change.

The directors' review of the year touches upon this:

"The Football Season 1973-74 was extremely disappointing from both the financial and playing points of view. The first team only just managed to avoid relegation from the second division after a tremendous effort led by our new manager, Steve Burtenshaw, and chief coach, Gerry Young.

The sickness we had at the club, together with some very severe injuries to key players, contributed in no small measure to the problems we had throughout the season. The Central League and Northern Intermediate League sides performed quite credibly, both finishing in the top half of their respective leagues. Our congratulations are due to T.B. Craig and R. Coyle upon receiving honours. Mr Eric Taylor, our general manager, retired on 30th June, and the Directors wish to place on record their appreciation of his exceptional services, loyalty and dedication to the club for 45 seasons since 1929.

Mr Eric England, who has been with the club for 38 years, was appointed secretary from 1st March 1974. Sir Andrew Stephen and Mr F.K. Gardiner resigned from the Board during the year and your Directors wish to place on record their appreciation of their services to the club over many years. Mr M. Sheppard was appointed chairman in succession to Sir Andrew Stephen."

> Report of the Directors, Sheffield Wednesday Football Club audited accounts for the year ended 31st May 1974

These final two points about the changes of personnel during the season perhaps underplay the changes that would be made and driven by the new board. Joining the new chairman on the board was Bert McGee, who in turn would become chairman himself. The two men, over time, would change the financial and playing direction of the club dramatically.

As we know, the season began with Sir Andrew Stephen as chairman. As results declined in the autumn of 1973, Stephen was faced with protests from fans which affected him and his family. These protests were both at matches and outside of them. His wife detailed the obscene phone calls and fear of attack when driving that faced the family. "I'm sick of this wretched game," she said. "You'd think my husband is responsible for the 11 men out there on the field. When I think about petrol rationing and everything, how can people get so worked up about football?"

What was effectively a boardroom coup in December saw Stephen resign to be replaced by Matthew (Matt) Sheppard. Sheppard was an accountant by trade, and financial consultant and business advisor. He was clear that he knew what to do and how to do it. "I know I have a very substantial job to do," he said. "I am going to use every ounce of my power and knowledge and diplomacy... to start the climb back."

In his address to supporters he suggested that the challenge might not be a quick one to solve: "We know we can bank on the support of you who have the long-term interests of Wednesday at heart," he said, adding: "We can and will turn the tide." Sheppard's name is associated by many Wednesday fans with the decision to sack Derek Dooley on Christmas Eve that season.

This decision was at best timed badly but should not, though, affect our understanding of Sheppard's efforts to regain control over the club's finances and ensure that the club was able to move forward on a secure financial footing. "I know these are difficult times," he said. "And we have a difficult job to do. But it is a job that will only be carried out with the maximum enthusiasm from all quarters – and the support of all true Wednesdayites." Such enthusiasm would be tested to the limit over Sheppard's time in charge.

Sheppard immediately put into place policies to reduce expenditure and to support the development fund. He also pushed forward policies to raise income – seeing season ticket prices rise from £16 to £20 in the centre of the South Stand for example (a considerable increase even with the rampant inflation of the time). The club had been pushing season ticket sales during the season, suggesting even as late as October that fans buy the tickets at the full rate.

In a nod to modernity, the tickets could be paid for in instalments (with a Provident Check), or on credit facilities offered by John Paget & Sons Limited. The matchday ticket prices also rose the following season.

Eric Taylor, "Mr Sheffield Wednesday" retired during the season. Taylor had been a hugely influential figure at Hillsborough for decades. He was suffering from cancer, and unfortunately died in September, at the age of 62. Taylor's career is expertly detailed by his biographer, Andrew Cooper, who wrote: "It is no coincidence...that when his guiding influence disappeared, the club entered a disastrous downwards spiral." Whilst this is true in terms of performances on the field *(Our Lowest Ebb)* – the evidence suggests that financially, the club were about to turn a corner at the time of Taylor's retirement.

The 1973-74 season therefore ended with a comparatively new management team, a relatively new chairman and secretary and an understanding that strict financial controls were needed to bring the club's accounts into order. The team were struggling and this attempt to control spending, raise income, and ensure improved performances on the pitch was to prove to be an impossible one the following season. Put simply, it was not possible to do all those things at once. Something had to give. That something was the performances on the pitch.

Sir Andrew Stephen

In terms of our period, Sir Andrew played a somewhat minor role – suffering the brickbats of fans as the club struggled in the autumn of 1973, before resigning. In the wider history of Sheffield Wednesday, and of football more generally, he was a much more important figure. Stephen was born in Aberdeen, qualifying in medicine at the University in his home city in 1928. He moved to Sheffield in 1930 to become a partner in a local general practice. In 1946 he became the Owls' medical officer, joining the board in 1950. He was chairman of the club from 1956 and was elected chairman of the Football Association in 1967 – the first-ever Scot to fill that post.

He was knighted in the Queen's Birthday Honours of 1972 for his services to football and to medicine. Sir Andrew knew that he was lucky to work alongside Eric Taylor, "who knew exactly how I would wish to deal with any matter which arose while I was absent on F.A. matters." He was therefore confident in fulfilling his roles, both at Hillsborough and nationally, in an effective way.

Stephen himself was also well regarded by colleagues, and his obituary in the British Journal of Sports Medicine described him as "a modest, gentle and kind man, much loved by his patients and colleagues." He was described in the club programme as a man of "integrity and considerable stature" on his resignation from the club's board. Stephen's career at Hillsborough ended in a disappointing manner. He should not be remembered only for the failings of the later years, though, as his time with the club also included a long period of success both on and off the pitch.

Eric Taylor

In a similar way to Sir Andrew Stephen, Eric Taylor's contribution to our period is a relatively minor one. He was general manager during the early part of the 1973-74 season before his retirement. Taylor officially retired from his duties on June 30, 1974, though in reality he had passed on the work to new club secretary Eric England well before then. Taylor's contribution to Sheffield Wednesday over his 45-year career at the club was immense. He began as an office boy at the club, working his way up to secretary-manager and team manager. Initially on a temporary basis, he ended up "standing in" as manager for 16 years!

Taylor negotiated the transfers of some of the Owls' most successful players of the post-war era – breaking the club's transfer record with the £34,500 buy of Jackie Sewell from Notts County in 1951. After handing over team duties to Harry Catterick in 1958, Taylor concentrated much of his energy on developing the stadium – with the cantilever North Stand opening in 1961 and the redeveloped West Stand in 1966. Hillsborough held 20 FA Cup semi-finals and other big games, including those of the 1966 World Cup, during Taylor's career.

Both his biography ("Without doubt, Eric's greatest legacy is the stadium that all Wednesdayites hold dear to their hearts") and his testimonial brochure ("This magnificent stadium will stand as a lasting memorial to the man whose vision inspired it") agree that Hillsborough Stadium is Taylor's greatest achievement. There is a counter argument to this, suggesting that Taylor's dedication to the stadium came at the expense of the team. As Harry Catterick achieved great success at Everton following Taylor's refusal to sanction the expensive signing of centre-forward Joe Baker from Hibernian, there is some fuel to this argument. It should not be forgotten however that Taylor was prepared to invest in the team at times, including the record-breaking signing of the teenage Tommy Craig.

His involvement in the appointment of Derek Dooley as manager has been suggested as one that was designed to excite the fans and increase ticket sales, over the need to appoint someone who could galvanise the team. Harry Catterick certainly had his differences with Taylor, who was clearly a strong-minded character. Taylor's biographer, though, feels that he did not entirely agree with the appointment of Dooley as manager and that the struggles of the club both on and off the pitch in his later years greatly saddened him.

His later years were also impaired by the effects of a serious car crash. Despite this, Taylor said that his choice to retire was the hardest decision of his career before adding that he had loved every minute with "this great club". Taylor should not be remembered therefore as responsible for the difficulties of our period – rather, as former FIFA President Sir Stanley Rous recalled: "A man of vision and a most capable administrator and organiser."

A testimonial game was played in Taylor's name shortly after his death and in Don Revie's first "game" as manager, he led an England XI to a 5-0 victory over a Sheffield Wednesday team. It was testament to Taylor's standing in the game that such a match was played. Some fans expressed their frustration at the club and its situation in the 1970s directly at Taylor, and chants of "Taylor Out" were not entirely uncommon. I argue that Taylor was never on the board; he was instead an influential and outstanding administrator. If there was anyone to blame for the club's decline from the late 1960s, it was not him. Taylor left a legacy of a world-class stadium. The responsibility for the team's decline lay elsewhere.

1974-75

The second season in our period was another difficult one financially for the club. The club's accounts show an operating deficiency for the year of £129,507; a figure improved by a £48,000 donation from the development fund to give an overall deficit for the year of £81,507. Behind these figures were some positives. The deficit was over £20,000 lower than it had been the previous year. Income had risen, including that for match receipts and for season tickets.

Expenditure had fallen. A closer inspection of the accounts clearly shows the club making cutbacks in several areas. Costs for items such as stationery, for example, had dropped from £26,847 the previous year, to £17,812. Match expenses fell, so did travelling and training expenses, and so – slowly – did wages and salaries. The club were trying to take control of finances, and every area of expenditure now seemed more closely monitored. Despite these improvements, though, the club was still losing money. That money needed to come from somewhere – and both the club's overdraft and its liabilities to other creditors both rose. The club now held a secured overdraft of £183,882 with the NatWest Bank, and owed other creditors £134,697. On the pitch, the season was one of relegation for the Owls and the directors' review of the year reflected on the financial and playing difficulties:

"The football season 1974/75 was a disaster; the first team being relegated to the Third Division for the first time in its long history. Consequently, the resultant financial results were also unsatisfactory. The directors share with the shareholders, supporters and staff their bitter disappointment at these events and are more than ever determined to reverse the events as soon as possible. In the view of the financial situation at the club, the directors are concentrating their efforts on producing players through the youth policy, although it is the intention to seek additional funds from shareholders and supporters in the near future for the purpose of reinstating the club to its former position. The Central League and Northern Intermediate League sides performed quite creditably, both finishing in the top half of their respective leagues. Our congratulations are due to H. Dowd, Esq., upon receiving honours. Mr Eric Taylor, our former general manager, died on 23rd Sep-

tember 1974, shortly after his retirement. The Directors wish to place on record their sympathy and sincere condolences to his family and their appreciation of his 45 years exceptional service with the club."

Report of the Directors, Sheffield Wednesday Football
Club audited accounts for the year ended 31st May 1975

In February of 1975, Matt Sheppard spoke directly to the club's supporters through a two-page letter in the match magazine. In his message he starkly laid out some of the problems: "This club is losing money – at the rate of around £2,000 a week," he told the fans: "Stringent economies – not necessarily apparent to our fans on the terraces – have been made during the past 12 months." This time had seen the signing of Phil Henson from Manchester City. Sheppard detailed how the club could not spend huge sums on players but that the board had made "as large a sum as possible available for… a new face."

As we saw in the end of season report above, the club's deficit was reduced this season, but Sheppard was clear on the need to further increase income. He urged all season ticket holders, shareholders and supporters to turn up for the remaining games of the season; thanked the development fund and those supporting it for their "tremendous efforts" and accepted that he was prepared to talk to any Sheffield businessmen who were "interested in assisting the club during this difficult time". Sheppard knew that the club was in great financial difficulty. It was also in difficulty on the pitch.

The financial and playing difficulties prompted the 'Save our Owls' campaign, and The *Star* reported about the fans, companies and sportsmen who supported the project. There was even a tale doing the rounds that Bruce Forsyth might make an appearance at Hillsborough as he was due to appear in Sheffield around that time.

Urban myth says he thanked the club for the invitation but claimed to be too busy! The club welcomed the campaign and the "Voice of Hillsborough" in the matchday programme said: "The support that Sheffield Wednesday are receiving at present illustrates just how many people care about the club. It is up to us to try and justify their faith in us… Wednesday's genuine friends are rallying around the flag for the major offensive to beat off the thought of relegation."

The York City game ended in a disappointing defeat. As one fan told me: "We played York away on a Friday night and there were SOO posters and patches by the thousands. We took 3,000 up that night and got behind the lads who as usual put in an inept performance and lost 3-0." Another told me simply: "I was one of the muppets that went to that!" The Blackpool game on the following Saturday did see an increased attendance (14,342), as did a game against Notts County two weeks later (14,736).

The Owls drew the first game 0-0 and lost the second 1-0. A third fan told me the story of how he was interviewed by Radio Sheffield coming out of one of the games and was asked what it would take to save the team. "Half a million quid to spend on decent players," came the response, and the Radio Sheffield interviewer simply laughed. Three more defeats followed, and the campaign was quietly dropped.

As we know, 1974-75 ended with relegation. The team struggled to score goals, and attendances dropped to around 7,500 for many games. The club remained in great financial difficulty and now found itself in Division Three. Spring 1975 had seen further changes to the board with Bert McGee promoted to vice-chairman and Clifford Woodard and Stanley Speight joining the board. There would need to be many more cuts yet before the financial situation could begin to improve.

The new boardroom team still had plenty of work to do.

Development Fund
As we have seen, the club's development fund made a huge contribution to funds during these years. In a way, this was nothing new. Under Derek Dooley's stewardship the fund had contributed £55,000 towards the building of the new West Stand, opened in 1961. This was half of the total cost. After Dooley's appointment as team manager, the organisation of the fund was passed to his assistant, Dennis Woodhead.

Woodhead first came to Hillsborough as an amateur player in 1941. He joined the RAF later in the war, signed professionally for the Owls in 1944, and made his debut for the first team at the end of the 1946-47 season. He was a regular for the club until 1955, before moving on to Chesterfield and Derby. After spending time in non-league – including managing Retford Town – Woodhead was named Pools manager for Chesterfield.

On Derek Dooley's appointment as manager, Woodhead was appointed to his official role of "Pools Organiser" at Hillsborough. In 1975 this role was expanded to commercial manager – the role encompassing, in his own words, "just about everything at Hillsborough where the raising of money is involved, the pool, the shop, this magazine, etc."

The commercial office was a one-storey brick building towards the Penistone Road end of the South Stand and was labelled "Sheffield Wednesday development fund" even after the role of the commercial team developed. The development fund raised money, simply speaking, by using agents to sign up fans to a regular prize draw. One such agent, David Hebblethwaite, described the details to me:

"I was an agent for the development fund from 1967 until about 1983. The fund was run by Derek Dooley and his staff. Then after Dooley was appointed manager of SWFC, Dennis Woodhead took over. The development office was inside the South Stand car park. I think that it was underneath the Ozzie Owl Club. And where the electric sub-station is now, that was where the club shop was. The development fund was for use by the club for improvements to the ground and the development of young players for the club. The first one that I remember, agents had to find their own customers and sign them up to a monthly draw that gave amounts of money as prizes. Not sure but I think that the top prize was £100. There were also other prizes, but I can't remember them all. By the 1980s the top prize was £500. Two of my customers won £80 each and one won £350. The agent got 10 per cent of the money they raised and one or two free

tickets on the Kop depending on the number of customers that you had."

A very clever system therefore – with something in it for the agent, for the club and potentially those who played. Another supporter, whose father was an agent, picks up the detail: *"I remember taking the money to the development fund office with my Dad who was an agent and later on his behalf. He collected the money from his work colleagues and friends and as I recall it was a form of raffle where people kept the same numbers each week. In return for doing this he got two tickets to each match... I assume the number of tickets was proportional to the money collected."*

Development agents, as they were known, were also rewarded with a Christmas dinner dance, held at the Phoenix Rooms in Rotherham. Here they found, as one former agent told me: *"The typical 70's dinner dance: meal, speeches thanking everyone involved, music, dancing, beer, and a few Wednesday players there too. What more could you ask for!"*

As we know, the scheme was very lucrative for the club. In 1974, the club received £47,205 from the scheme, in 1975 exactly £48,000 was paid into the accounts and in 1976 it was £47,000. A total therefore of £142,205 across the three years. This was higher than the income from season tickets in each of the three seasons – so Sheppard was understandably keen for fans to join. Around the time of the Save our Owls campaign he said: "I would particularly commend these people with Sheffield Wednesday's interests at heart to join the development association, preferably as an agent, but equally importantly as a subscribing member." As the 1970s dragged on, the development fund took on even more importance for the Owls, with huge donations of £144,460 in 1978 and £233,500 in 1979. Much of this rise followed the development of a club lottery.

The 1977 Lotteries Act had allowed for this and following the example of clubs such as Plymouth Argyle, the Owls soon launched their own version. Dennis Woodhead and his agents still worked hard in selling the tickets, and without the system developed by Dooley and Woodhead, it is debatable whether the lottery would have been such a success.

In the 1960s and then again in the later 1970s, the development fund made a huge contribution to the success of the club. In our period, it helped to keep the wolves from the door.

Matchball Sponsors

The club needed to increase revenue as well as cut expenditure if it was to claw its way out of the financial hole it found itself in. One example of how this was done, was through the sponsorship of the matchball, and an advert in the programme in 1973, tucked away near the back, showed how this was available for "just" £12.50. By 1976, it was much different. A full-page recognition of the sponsors' generosity was given in the programme, along with a much larger and clearer reference to the company name. This focus on what we nowadays would describe as marketing bore fruit in the accounts. Income from advertising rose from a mere £2,230 in 1974 to £8,268 in 1976. Not enough to solve the club's problems, but representative of the determination of the board to move the club to a secure financial footing.

Eric England

Eric England was already club secretary before Eric Taylor's retirement. He was promoted to the role during the 1973-74 season as it became clear that Taylor would be retiring. The two had worked as a team for a long time – for many years as secretary and assistant secretary. Taylor's job title by 1974 was general manager. Regardless of the titles, in 1974-75 England was left to complete the work alone; partly as a money saving exercise, but partly also due to England's undoubted competence and knowledge of the club and how it worked.

Eric England joined Sheffield Wednesday in 1936. Similarly to Eric Taylor, England began his career at Hillsborough as an office boy. The two Erics worked alongside each other for many years and built up a close friendship both in and outside of the offices at Hillsborough.

During the Second World War, England served in the Royal Air Force and on his return found himself promoted to assistant secretary with the Owls. In that capacity he served the club and the game effectively – playing his part in the organisation of 19 FA Cup semi-finals and other big games. He was introduced in a match day programme profile as "one of football's most experienced and efficient administrators." He would need every ounce of those skills as the Owls cut back over the following seasons.

1975-76

The 1975-76 season was again a difficult one for the club financially. A careful study of the accounts does though suggest that the green shoots of recovery were, if not growing, then at least beginning to germinate. The accounts show an overall deficit of £55,807. This was the lowest of the three seasons in this book and had almost halved since 1974. Income had risen and expenditure had fallen.

As we have seen, it was again aided by a large donation (£47,000) from the development fund. Although income from season tickets had fallen (perhaps unsurprisingly given the team's fall into Division Three), income from match receipts and other areas had both risen considerably.

Expenditure fell slightly, though it seems clear that in many areas it was cut to the bone already. Interest payments to the bank continued to rise – to £28,641 – more than the total income from season ticket sales.

The club revalued Hillsborough stadium to a round £1,000,000. The total overdraft value is not listed, as instead the accounts show that debentures were outstanding to the NatWest Bank providing security for borrowing facilities.

I am no accountant, but it seems that the stadium was being used as security for a more preferential rate of borrowing. A risky strategy, as the club would find in more recent years. The club also listed a long-term loan of over £19,000 from the Football Association – to be repaid in 1981. The directors' review of the season was shorter and much more to the point than in the previous two years.

Once again, we have to record a most disappointing season from a playing point of view, the first team just avoiding relegation to the Fourth Division after a tremendous fight by our players most ably led by Manager Len Ashurst and his assistant Tony Toms. Our last five home games brought maximum points, and your directors are very confident the changes made to our playing staff, allied with the need for success prevailing throughout the club, the future looks far brighter.

To our very loyal supporters, may we say a very big thank you for being so staunch during a most unsuccessful season. The Central League and Northern Intermediate League sides did quite well, when it is realised how many young players were played and the likes of D. Cusack, I. Nimmo and G. Hull were promoted to first team duty with unquestionable success.

Report of the Directors, Sheffield Wednesday Football
Club audited accounts for the year ended 31st May 1975

There is no reference at all in the statement to the financial situation at the club. Nor is there mention of the September 1975 switch of Matt Sheppard and Bert McGee; McGee to chairman and Sheppard as vice-chairman. This is somewhat surprising as the boardroom team had begun to turn the financial situation of the club around. The percentage of wages to turnover fell in each of the three seasons, from 86 per cent in 1974 to 74 per cent by 1976. The club were still making a loss, but the cuts to expenditure and rises in income boded well for future seasons.

McGee did comment in the press, however: "The position is a lot better than last year. In a time of rampant inflation, we have been able to cut our coat according to our cloth, hold our expenditure and reduce our operating deficiency." The club were also planning a share issue which in later 1976 was very successful in bringing money back into the club.

As we have already seen, the development fund also went from strength to strength in the following years. The club's finances improved considerably in the years after this. By 1978 the accounts announced a profit, and in 1980 that profit reached £450,180.

Bert McGee

H.E. (Bert) McGee was born in 1917 and was raised on Langsett Road, close to Hillsborough Stadium. He was a boyhood Wednesday fan and attended games with his father, Bernard. His father's sudden death at the age of only 48 – after suffering a heart attack at an Owls match – altered Bert's career plans. He put on hold his ideas of studying medicine to begin an engineering apprentice. His career took him from that apprenticeship to become head of a tool-making firm and eventually Sheffield's most coveted industrial role – that of Master Cutler.

McGee almost joined the Owls board in 1971, and as we know did join the board in December 1973 – filling the vacancy left by Sir Andrew Stephen's resignation. McGee was soon promoted to vice-chairman and in September 1975, another boardroom re-shuffle saw he and Sheppard swap positions. McGee was quoted at the time as saying: "I intend to try and make sure that the supporters of Sheffield Wednesday see the sort of football which will take the club back to Division One."

McGee was of course successful in this quest – with the Owls promoted from Division Three in 1980 and finally back to Division One in 1984. McGee explained how this was achieved in 1981: "We stopped spending and started earning. We kept a tight control on all overheads, instituted rigorous, sensible housekeeping, appointed sound management and let them get on with it."

McGee remained as chairman from September 1975 until March 1990. The arrival of Jack Charlton is often seen as a turning point, but McGee also often praised the work that Len Ashurst completed in mid-1970s.

McGee remained chairman throughout the reigns of Charlton, Howard Wilkinson and Peter Eustace. After Eustace's short lived and ill-fated term in charge, McGee was instrumental in the appointment of Ron Atkinson. He retired, accepting the need for new men and new ideas, but knowing that the club remained on a secure financial base.

McGee died in April 1995, at the age of 77. His tribute in the matchday programme sums him up as follows: *"He will be remembered with affection by a generation of Wednesdayites ever grateful for what he achieved when it was vital that he should succeed in exactly the way he did. He was indeed a wise Owl!"*

Conclusions

These were certainly difficult times for the Owls financially, and the struggles on the field did not help in lifting the financial gloom. The various changes in the boardroom are emblematic of the club's struggle to find its way in the mid-1970s. Matt Sheppard will forever be remembered by some Wednesdayites for the brutal sacking of Derek Dooley. Some fans would never forgive him for that. However, the financial makeover that he began, and that Bert McGee continued, was vital in helping bring success back over the next decade or so.

As our period moves on, we see an almost complete change in the hierarchy of the club – from the chairman and general manager who had so much success in the 1960s to a new team who accepted what needed to change and began to set about that change. This was not a painless process and we see elsewhere in the book examples of how the management, team and club were being run on the proverbial shoestring. This book aims to "rescue" the era. In terms of the finances, on paper there is very little to rescue. The club lost money. Lots of money. However, the building blocks were put in place by people who knew what needed to be done and were prepared to take the hard decisions necessary to do so. This may have been the *"Lowest Ebb"* financially, but the decisions made in these years would help lead to the revitalisation of the Owls.

AN INTERVIEW WITH DAVID CUSACK

David (Dave) Cusack played for the Owls in the final of the three seasons covered by this book. He made his debut against Millwall in October of 1975, going on to play a total of 40 games that season. He continued to play for the Owls until 1978, appearing a total of 109 times and scoring one goal. He is remembered by the fans in my survey as a "tough, no nonsense centre back", who was "built like a brick out-house" and who "took no prisoners".

I was a little nervous therefore when contacting him. Partly because of this fearsome reputation, but also because I knew of problems he had with his memory – which he puts down to being elbowed by opposition strikers during his playing days. I had no need for either of those worries as David was friendly, helpful and had a very clear recollection of his time at Hillsborough, and elsewhere in his footballing career.

I began our conversation by introducing myself and reminding David that I was researching and writing a book about Sheffield Wednesday in the 1970s. "Well, someone has to!" he replied with a booming laugh. He went on to tell me that he is a Wednesday fan. "Once you're Wednesday, you're always Wednesday!" he told me. I laughed at this and talked for a while about how long I'd followed the Owls and my hopes that my children will keep it up, even though we live at a distance from Hillsborough. The ice was broken, and we began to talk through David's career.

What memories do you have of the various managers at Hillsborough?
Derek Dooley was my first manager. He signed me as an apprentice in 1971. I started as a left-winger, but they soon found me out! Derek was a great man, and a real shame that he left in the way he did. Steve Burtenshaw though... Listen, I don't dispute his coaching abilities, but man management? He didn't have any.

Shocking. He'd come up from Arsenal or QPR and did not know how to deal with a bunch of northern lads. I made my debut though for Len Ashurst. He brought Tony Toms with him. That fella could not kick a ball! Ex-military and P.E. trained; I think. But he knew fitness. He had us running up and down the Kop and doing laps of the Hillsborough pitch. It was all about fitness.

Did you go up on to the Moors with him?
Yes, we did! **What was that like?** Cold! But it was great publicity for the club. We got in all the papers. Tony Toms is probably still living out on the fact that we won the next game. Doesn't mention that we then lost the next five or six! Talking of managers, I would have stayed at Hillsborough for much longer, but for money and for Jack Charlton. I got wind that some players who had dropped out of the first team, and were never getting back in, were on more money than me. So, I went to see Jack about it, because I thought it was unfair. It was Jack's way or the highway though, and he wouldn't budge. I have a lot of respect for Jack, but that's why I decided I had to leave.

Are there any players you particularly enjoyed playing alongside for the Owls?
Oh, lots. Prendo was excellent. Potts another one. Willie Henderson though, he was different class. He could land the ball on a sixpence. Great fella too. I used to babysit for him. I was still a young lad in the reserves, and after a match Willie would contact my girlfriend and get her and me round to babysit while he went around town. The Fiesta Club was a favourite of his. All the bouncers were Scottish in Sheffield at the time. So, Willie knew them all, and never needed to buy a drink!

What about when you broke into the team – who helped you along?
Dowdy. Hugh Dowd. Me and him made a good pairing in defence. He was the best man at my wedding and godfather to the kids. He married a childhood friend of mine from my village, and I still see him once a week or so.

How about particular games? Are there any that stand out?
Well, the Southend game was a big one. I remember that. Big crowd and we needed a result. Great goal from Prendo from a Potts cross, I think. I remember that Southend also brought a few and it was a great atmosphere. The crowds kept up reasonably well I thought, though Hillsborough is a huge place.

Let's ask about fans then. How was it to play at such a big stadium in front of low crowds? Well, the fans that did go were dedicated. It was still standing at both ends, and they could get an atmosphere going. The problem was that all the teams that came to Hillsborough treated it like the FA Cup final! The opposition would up their game every time we were at home, and we had to try and deal with that. **How about away games – I gather the Owls had a large away following even then?** Yes, we did, they travelled in huge numbers and that is something that the players really appreciated.

You signed for Southend after leaving Hillsborough?
I did, for £50,000 which was a big fee in those days. I soon moved on to Millwall though and stayed there a couple of years before moving back up north to Donny. It was Billy Bremner who brought me to Doncaster. George Graham was the manager at Millwall and the two of them couldn't agree on the fee. So, it went to a tribunal. The two of them ended having a stand-up row in the street outside the hotel in London where it was all discussed.

Funny, really… two Scotsmen arguing about who can spend the least money! It was Doncaster where I moved into management, as Billy went back to Leeds. I also managed Rotherham for a while. After that I moved back down south. **Yes, you were at Basildon for a while?** I owned the club! It was a good standard and a good bunch of people.

And where are you now?
I've moved back north. You know about the memory problems? **I do, yes.** Well, I was coming up to retirement anyhow, and felt that

coming back home I can be much closer to family and friends. So, I'm back near Thurcroft. I have family and friends and they keep an eye on me!

I ended by thanking David for his time and offering my appreciation for his thoughts and memories. He told me that I was most welcome, and that he hopes he'll be able to get a copy of the book for his birthday in the summer of 2020. I promised to do my best!

1975-76

A season of two managers and two chairmen. A slow start followed by a dramatic change in style and outlook. Illness hits the club again. Crowds stay low until another "great escape". The season finishes with the club at its "Lowest Ebb" but with a feeling that better things were to come.

The summer of 1975 saw the Owls attempt to rebuild after the disastrous season that preceded it. Several players left the club and, owing to the club's difficult financial situation, so did several members of the backroom staff. At the club's Annual General Meeting, (held less than 72 hours before the first game of the season) chairman Matt Sheppard announced that "Wednesday are in serious trouble, both from a financial and a footballing point of view."

The local papers were filled with angry letters about the state of the club. In the first matchday programme of the season 'The Voice of Hillsborough' told fans: "Last season left a bitter taste – we are determined that it is wiped away... this demands the consistency of good performance that was so lacking in 1974-75." Pre-season games had not demonstrated an obvious improvement – in results at least. Steve Burtenshaw took the squad (including many youngsters and reserves) to a training camp in Troon, Scotland. Alongside the chance to play golf, the team lost their two matches. Despite the defeats, the club felt the tour had gone well and Wednesday did pick up a pre-season win at York City, but lost their final game 3-0 to Division One side Coventry City. Burtenshaw felt that his team could produce the performances when it mattered, though. "I believe that the alterations in personnel have given my available squad the qualities the club require from the players that must take us through this important season," he said.

Those qualities were to be tested in the first game of the season, a trip to the seaside to face Southend United. The Owls were followed in huge numbers by their fans who saw Colin Harvey captain the team in their new yellow and green away kit. Wednesday took a half-time lead through Mick Prendergast but, unfortunately for the travelling fans, that was as good as it got for the Owls. After what appeared to be a regulation 2-0 win in the first leg of their midweek League Cup tie at Darlington, Wednesday faced their first home league game of the season against Brighton and Hove Albion.

Burtenshaw spent 17 years with Brighton as player and coach and may therefore have had his own reasons for wanting a successful outcome from the game. In advance of the game he said: "My players have got to be out there competing for themselves and for Sheffield Wednesday from first kick to last." A crowd of 10,326 turned out to watch the Owls take a 2-1 half-time lead (Prendergast and Joicey) before falling 3-2 behind and relying on a late own goal to claim a point.

The result at least showed that the team were prepared to compete until the end as Burtenshaw required. This competitive edge seemed to be missing in the next game though – the second-leg League Cup tie against Darlington. The Quakers had needed to apply for re-election to the Football League at the end of the previous season and few in the 7,452 crowd would have foreseen any difficulty in the Owls progressing to the next round. Despite a couple of early chances for both sides, the game reached half-time goalless.

The second half was different. The Quakers grabbed the lead after 50 minutes. Steve Holbrook robbed Jimmy Quinn. He moved into the area while holding the defender off and fired an unstoppable shot into the roof of the net from an acute angle, giving Owls goalkeeper Neil Ramsbottom no chance. Things got even worse for the Owls ten minutes later when Colin Sinclair added a second. Eric Young won the ball in midfield and advanced towards goal before sliding the ball to Sinclair. His first time shot from the edge of the box screamed past Ramsbottom into the net. Despite late attempts from Prendergast and Herbert, and a Henson header cleared off the line, that was how the score stayed.

There was to be a third game to decide the tie. The venue (decided on the toss of a coin) was to be at Hillsborough again, one week later.

Before then, though, Wednesday faced their first-ever league game against Hereford United and Wednesday were again followed in huge numbers. One fan remembers Owls goalkeeper Ramsbottom joining the queue to get in and handing out free tickets as a thank you for the support and The *Star* suggested after the game that well over 1,000 of the 7,017 crowd were Wednesdayites. Hereford finished the season as champions of Division Three, and they showed some of their quality in defeating the Owls 3-1 – Wednesday's second-half consolation scored by Henson (his first goal for the club). The result left the Owls in 22nd place (out of 24) in the early season table at the end of August.

The club's first game in September was the third match against Darlington. After playing out a goalless draw in front of a crowd of 6276, the Quakers won the penalty shoot-out to advance into round two. They successfully converted all five of their penalties, while for Wednesday Mick Prendergast fired wide and Ogley saved from Danny Cameron. "Darlington will not be the only club this season to come to Hillsborough and find themselves lifted by the splendour of the ground and the facilities," commented Burtenshaw before the match. Whether lifted by playing at Hillsborough or not, this was a disappointing result for the Owls who needed to find some early season form in their next match – a home game with Wrexham.

The game was Wrexham's first-ever against the Owls – "an auspicious occasion indeed", as the club programme put it. "Everyone wants to see beautiful attacking football from their team," said Burtenshaw, "but they also want to see it win... sometimes that means we have got to be effective rather than exciting." The game itself was not a classic, though the crowd of 7,585 did see an Owls win as David Herbert's 79th minute goal was enough to ensure a 1-0 victory.

"Owls win at last," was the *Green 'Un's* accurate headline after Herbert's first goal for the first team, and a second swiftly followed a week later at the County Ground against Swindon.

The goal gave Wednesday a half-time lead before two goals from the hosts send Wednesday back up north on the back of a 2-1 defeat. This was despite former Owls defender Colin Prophett playing the whole of the second half in goal for Swindon after an injury to their 'keeper Barron.

After the underwhelming start to the season, few Owls fans would have been expecting the result of the following game. "Tonic Owls Win!", "Shoot on Sight Owls Pile Up Goals Galore," shouted the headlines in the *Green 'Un*. The team had played Grimsby Town where goals from Prendergast, Herbert, Gray (own goal) and Potts in front of 11,345 fans saw the team win 4-0. This was the highest crowd of the day in Division Three and a dominant Owls performance with two goals in each half. The revitalised Owls then faced the short trip to Saltergate to face Chesterfield in a midweek game – but the outcome was a disappointing 1-0 defeat for Wednesday with Darling's first half goal the difference between the two teams.

Two days later it was announced that chairman Matt Sheppard had stepped down – citing pressures of work. He was to be replaced by vice-chairman Bert McGee who quickly announced that Sheppard would now act as vice-chair; the two men effectively swapping roles. "My intention is to provide all Sheffield Wednesday supporters with the kind of football that will take this club back to their rightful place in Division One," announced McGee.

Wednesday then had a chance to show the footballing world that they could play the right kind of football, with their next game against Crystal Palace shown on that evening's *Match of the Day*. Footage of the game shows the Owls playing some flowing football, passing their way through Palace's defence on the way to a 1-0 half-time lead through Eric Potts. Although Palace equalised in the second-half, this was a creditable performance. Ten million television viewers watched the game, and the Owls in their yellow and green kit, as Wednesday were left 16th in the table at the end of September – their highest position of the season to date.

But McGee, it seems, was not satisfied. The *Star* reported at the time that manager Burtenshaw had demanded "showdown talks" with the club after the Owls apparently approached Cambridge United for permission to talk to their manager – a certain Ron Atkinson. Although Cambridge announced that they had turned down an approach from an unnamed club, Burtenshaw's days at Hillsborough seemed numbered.

The following week saw the inevitable happen. Burtenshaw was sacked, along with coach Gerry Young, and Jim McAnearney was placed in temporary control of the team. "Results, lack of success and our determination to succeed is why the decision was taken," announced McGee. "The directors feel that it is in Wednesday's best interests long term for a new man to come to Hillsborough." Whatever the long-term plans, the Owls faced a game two days later, with Peterborough the visitors. The Owls rescued a 2-2 draw with a late own goal from Peterborough's Lee, Prendergast having scored for Wednesday in the first half.

McAnearney suggested that the team lacked confidence, saying: "We have got to have confidence in our own ability to play our full potential," and Wednesday certainly appeared confident in McAnearney's second and final game as caretaker manager when Milwall visited Hillsborough the following Saturday and were convincingly defeated 4-1, in front of a 10,144 crowd. The result left the Owls 13th in the table in time for Len Ashurst's first game as manager – a trip to Ninian Park to face Cardiff City.

Ashurst was quoted in the press as saying: "No stone will be left unturned and there will be a whirlwind which will go through the club." Ashurst spent the coach journey to Cardiff in discussion with McAnearney and physio John Haselden and although Ashurst was appointed manager by this stage, McAnearney had selected the team. Ashurst began the game sat in the directors' box but moved to the trainer's bench midway through the second half. By this stage, the Owls were losing the game and ended on the wrong side of a 2-0 defeat.

"We were in effect a disgrace," Ashurst said. "Generally speaking, the side is very, very undisciplined." Ashurst then spoke to each member of the squad individually on the front seat of the coach back from Cardiff. It certainly appeared that times were to change for the Owls. Ashurst's first home game came the following Saturday, with 12,045 turning out to see the Owls face Shrewsbury Town. Allan Thompson was recalled to the side – the day before his wedding! – and Brian Joicey opened the scoring, after an effort from Hugh Dowd had rebounded off the post. Wednesday couldn't hold on, conceding a second-half equaliser and drawing 1-1, but Ashurst did not seem too disappointed with the result.

"I am certainly not going to criticise the players for not winning the day", was his immediate post-match reaction. Ashurst was left frustrated for different reasons when Wednesday's next fixture, away at Walsall, was abandoned after 26 minutes due to a waterlogged pitch. In that time, Prendergast damaged his hamstring and would miss three games. Ashurst had brought in Neil O'Donnell from Gillingham before the game, and his debut was curtailed with the early abandonment of the game. A frustrating afternoon indeed.

Some of that frustration was tempered by a 1-0 victory in Wednesday's next game, against Ashurst's previous employers Gillingham. A goal from Joicey in the second half was enough to send 8,235 fans home happy. "It was a win to savour," said Ashurst. "It will be a great morale boost for the players."

Wednesday, though, couldn't build on that win as they suffered a disappointing 3-0 defeat at home to Port Vale. Although he didn't quite know it yet, the game was also to be Colin Harvey's final appearance for the Owls before his enforced retirement through injury later in the season.

Harvey's place as captain was taken by Thompson as Wednesday drew 1-1 with Aldershot – future pantomime villain Neil Warnock taking his place in the Shots' line-up – before a break from the league for the club's first FA Cup first-round game since 1925. Non-league Macclesfield Town were the opponents. Not only was the game the first-ever meeting of the two sides, it was also notable as the first ever game at Hillsborough to be sponsored (incidentally by Portland Autos, who described themselves as "Britain's first Datsun main dealer"). "Macclesfield will be as tough as any Football League opposition we could have met,"

Ashurst said before the game. And although the two sides could not be separated at half-time, Wednesday's quality told in the second period in a 3-1 victory. Ashurst, though, was not entirely pleased. "We tried to play to the gallery with possession football, when we would have really pleased the crowd [of 12,940] with more goals and direct play," he said.

Then followed a frustrating run, which saw Wednesday draw 0-0 with neighbours Rotherham United, tie 2-2 with Walsall and lose 2-1 in their first-ever visit to Layer Road to face Colchester United. Wednesday were now in the relegation places in Division Three, and Ashurst went to the press with his ideas of how things must change.

"The Old Order Changes – So Now We'll Do Things My Way," announced the headline in the *Sheffield Star*. Len Ashurst's words were printed in full. Here is an edited selection: *"I HAVE now had over two months to get "bedded in" at Hillsborough and I think it is an opportune time to put into print my thoughts on the situation at the club.... The biggest factor which is stopping a lot of the players from doing their stuff is that they are used to losing. If you check up on some players, they have not won more than half a dozen times in the last 18 months. There is an acceptance of defeat in the dressing room with certain players because that's what they are used to, and so, for this reason alone, a change of club for some and new faces in the team... will help eradicate this particular cancer.*
It is not easy to effect change overnight... but from our point of view we are effecting change in the attitude of the individual in the team. The morgue-like pre-match dressing room has gone and, in its place, we have a professional, bubbling atmosphere with 11 lads ready to put everything into the 90 minutes.
I am trying to establish a pattern of the way I want everyone to play throughout the club and top of the list is that they have to be competitive and hard to beat. Then, if you have the quality you are in with a shout. At the moment we are starting to compete well... but it's obvious that I am not happy with the quality. We have too many players on par with each other in ability and foot-

ball sense as well as having a few who are past their best days. This all needs to change before we see a rise in our fortunes.
I have not mentioned finance… To put the team on its feet I will need a few new faces… There will be no big money signings at the moment, but we will have new blood."

Ashurst was as good as his word and, ahead of Wednesday's FA Cup tie against non-league Wigan, he circulated the names of four men the club were making available for transfer: Eric Potts, Jimmy Mullen, David Sunley and Ronnie Ferguson. Ferguson was available on a free transfer with fees being sought for the others. Len Ashurst told me in 2020 that he needed to change the changing room at Hillsborough. He felt that the team needed a major shake-up. Despite having very limited funds, this was his first attempt to do so. Potts and Mullen remained at the club until 1977 and 1980 respectively, but Sunley and Ferguson both left in the weeks that followed. Ferguson left for Darlington where he was to score the winner in a League Cup tie against the Owls in 1976 and, as we have seen elsewhere, Sunley moved to Hull City.

For the cup tie, Ramsbottom was replaced in goal by Peter Fox – a position he would keep for all but one game for the remainder of the season, while youngster Ian Nimmo was named as the substitute. As Ashurst predicted beforehand Wigan did provide a stern test, before second half goals from transfer-listed Sunley (his first for the club for over a year) and Nimmo, on his professional debut, sealed a 2-0 win.

Ashurst's restructure of his squad continued when it was announced that Prendergast and Thompson were to sign new contracts, with Thompson's new deal a reward for improved form under Ashurst and his taking on of captaincy duties.

Three games over the Christmas period, against Preston, Bury and Mansfield, yielded three points, with a crowd of 8,553 watching the Preston game. That number led to a piece in the following game's programme, which read:

"WHERE WERE YOU? All right, all right – don't tell us. At 3p.m. last Saturday you were half way up the Moor, lumbered with the missus, screaming kids, and your arms full of Christmas

presents… We know you have to help with the shopping SOME-TIME, but NEVER when the Owls are at home, surely. Hope to see you all in the New Year… if you can get away!"

The sexist nature of the previous comments aside, attendances were low, although the Mansfield game did attract a better crowd of 15,430. Still, Wednesday were left in the relegation places as 1975, a year described as one "that will be remembered for largely the wrong reasons" by the "Voice of Hillsborough", came to an end.

The new year began with the Owls in FA Cup action, their reward for defeating two non-league opponents a trip to Division Two Charlton Athletic. The 12,284 crowd included a large and noisy contingent of Owls supporters but Charlton went 2-0 ahead, before Sunley's last ever goal for the club brought late consolation in the 2-1 defeat.

Ashurst had returned to the transfer market before Wednesday's next league game, bringing in right-back Richard Walden on a free transfer from Aldershot (Walden had previously attended tribunal meetings to negotiate his release). The next fixture was against high-flying Hereford United, and Ashurst was still looking positively on his side's chances. "If we can have a sustained run of good results, we could be right up there," he said. Walden made his debut against the city of his birth but was not able to prevent the Owls falling to a 2-1 defeat.

More changes were to follow, although they came off the pitch with the announcement that long-serving backroom duo Jim McAnearney and Ron Staniforth would depart Hillsborough. "We have got to cut our coat according to the cloth we have got," said McGee, while the Voice of Hillsborough added: "These are not measures that Wednesday wanted to make willingly. They were forced on the club by the sheer economics of football today."

On the playing staff, Nimmo signed his first professional contract, having passed 18 that week, and goalkeeper Barry Watling signed from Hartlepool. Watling made his debut, and his sole Owls appearance, at home to Swindon Town, but it was not a happy occasion. A 2-0 defeat left Wednesday firmly in the relegation places, and without a win since Bonfire Night. Ashurst and Tony Toms decided that drastic action was required.

★★★★★

Key Game: Sheffield Wednesday 2-0 Chester City, January 31st 1976

This fixture is included as a key game not so much for the result – although it was a long overdue win – but for the infamous methods used by Len Ashurst and Tony Toms to prepare their team for the game. The technique used was to take the players on to Broomhead Moor, near Stocksbridge, Sheffield for a night of survival training and "team bonding".

This idea was not a new one, as Ashurst and Toms had used a similar idea when in charge of Hartlepool and Gillingham.

What was perhaps different this time was the winter setting. In fact Ashurst, feeling under the weather as he described it, left the organisation to Toms and later claimed: "I thought it was madness as winter was entrenched." 'The Voice of Hillsborough' described the reasoning further: "One league win since Millwall were well beaten in October is the reason why Wednesday are where they are… and the exercise on the Moors was designed to help the players get into the right frame of mind for the battle ahead. Coming to terms with the elements can help them come to terms with the harsh realities of the life that faces themselves and this club should they fail to climb out of the bottom four positions."

Bernard Shaw, the Owls' full back, collaborated with the *Sheffield Star's* Tony Pritchett to write a report that was published later in the week. The report gave a no-holds barred account of what happened.

Wednesday 4:00pm: Shaw gets kitted out in in his camping gear… "I was luckier than most," he said. "I had a sleeping bag designed for a chap seven foot tall. That meant I could get right down inside it."

Wednesday 4:30pm: Leave Hillsborough for the Moors. Said Shaw: "We left the cars and set off walking. By, but I was bloody

170

cold, I've never known it so cold in my life as I was there. We tried to light a fire, but there was only heather to burn and it just smoked."

Wednesday 5:00pm: It's dark. "We tucked into our soup and sandwiches. Best soup the Lord ever made it was. We set off walking ...we must have walked an hour and then Tony Toms said: 'This is the spot.'"

Wednesday 6:30pm: The players are looking for the best spot to kip down, but there is no best spot. "Had a sip of whisky. It tasted like water, it were so cold."

Wednesday 7:00pm: Off for a walk. "Talk about the Grand Old Duke of York marching us up the hill, it was even colder up there."

Wednesday 8:00pm: "Rest for an hour and then up that hill again... Tony Toms advised us when we got back to get into bed."

Wednesday 9:00pm: "Settled down. One of the press lads with us helped us. Cyril Cusack and I kipped down together and I reckon we had the best night of any of the lads."

Thursday 7:00am: "Tony Toms woke us up. I couldn't open my eyes. Maybe the lashes were frozen together."

Thursday 8:00am: "Tony Toms has us on circuit training. We never expected to be training as well as sleeping but it was hard work and made us forget the cold."

Thursday 9:00am: "'That's it lads', said Tony Toms and I couldn't believe it."

"Now it's all over, I can look back on it objectively. Frankly, I'm glad I did it. My chief memory is of the bitter, unbelievable cold, and the relief of getting home but, like the other lads, if it's done us good, then it's been worthwhile. I wouldn't really fancy doing it again at this time of year.... but if the manager suggests camping out for pre-season training in July or August, I'm all for it."

It turned out that the night was the coldest of the year. It had been a brutal evening for some. Allan Thompson was quoted in the local press as saying: "It kept getting colder and colder. It was murder." Brian Joicey felt "it was absolutely terrible" and Mick

Prendergast described it as "the worst night of my life". Tony Toms however felt that the trip was a success.

"They did very well, they worked for each other, they helped each other," he said. The proof of the pudding would be found in the next few results." The reaction from supporters to the "escapade" in that week's *Green 'Un,* however, was far from positive: "What did Toms hope to do?" asked E. Alllison of Sheffield. "If the spectators think it paid off, why don't they sack Ashurst, and bring in Chris Bonington of Everest fame?" asked G.W. (name and address supplied). Given the less than enthusiastic reaction, there was some pressure for a positive result from the next game. This was Chester's first ever season in Division Three and their team were still relatively confident after their promotion the previous year. Ashurst named the following team:

1 Fox
2 Shaw
3 Mullen
4 Thompson
5 Cusack
6 O'Donnell
7 McIver
8 Henson
9 Prendergast
10 Nimmo
11 Potts
Sub: Wylde

With reference to the trip to the Moors, the *Green 'Un's* headline that evening was: "Owls Turn On Heat, Grab 2-Goal Lead". The Wednesday team did indeed take a two-goal advantage as strikes from Nimmo and Prendergast saw them lead by 2-0 as early as the 15th minute. Nimmo took advantage of a poor back-pass, and Prendergast blasted home a 25-yard drive after Henson tapped him a free-kick. That was the end of the scoring, but the crowd of 7,558 (the lowest of the season) went home having witnessed the first Owls victory in 13 league games.

The win also lifted the Owls out of the relegation places for the first time in 1976. The impact of Toms and Ashurst's pre-match excursion on this success is of course debatable, though, as David Cusack told me in 2019, Toms may well still be living out on the story! Ralph Whitworth, the *Sheffield Star* artist, drew a cartoon that went down in Owls folklore in the week following the game. Picturing two sheep on the Moors, it was labelled: "I've been roughing it on these Moors for years and I'm STILL no good at football."

Chairman Bert McGee took the joke in good humour and asked for a copy of the cartoon – with the comment: "I intend to put the cartoon up in a prominent position at Hillsborough. It was very funny and witty, and tickled the players no end." Whitworth himself added: "Whatever the merits of the project, I feel I've got to pay tribute to Len Ashurst and Tony Toms for having the courage of their convictions… and to cap the week off, of course Wednesday won on Saturday!" That win should have provided the team with confidence going into the last 20 games of the season.

Those final games were to be squeezed into a three-month period – a fixture pile-up that meant the team were to play nine games in March, and a further eight in April. The Owls returned to league action for their first game in February with a trip to Ashurst's former employers, Gillingham. Bernard Shaw was named as captain for this fixture, with Allan Thompson ruled out with an injury. Jimmy Quinn also returned to the line-up, with Roger Wylde dropping to the bench in what appeared a more defensive minded team. Perhaps unsurprisingly, then, the game finished goalless, before a 1-0 defeat at Port Vale on a Monday evening.

That game was notable otherwise for the debut of Peter Feely, who signed for the Owls for £10,000 after protracted negotiations with his previous team Gillingham. Feely scored 16 goals in 27 matches for Gillingham under Ashurst the previous season, after beginning his career with Division One Chelsea. Ashurst had high hopes that Feely would help improve the Owls' goalscoring record.

Feely made an immediate impact on his home debut, scoring the Owls' third goal in a comprehensive 3-1 victory against Aldershot. In front of 8,286 fans Nimmo and Prendergast had given Wednesday a 2-1 half-time lead. The result was more impressive as the Owls were missing Potts, Quinn, Mullen and Henson through flu, and the Owls' following two games (at home to Chesterfield and away at Shrewsbury) were postponed as a result of what was described as an influenza bug epidemic. The postponements meant that the Owls had up to five games in hand on most of their relegation rivals, though had to play these fixtures in quick succession. Next up, as March began, was a trip to Halifax and a game that finished as a goalless draw and Tony Toms described as "terrible".

There was more drama on show in Wednesday's trip to Peterborough, a game that saw the Owls go into the final few minutes leading 2-1. Then Jimmy Quinn was sent off, Posh scored a very late equaliser and, after the final whistle, what the Owls' matchday programme described as "a horde of irresponsible Wednesday fans" spilled on to the pitch. Wednesday remained without an away win all season, but the single point was the ninth that they had gained since the trip to the Moors. The Owls were now 18th in the table and could take some confidence into their remaining games.

After a 1-0 defeat to Millwall at The Den, Wednesday dipped into the transfer market with the signing of 19-year-old striker Derek Bell from Halifax Town before the deadline. The intention was for Bell to join permanently if his initial loan spell went well, while the Owls also had offers for other players rejected and a deal for Brian Joicey to join Port Vale fell through. One defeat quickly became four as Wednesday lost to Millwall (1-0), Rotherham United (1-0) and Chesterfield (3-1), to understandable disquiet amongst the fanbase.

"I was disgusted and outraged by the disgraceful tactics of Sheffield Wednesday last Saturday," said one fan in his letter to the Green 'Un after the Rotherham defeat, which was again followed by outbreaks of hooliganism. "The events on and off the field against Rotherham United a week ago did not do many reputations much good," admitted the Voice of Hillsborough. Against Chesterfield, Wednesday actually took the lead before capitulating and losing 3-1. "Where now for Sheffield Wednesday?" asked the following day's *Star* newspaper. "On the evidence of the home failure against Chesterfield, there's only one answer – Division Four."

Just 6,905 fans turned out for Wednesday's next game, at home to Colchester United – the lowest league attendance of the post-war period and a record that is still to be broken. In his programme notes, manager Ashurst wrote: "It has got to be better than against Chesterfield" and he was right, in terms of the result at least; a 1-0 victory for Wednesday, courtesy of a 77th-minute winner. The goal was credited to Phil Henson, but many felt that the deflected half-struck effort should have been given as an own-goal.

It was an important result, which lifted some of the gloom around Hillsborough, but could not lift Wednesday out of the relegation zone ahead of a heavy 4-2 defeat away at Preston. Derek Bell scored his only goal for the Owls in that game, and Ashurst decided against making his move permanent. With Wednesday in the drop zone going into the final month of the season, he had more pressing matters at hand.

That month was to feature eight games, the first of which saw Wednesday defeat FA Cup semi-finalists Crystal Palace at 1-0 at Hillsborough, the goal from Mick Prendergast. Curiously that result meant Wednesday had now gone seven games without defeat against Palace but, more importantly, lifted them out of the relegation places. That was to prove short-lived, however, as a 3-0 defeat at Wrexham dragged them right back into trouble again.

Wednesday's season-long wait for an away win continued when they could only manage a scoreless draw at Shrewsbury, with Eric Potts missing a penalty, but there was some joy on the home front at least when 'super-sub' Ian Nimmo scored in the final few minutes to beat Bury and secure what the *Green 'Un* reported as "two priceless points". A heavy 3-0 defeat at Mansfield did Wednesday's survival hopes no good but results elsewhere gave fans some hopes as relegation rivals Halifax and Southend lost and drew respectively.

In a remarkably quick turnaround, Wednesday faced Halifax the following day and won 1-0 against the division's bottom club, thanks to Phil Henson's winner. Henson told me in 2019: "My outstanding memory (*of the period*) was the game vs Halifax. We needed to win and fortunately we did." Henson's winner sent Wednesday up to 19th in the table and, crucially, left their battle against relegation in their own hands. A pitch invasion followed the game, with Henson carried from the pitch by jubilant fans.

Wednesday then had the chance to guarantee survival with victory over Brighton and Hove Albion, and things looked promising when Potts put the Owls ahead in the first half. But disaster struck in the final minute when Paul Ward crashed home a volley to equalise for Brighton, ensuring Wednesday's survival bid would go down to the very final game of the season. Southend still had a game in hand at this stage but drew 2-2 at Wrexham, setting up a winner-takes-all tie at Hillsborough between the two sides on April 29.

A season where the final 17 games had been squeezed into just two months with a mixture of postponements due to the weather, illness, and Hillsborough's use for other games, and with the Owls in and out of the relegation positions, came down to just one game.

* * * * *

Key Game: Sheffield Wednesday 2-1 Southend United, April 29th 1976

The game against Southend was played after the end of the regular season, after being postponed because Hillsborough was used for the FA Cup semi-final between Manchester United and Derby County. Southend's result against Wrexham left a simple scenario; a Southend victory would keep them up and relegate Wednesday. A draw or Wednesday win would save the Owls and send Southend down. Do or die.

"They will fight like Trojans," said manager Ashurst of Southend, who he had watched in their draw against Wrexham. "We've just got to do it; I've said this all along… The odds are in our favour and we are confident." Mick Prendergast was in no doubt about the importance of the game. "I think this must be the most important match I have played for the club since I've been at Hillsborough," he said.

"We've got a hell of a manager and I think this man is the best I've played under at Hillsborough… We shouldn't be in this position. We've had the breaks at home, and I hope we do it tonight."

Wednesday, Ashurst vowed, would not be playing for a draw. "It's the crowd plus eleven players," he said. "We are all in it together and everyone will have the adrenalin pumping. It's nice to know the crowd are behind us." The 'Voice of Hillsborough' in that evening's match programme also made mention of the fans: "There will be no half measures on the pitch or terraces tonight; give the team all the vocal support you can muster. Wednesday Need You!"

The Owls' fans certainly did turn out in good numbers, with a season-high attendance of 25,802 recorded. Southend were rumoured to have booked six supporters' coaches, to try and boost support for their team. There is little evidence of a large contingent of opposition fans making it to Sheffield, but Southend could still approach the game with some confidence, having lost only one of their last six matches (they had also, it must be said, only won one of those games). Their manager, Arthur Rowley, (a former Sheffield United boss), expressed some of that confidence: "Our salvation is in our own hands… I think we shall escape, but it won't be easy."

Len Ashurst selected an unchanged team from the one that had drawn at Brighton. Mick Prendergast characteristically played despite suffering the effects of an ankle injury:

1 Fox
2 Walden
3 Shaw
4 Mullen

5 Cusack
6 O'Donnell
7 Wylde
8 Henson
9 Nimmo
10 Prendergast
11 Potts
Sub: Hull

The *Star's* match report the following day described the action:

"SUPER GOALS CHASE BLUES AS OWLS AVOID THE DROP. Scenes fitting for a promotion-winning side followed Sheffield Wednesday's 2-1 win over Southend at Hillsborough last night – a victory which, at the last gasp, kept Wednesday in Division Three and relegated Southend. Hillsborough's best crowd of the season turned up to cheer the side on... The match had a nervy kind of start – hardly surprisingly – but Wednesday roared into the driving seat with two goals inside 35 minutes. The scorers, Mick Prendergast and Eric Potts, constantly tormented the Southend defence and with captain Jimmy Mullen and Dave Cusack decisive at the heart of the defence, and Phil Henson cool in midfield, Wednesday had the men where it mattered... On the quarter hour Neil O'Donnell crossed from the right and Henson came so close to giving Wednesday the lead – his header struck the bar. At this stage it was a case of Wednesday pressure, though after 25 minutes they had faded somewhat.
Just when we were wondering if that early impetus might have vanished, Wednesday snatched the all-important first score through Prendergast... Wylde began the move with a fine crossfield pass to O'Donnell, he controlled it, rounded Southend left back Andy Ford, and when he crossed from the right, Potts flicked the ball on for Prendergast to tuck it into the corner... Seven minutes later came another Wednesday goal. Henson's free kick went via Ian Nimmo to Potts, who crashed in a cracking shot from the left for a superb goal...
Though Wednesday were in the driving seat with a two-goal lead,

*the tension of the occasion was shown when Potts and Henson
had a slight temporary squabble when forming a two-man wall
at a free-kick. The situation changed just past the hour when
Southend pulled back a goal. Allan Little drove the ball in low
and Alan Moody got a close-range touch to give Arthur Rowley's
side some hope... Southend substitute Ron Pountney miscued his
10-yard shot before Wylde might have put the issue beyond any
doubt at all but after Nimmo and Potts linked well he shot wide.
The whistle duly came, and with it joy and relief."*

The Owls dug deep to defend their lead, dropping further and
further back as the game went on in an attempt to protect what
they had. Len Ashurst spent the final few minutes urging his players to push out and avoid falling back. His attempts were successful, and the full-time whistle was met with jubilant scenes.

After the game, and despite Owls secretary Eric England's pre-
match request for fans to stay off the pitch, Owls' supporters
invaded the Hillsborough turf in their thousands. After surrounding the tunnel and chanting for the players to appear, the players
obliged to take to applause of the faithful. It was a happy end to
a very difficult season.

Wednesday finished 20th, one place and one point clear of the
relegation positions. This moment gives the book its title – this
was the club's *"Lowest Ebb"*. Ashurst, though, recognised the potential. "To finish so close to the bottom and get a reception like
that – it's fantastic," he said. "As a manager you could be on top
of the world with some success." The team had won 12 league
games, drawn 16 and lost 18, scoring 49 goals in the process.
They conceded 59 times and gained 40 points – which, Ashurst
admitted afterwards, was his target for the team.

But despite hitting that mark, and sealing survival in Division Three, it could by no means be seen as a successful season.
Ashurst accepted that in an open letter to the fans, written at
3am after the Southend game.

"YOU were fantastic! I write this letter in the early hours with

the adrenaline still pumping and my brain spinning. Not only from our 2-1 victory but by the fantastic vocal support given to the team in encouraging them to victory. A victory that owed as much to you as to the boys…. In my office I've got hundreds and hundreds of critical letters as testimony to the interest and concern that all of you have shown to the club. To crown it with an attendance of over 25,000 makes me all the more determined to give you a team to be associated with. Because, if I don't, I have lost the greatest football opportunity I shall ever have in my life and I don't want to be a forgotten name. Finally, thanks to all the supporters who have given time, money and tears away from home this season. I know thanks are not what you want, but a winning team… and so do I."

Ashurst immediately gave free transfers to nine players, including Bernard Shaw and former captain Allan Thompson (despite his new contract offer earlier in the season). Ashurst wrote in more detail in the following week's *Green 'Un* about some of his reasoning and plans for the future. "I've let players go," he revealed, "because of lack of playing ability, lack of interest in Sheffield Wednesday, lack of fight for the cause and also that one or two players are not good for the dressing room. Ashurst accused certain players of being late for training, of not giving 100 per cent in games, of attending dental appointments rather than training, of having lost pace, of having "failed him" and having come into training "smelling of liquor."

Shaw was the player accused of lateness to training, and he in turn responded in the *Sheffield Star* two days later. "I was staggered when, in relating a number of incidents that have occurred, he chose to single me out," he said. Regardless of the rights and wrongs of the situation, chairman Bert McGee was happy with Ashurst's efforts. "I've congratulated him, he's worked very hard," he said. "I can assure Wednesday fans they will see a better team next season – a team to match those wonderful fans." What followed is material for another book. Ashurst and the team had reached *"Our Lowest Ebb"* and, so far at least, the club has never fallen that far again.

AN INTERVIEW WITH NEIL RAMSBOTTOM

Neil Ramsbottom played one season for the Owls in 1975-76. He was hugely experienced at that stage, having previously played for Bury, Blackpool, Crewe, Fulham and then Division One Coventry City. He joined the Owls from the Sky Blues in the summer of 1975 and went on to play 22 games that season. He moved on at the end of the season to Plymouth Argyle and later spent time at Bradford City, Bournemouth and briefly Sheffield United, in between spells in North America. Neil is now retired and lives in his native Blackburn where he spoke to me in the summer of 2019. We chatted for a short while about football, and the West Midlands – where Neil was once based with Coventry – before moving on to talk about his time with the Owls.

Tell me a little about how and why you moved to Hillsborough?
Well, as you know I was at Coventry. They were in Division One and had been doing well at the time. I'd played a couple of seasons in the first team there and thought I'd done well. Anyhow, I lost my place in the team and I was disappointed by that. Steve Burtenshaw got in touch and sold Wednesday to me. I talked with him and all but agreed to join. I came up on a Saturday to sort the details – Wednesday were away at Southend that day, it was the first game of the season. Anyhow, I came up with my girlfriend, now my wife, we had a look around the area and at the stadium and facilities and I decided to join. I thought Hillsborough stank of success, somewhere like that was not the kind of place that would be in Division Three for long. So, I actually signed after the first game. I knew that the other goalkeeper, Peter Fox, was a young lad, so I'd have a good chance of making the team. They lost at Southend, so Steve Burtenshaw put me in the team for the next game, a cup tie up at Darlington, where I kept a clean sheet, and I was away!

How did you find working for Steve Burtenshaw?

He was a good coach, with great ideas about the game. He was very intelligent and very thoughtful about football, almost like a 1970s Jose Mourinho! Perhaps not quite at his level to be fair. The issue was he had been working in Division One with Arsenal and QPR. He wanted to play football where we passed it out from the back. This was Division Three though, and without being rude some of the players in front of me weren't cut out for that. One or two couldn't really control a ball! Anyhow, he didn't last long while I was there – I think about six weeks later he was sacked. Mind you, I was signed for Coventry on a Thursday as it was transfer deadline day, by a manager called Noel Cantwell. He was sacked on the Sunday. I think managers got a bit nervous in signing me after a while! There were a few managers sacked in my time at various clubs… it's something you get used to as a player.

Did things change for you under Len Ashurst and Tony Toms?

Put it this way, me and Len Ashurst didn't really see "eye to eye". I also didn't really respect Tony Toms. They came in and wanted to do things their way. Toms knew nothing about football. **It was all fitness wasn't it?** Yes, it was all fitness, but he thought he knew about football, but didn't. Len called me into the office on Christmas Eve that year and told me that he wanted me to sign for Gillingham. Christmas Eve! Anyway, I told him I wasn't going. I think it's probably not too strong a thing to say that I found Ashurst to be a bit of a bully. It was his way only. Anyhow, shortly after that I got ill and ended up in hospital for some time.

Yes,tell me about that – the club programme sent good wishes,but didn't say what the problem was.

I'd caught hepatitis! Ended up in Blackburn Hospital in isolation for three days. Even when I was let out, I wasn't allowed alcohol for a year, and had to really watch my diet. It left me very weak for a while. To be fair, I'd been not feeling well for a while beforehand, but it hit me hard. The only thing I got from SWFC was a bunch of flowers – which I think came from the office staff. I never heard a thing from Len Ashurst. It took me a long time to recover and at the end of the season I moved on to Plymouth. My reactions were okay by then, but I still don't think I'd recovered all my strength.

So, only one season at Hillsborough – would you say you made a mistake in signing?
It's easy to look back at any professional career and look at the choices you made. In hindsight, maybe, but I don't regret it. Shef-field Wednesday were a huge club. I liked the digs I was in, I lodged with a family out in Hackenthorpe, and they were lovely people. They had an Owls-mad son though, who was a great lad, but didn't half used to bother me with questions after training! I really enjoyed playing in front of the fans as well – we'd go away to somewhere like Hereford, say, and there'd be more Wednes-day fans than home supporters. It was great, hearing them all chanting your name and shouting for you. The problem was the opposition would often play out of their skin against us. It was the same when they came to Hillsborough. Opposition teams would have their best game of the season when they came. And we had to try and counter that.

Is that why you think the team struggled?
Well, we had some classy players. Colin Harvey for example, he was right out of the top drawer. Phil Henson was another one. We also had some good lads – Dave Cusack was just coming through. Jimmy Mullen would tackle anything. Rodger Wylde – I always felt he could have played at the very top. I suppose we didn't really have enough of the top-level players and we lacked confidence. It was difficult then for the young lads as they were coming into a team that wasn't doing well, and it was tricky for them to come in and do well.

Listen, I don't want to do Wednesday down, but I'll give you an example of where the club lacked professionalism at the time. At Coventry, for training, you'd turn up in the morning, and the kits would be cleaned and laid out ready for you, every day with-out fail. At Hillsborough, they put the kits through a tumble dryer to wear again the next day. There'd be a scramble for the kit, and the goalie kit would stay dirty from one day to the next! Also, I think the expectations were high – and that made it difficult for some of the players we had. Wednesday were a top club a few years previously, and there was an expectation that they'd get back there.

You came back to Sheffield later in your career I think, with United?

Yes, I did briefly. I contacted them, as I had been in the States playing in New Jersey and was back in England for a while, before I was due to go back to America. Anyhow, United signed me, then had injuries and before I knew it, I was in the first team! I went back to America after that and ended up playing and then managing a team called Miami Americans. They were owned by South Africans, who seemed to have plenty of money. It ran out though, the club went into receivership and I came back and finished my career at Bradford and then Bournemouth.

I thanked Neil for his time and asked him if he had anything else he'd like to add.

Only to say that I really enjoyed my time at Wednesday. I hope I haven't sounded unfair or harsh on the club or the team. I made some good friends there – I enjoyed working with and teaching some of the younger players, Chris Turner especially. It's a great club.

THE RESERVE AND
YOUTH TEAMS

A romantic tale of what might have been, or the story of what happens to thousands of young footballers across clubs and across time? One for the reader to decide.

Sheffield Wednesday struggled financially after relegation from Division One in the 1970s. As the decade developed and the team saw no sign of returning to the top-flight, the club put more and more faith into its youngsters. Between 1970 and 1975 the following players all appeared for the club's youth team: Danny Cameron, Jimmy Mullen, Roger Wylde, Allan Thompson, Eddie Prudham, Kevin Johnson, David Sunley, David Herbert, Gary Hull, David Cusack, Peter Fox, Ronnie Ferguson and Ian Nimmo. By the end of 1975-76 they had all also played for the first team. This was a core of talented players who had an obvious team spirit.

All of those who I have spoken to remembered others from the team with real fondness, some staying in contact with each other to this day, and all remembering David Cusack by his nickname of 'Cyril' derived from the Irish actor Cyril Cusack. It is easy to argue 'what if...?' in history, but there is certainly an argument that in different circumstances, these players could have formed the spine of a more successful Owls team than the one of this period. The youth squad were successful as a team during the early to mid-1970s. They finished third in the Northern Intermediate League in 1971-72 and again in 1972-73. They were also runners up in the League Cup in 1970-71 and 1971-72, before reaching the semi-finals in 1974-75.

They were twice winners of international tournaments – winning a competition in Parma, Italy in 1972 and the Zilveren Botton Tournament in the Netherlands in 1973. In the Dutch tournament, the young Owls did not concede a goal in five matches, including one against Ajax Youth. They won the final, with goals by Nicholson and Spacie bringing a 2-0 victory against Volendam.

The club also sent an under-21 team to a tournament in Venice, Italy in 1973 and creditably reached the quarter finals. The teams had regular goalscorers, with Ian Musson topping the charts in 1970-71 and 1971-72, followed by David Herbert in 1972-73 and Ronnie Ferguson in 1973-74 and 1974-75.

Musson never made the first team at Hillsborough, though he did play league football for Lincoln City after leaving the Owls. There were other good youth teams at the time, with Newcastle and Sunderland maintaining particularly strong youth set-ups. The Owls remained competitive throughout, usually finishing in the top half of the Northern Intermediate League, with their lowest finish being 10 in a 16-team division in 1976.

The reserve team played in the Central League. They were somewhat less successful in terms of results and league positions – though they managed a creditable sixth place (out of 22) in 1972-73. Many of the youth team quickly made the step up to the reserves. As far back as 1970-71, Danny Cameron, Eddie Prudham, David Sunley and Jimmy Mullen had all made the jump.

Sunley was in fact top scorer for the reserve team that season with 12 goals while Prudham scored a hat-trick in a 7-4 defeat to Huddersfield Town's second string in October. By 1972-73, Roger Wylde was top scorer with 26 goals, including six in a 7-0 win against Manchester City in September.

Prudham, Wylde, Ferguson and Herbert were regular goalscorers for the team throughout the mid-70s and Herbert finished as top goal scorer in both 1974-75 and 1975-76. It is not unexpected that the reserve team sometimes found life more difficult. Danny Cameron told me in 2019 that "most of the big clubs included household names in their reserves". Facts and statistics on reserve games are a little hard to come by, but one fan supports this view with his memory of seeing John Toshack and Kevin Keegan playing for Liverpool's reserves, in front of a crowd of around 2,000.

Francis Smith, who signed apprentice forms in 1975, said: "I played a lot of reserve matches from the early stages, but I loved it: going to big stadiums like Newcastle's St James' Park, Maine

Road, Old Trafford… it was heaven for me! Some teams such as West Brom and Aston Villa in particular had some good players in their squad then. It was a fantastic experience at that age."

Prudham remembers playing in front of relatively large crowds both at Hillsborough but also away at grounds such as Elland Road, and Smith supports this view – remembering a one large crowd in particular.

"There were something like 13,000 at Old Trafford," he said, "because you got tokens towards the European Cup games…" Success in reserve team football was success in a man's league, and the Owls had players who were successful at that standard.

In 1975, the club also set up an under-16s team who played at the Owls' Middlewood Road training ground and were called the Middlewood Rovers. Their first game was against Springfield Juniors on September 7, 1975. Owls fans were encouraged to attend. As the matchday programme said: "Don't laze around in bed – get off to Middlewood Road and give 'em some support. There'll still be time for a couple of pints afterwards."

The players in this team were too young to get near the first team during the years covered by this book. As time progressed, however, several players did come through and play for the Owls. The creation of Middlewood Rovers is perhaps one of Steve Burtenshaw's main legacies as manager.

The team was successful on its own merits and, by March 1976, the club programme was encouraging fans to attend the game against Greenhill Park who "…like themselves are unbeaten in the League and the match will virtually decide the championship." The team kept schoolboys under the watchful eye of the Owls for one full season before they signed as apprentices. Their manager was Albert Phelan, who remained with the Owls into the 1990s and, among other players, Peter Shirtcliff, Mark Smith, Charlie Williamson and Mel Sterland came through their ranks.

Others, such as Steve Charles who played for Middlewood Rovers' under-16s team in 1976, had successful careers elsewhere. Charles played over 100 games for Sheffield United, and 200 more for Mansfield Town.

George McCabe oversaw the youth set up at Hillsborough. At various times he was titled coach, trainer, youth administration officer and simply he who "looks after the youngsters". McCabe was a former referee who had officiated at the 1966 World Cup and the 1969 FA Cup final (his last game in English professional football). He was initially employed on a part-time basis at Hillsborough while Gerry Young ran the reserve team in the period after his retirement from playing in 1971. Young also offered further support to the youngsters.

At other times Ron Staniforth, Jim McAnearney, Ken Knighton and others also helped with the coaching and development of the youngsters and reserves, while Wednesday also maintained a scouting network under chief scout Jim Scott until 1975, when he was released for financial reasons. The network helped bring in players from outside the local area – Stan Shaw and Paul Swann for example being responsible for Leicestershire and Lincolnshire (and recommending Ronnie Ferguson to the club). McCabe was not an experienced or natural coach, but he was determined to develop a system that would bring youngsters through into the first team.

David Barker, who played as goalkeeper for the youth team in the early 1970s, recalled the training they received. "George McCabe was rubbish but was one of Derek Dooley's mates!" he said. "Hugh Swift, Keith Bannister and Ron Staniforth used to help with the training. We trained and usually played our home games on Saturday mornings at 11am, at Mortomley High Green where the new swimming baths and hub is now".

David Herbert, interviewed as a 16-year-old in 1972, described the set up as "just great" and the article, in The *Star*, added how a player like Herbert had "the opportunity for advancement at a modern football club which runs on smooth and well-oiled lines."

Propaganda perhaps, but the article did add that, through McCabe, the players would be taught "a strong set of values". That's a view supported by Danny Cameron, who told me: "We called George McCabe 'the penguin' because of his running gait and whilst we learned that discipline was a key asset for a footballer,

I'm afraid that his coaching abilities were extremely limited. He was though a thoroughly nice man."

McCabe demonstrated his "nice man" qualities in many ways, like the personalised Christmas card he sent to all youth team players every year. He did need, though, the support of experienced football men to help build the teams and the players to the standard necessary for reserve and first team football. It is a plausible argument that the training and coaching provided was not of a high enough quality to ensure that players made the jump to first team standard. Tommy Craig, interviewed after he left Hillsborough, certainly thought so.

"Look, Allan Thompson was a great player when I first saw him. Like Jimmy Mullen, Allan could, and should, have been a top defender – but their early promise was never given the correct encouragement or coaching," Craig said. "Sure, Allan had his bad points – but it was hardly his fault that he never made the top grade." Here perhaps lays the root of the Owls' inability to ensure that this group of talented players made the step up. A changing group of coaches, under three managers in a short period, with the stability provided by McCabe who several accounts suggest was not an effective coach (though a thoroughly good man). McCabe needed support, and at times he got it.

One example was the Parma tournament of June 1972, when McCabe and Gerry Young took charge of a young Owls side who won the tournament with a 1-0 final victory over Partizan Belgrade. Jimmy Mullen was also named man of the match in the final and Danny Cameron was awarded defender of the tournament while Garry Hull won best young player of the competition, and Roger Wylde won player of the tournament. The Owls made much of that success, with pictures and articles featuring in the match day programme, in the *Sheffield Star* and the Supporters' Club yearbook.

Derek Dooley was quoted in the programme: "We sent the team for experience and they returned victorious. Their performances do great credit to Gerry Young and George McCabe who accompanied the juniors to Italy and prepared them for this tournament." Dooley clearly had great respect for McCabe. After a period of success in 1971 which saw the youth team thrash Hull City's youth team 5-2 and five youngsters promoted to the reserves, Dooley said: "A great deal of credit belongs to George McCabe. He has done a tremendous job with these junior footballers."

McCabe was allowed a short slot in the matchday magazine at times. In the programme for the famous 4-4 game against Manchester United in 1974, he wrote: "We congratulate our youngsters on reaching the semi-final of the League Cup... The pleasing thing is that nine of the players are products of the Sheffield area. Well done to you all." In August 1975, the centre page of the club programme focused on a piece about the Owls' 'Super Apprentices' and a picture of eight of the club's youngsters (featuring future first team players Ian Nimmo and Chris Turner) was included along with a quote from Ron Staniforth: "Opportunities are unlimited for the progression of apprentices at Hillsborough... they are players of quality." Kev Lancaster was part of this group. "I've got good memories of my time as an apprentice at SWFC," he told me.

"They were very different times, almost amateurish compared to today. Our days started with cleaning boots and laying out kit for the pros. Then training, then cleaning up when the first team and reserves had finished. Hard work but we managed to have some great laughs. We weren't really aware how bad the first team situation was and concentrated on our own matches in the Northern Intermediate League and reserves." McCabe was always very pleased when one of his charges made the step up to the first team. After Ronnie Ferguson's first team debut, McCabe said: "Years of hard work go into producing the sort of thing we saw this afternoon – let's hope there will be more, because rearing our own talent is the club's passport to a brighter future."

McCabe remained at Hillsborough until he was dismissed in October 1975 for "financial reasons". His dismissal coincided with the appointment of Len Ashurst as manager. Jim McAnearney and Ron Staniforth continued working with the youth and reserve teams until they in turn were dismissed in January 1976. Ashurst and his trainer Tony Toms then took control of the training, coaching and football at all levels at Sheffield Wednesday. Much would change.

Prior to Ashurst's arrival, and particularly during Steve Burtenshaw's time as manager, there were regular messages from the club about the importance of developing young players. "We have got to push our teenagers through, carefully of course, so we can see if they can shine as the level of competition rises," said Burtenshaw in 1974. The directors' report for 1974-75 suggested that "in view of the financial situation at the club, the directors are concentrating their efforts on producing players through the youth policy". As early as 1972, Sir Andrew Stephen is said to have spoken at the club's annual meeting about the necessity and importance of developing young talent.

The club had deliberately extended their youth policy from the very early 1970s, as Owls historian Daniel Gordon, comments, "perhaps in the hope of following Scunthorpe and discovering the next Kevin Keegan." They may not have found the next Keegan, but the club had uncovered a series of players who had broken through to the first team. The club's programme recognised the success of the youngsters by putting Ian Nimmo on the cover and commenting on how he "shot in five golden goals in our 5-0 victory over Grimsby in the Northern Intermediate League, and who scored on his first team debut last month – a flying start to the New Year!"

Some fans, though, expressed frustration that the club had not provided more opportunities for first team action for the youngsters. One letter published in The Star in 1973, after the reserves thrashed Manchester City 7-0: "The standard of the young Owls' play was amazing…These players, allied with the methods and unselfish team work displayed by the reserves would, I feel sure, bring the desired results for the first team." Another letter, from the 1973-74 season, suggested that: "If ever there's a lad who's had a raw deal it's Roger Wylde… Prudham is another who gets a game now and again… It's time Cameron, a young "tiger", and Roger Wylde be given an extended run in the first team." The authors of these letters were correct, in a way. A series of youngsters had broken through into the first team but by 1975 at least, none had fully established themselves.

The first team that these players were looking to cement a place in was struggling, falling down the leagues, and was on to its third full-time manager in as many years by the time of Ashurst's arrival. Ashurst would look to change things after arriving at a club that he described as "overstaffed and lacking in quality". Ashurst was keen to clamp down on what he saw as negative habits around the club, and once took off David Herbert in a reserve game in 1975 because he felt the player had ducked out of a situation in the opposition goalmouth which could have resulted in a goal for Wednesday.

"I pulled him off to teach him, and everyone else, a lesson," Ashurst said. Herbert was subsequently released at the end of that season, along with many other youngsters who had looked promising in the early 1970s. Danny Cameron, Ronnie Ferguson, Allan Thompson and David Sunley all left at the end of the season or before. Eddie Prudham had already gone, as had Kevin Johnson – who, despite "murdering the first team in training" (according to Danny Cameron at least), only made one substitute appearance for the first team. Gary Hull stayed one further season, and other players survived the cull.

Jimmy Mullen was placed on the transfer list but was removed from it and returned to the team with a good degree of success. Roger Wylde stayed until 1980 and eventually scored 66 goals for the first team. David Cusack, Peter Fox and Ian Nimmo all stayed for several years and contributed to a greater or lesser extent to the Owls' revival of the later 1970s. Of those who left, Cameron, Prudham and Johnson continued to have successful careers in the game. The others drifted away somewhat.

In conclusion, it is possible to argue that the end of this story is what happens at most football clubs, most of the time. The club signed a bunch of lads as apprentices and some were released at 18 and drifted into the non-league without even playing for the reserves. Others were kept on, some made it through to the first team. Of those who made it, some had a short career, others were more successful.

All this is true about the lads who were playing for the Owls youth team in the early 1970s.

And yet... The romantic in me feels that there was something about a number of these players. Watch Danny Cameron bombing down the wing on footage from the time or see the look of delight on David Herbert's face on scoring in front of the Kop. Read Allan Thompson's heartfelt letter to fans as he explains his frustration with the team's position in early 1976: *"I doubt there is a single person in Sheffield who doesn't know the shambles this club has got itself into."* Each of these suggests to me that these were men with talent who wanted themselves and the club to succeed.

It didn't quite happen. Some of this seems to me to have been a product of the circumstances. These talented players came through at a time when the team and club were struggling. The club aimed to provide opportunities for young players, and these were available, but it is difficult to make your mark in a losing team. In altering that losing team, Len Ashurst changed much. He, and Wednesday, eventually succeeded. It was maybe at the cost of some of our young players' careers with the Owls.

AN INTERVIEW WITH LEN ASHURST

Len Ashurst was Owls manager for 11 days short of two years between October 1975 and October 1977. As we know, he took on the job after the disastrous relegation of 1975 and a slow start to the following season under his predecessor, Steve Burtenshaw. Born in Liverpool in March 1939, Ashurst was 36 when he took the post at Hillsborough. Now into his 80s, he spoke to me from his home on the North East coast in early 2020.

Thanks for taking the time to talk to me Len.
No problem young man. I enjoyed my time at Hillsborough, and think I did a good job in the circumstances.

Tell me firstly, what attracted you to the job at Hillsborough?
Well, it's a massive club. It was facing hard times, but I felt I could help turn it around. I also felt that I'd taken Gillingham as far as I could and that it was time for a new challenge. Mind you, it became very bitter with Gillingham, as they didn't want me to leave. When I went back with Wednesday in February the next year, they wouldn't let me, Tony Toms and the rest of the team stand in the dugout next to Gerry Summers, the new Gillingham boss. Instead they moved us to the opposite side of the pitch, next to an area of hardcore fans called 'The Paddock'. We faced dog's abuse! The players couldn't hear what we were saying to them! A very bitter day. We did come away with a goalless draw though.

The Owls were struggling before you arrived. How did you find the situation when you started?
Sour! The crowd were very frustrated and "anti" if you know what I mean. There was a big squad, I know I said in my book that there were 60 players on the books – I may have exaggerated a little, it was more like 30 senior pros. Of those there were

15-20 who felt they should have been in the team at any one time. There were also some "hangers on", people who I felt were just there for a pay-day.

The attitude in the dressing room was not very positive either. They'd grown used to losing. The chairman was not very generous to the players, so they were pretty fed up. It needed a good shake up all round. But then that's what me and Tomsie were there to do.

You mention Tony Toms there. Tell me about your relationship with him.
Well, me and Tomsie were big pals. He was a formidable character; he was strong and knew about fitness. We'd worked together at both Hartlepool and Gillingham. I first came across him at Hartlepool when he was with the military – and they did some training with us. The players liked him as well, I think. He's a good guy.

How did you begin to shake things up at Hillsborough?
I knew that I would need to be my own man and that my management style and the style of football that I wanted the team to play would be different to my predecessor's. There's no point trying to ape other people in anything you do. So, it was all about discipline. I was disciplined in myself and I expected that from the players and the team. It was difficult to motivate everyone that first season given where the club had come from, but we worked at it and worked at it. It was a shock to the system for some!

What impact do you think the famous night on Broomhead Moor had?
Well, we won the next game! Here's a quote for the book for you. I claimed to be ill at the time, but the truth is I bottled it! I didn't go, Tomsie did. He thought it would be good for team bonding. He let the players take a certain amount of food and drink with them and a sleeping bag, I think. We'd done similar sessions at Gillingham and Hartlepool. Possibly not on the coldest night of the year though! Anyhow, like I say, we won the next game, so

I think the exercise was worthwhile. It was another shock to the system of some though.

How was the situation behind the scenes at Hillsborough?

The finances were not great. In fact, it seemed like the club didn't have two pennies to rub together. The chairman was not prepared to spend any money. So, I had to do the best job I could with what we had. Did that affect your transfer policy? Well, as I say, there was no money in the kitty, but the expectations of the chairman and the fans were still high, so I had to do the best I could. I brought in free transfers, but listen, some of those players were a darn sight better that what we already had. Richard Walden, for example, he was an excellent right back – he went on to play lots and lots of games at a good standard.

How far do you think your work set the scene for future improvements at Hillsborough?

It was a sour club when I began. The whole place needed a tidy up and a clean-up. I had to revamp the squad with limited money and improve a dressing room attitude that wasn't great. By my second season I think we had a top half finish and could have had a shout at promotion.

The squad just fell short that season, I felt that if we'd been able to bring in another player or two – we might have been somewhere near. I didn't quite achieve what I wanted at Hillsborough, I really wanted a good cup-run and promotion back to the Second Division. We did though get the crowd back on side and develop the team. So, all in all, I think I did a good job with what I had.

One last question... how did you mark the win over Southend that kept the team in Division Three?

To be honest I was knackered! We'd played lots of matches in a short period of time. There was a lot of pressure and that takes it out of you. So, it was a time of relief and recollection. There wasn't a celebration. No champagne in the dressing room (laughs) not that the chairman would have bought us some anyway!

Thanks Len - is there anything else you'd like to add?

Only that it was a difficult job, but I enjoyed it, and I think we managed to change things eventually. Good luck with the book, I'll certainly be interested in having a read when it's out. Now, let me get you Tony Toms' number, he might have a story or two for you as well!

AN INTERVIEW WITH TONY TOMS

Len Ashurst was as good as his word, and in the late winter of 2020 I contacted Tony Toms. As we know, Toms was Ashurst's trainer and right-hand man. He had an interesting background but was still only 30 years old when he joined Ashurst at Hillsborough in 1975. Now in his mid-70s, Toms is retired and living in South Wales. It was from his home in Carmarthen that he spoke to me about his time at Hillsborough. He was keen to help and told me that he "usually got on well with everybody!" We talked a little about football and my reasons for writing the book, before turning to his time in Sheffield.

Tell me firstly about your relationship with Len Ashurst.
I was honoured to work with Len. I had never met someone of his ilk before or since I think. A great guy. I was shocked at his honesty when we met. He was absolutely determined to succeed.
So, how did you meet? It seems a big step from the military into football. Well, I'd been doing a TV programme you know. All about fitness, we'd get various celebrities on and work with them doing military style exercises. Anyhow, one week we got a football team on. It was a team that were bottom of the league, struggling. Turns out it was Hartlepool United, and Len was the manager. Well, we got them working hard and running. Len was impressed with how hard we got them to work. A short while later he asked me to work with him at Hartlepool. I moved with him from there to Gillingham and then onto Sheffield Wednesday.

How did you find the situation when you arrived at Hillsborough?
Well, what I'd say firstly is that Len was very unlucky at Hillsborough. He worked so hard for success there without a scrap of luck. He had injuries to cope with and a chairman, who was a great guy, but also tight as a duck's arse! We had no money for

new players and had to manage with what we had along with the odd free transfer. **How about the fitness of the players?** I'd say that overall, the fitness of the players was very poor. They had a recovery rate that was well below average for an athlete. Not all of them obviously, and it wouldn't be right to name names now, but I'd say that most of the players were simply not fit enough.

What did you do to try and rectify that?
Lots and lots of fitness work! We increased repetitions in everything we did. We worked hard on stopping and turning – running to one cone, stopping, coming back, turning again. We did that again and again until the players could do no more, when their lungs were bursting and hearts burning! **Did it work?** In terms of fitness, yes - after six to eight weeks, the players were a lot fitter. We couldn't do a lot about the footballing side of things, but increased fitness helped the team be more competitive. I told you we were unlucky though, soon after I felt we were sorting the fitness, we had a flu outbreak at the club, and that knocked us back again. As I said, we couldn't sign anyone, so we just had to get back at it after the flu with who we had.

It must have been around that time you took a group up onto Broomhead Moor?
I took all of them up onto the moors! No overhead protection. It was pitch black, we couldn't see a thing, it was p***ing it down and they really didn't know what had hit them! I made them run and run and then complete more running because there was nothing else to do. **Was that the aim, fitness again?** Partly, yes. But also, togetherness, comradeship. I never had as many letters as after that! Some from Owls fans, others from Blades, nearly all of them complaining and wondering what the point was. Did it work? Well it helped a little bit; we won the next game I remember. As I say, we couldn't do much about the standard of football, but we did become more competitive through working hard.
A couple of questions now that fans have asked me to ask. Firstly, can you explain how you managed to persuade fa-

mous Sheffield United fan Bobby Knutt to appear on your shoulders at Hillsborough wearing an Owls shirt?

Bobby was a mate of mine. He was a big guy, strong. He did though love his publicity, so asked me if I'd mind doing it – thinking it might end up in the papers. As it happened, it ended up in the programme for the Sheffield derby in 1979 I think, and he struggled to live it down! I know that Owls fans sung about it at the derby games for years afterwards!

Finally, it is true that you worked as a bodyguard for Madonna?

Yes, it is! We worked with her in the early 90s. She was hugely famous you know, and wherever she went there would be hundreds if not thousands of people about. I nearly got in a lot of trouble the once in Madrid – for telling a policeman there to f*** off when he wouldn't get out of the way so I could keep Madonna safely away from all the people who were round and about. We appeared in the papers when she came to London – they got pictures of her running around Hyde Park. Mind you, I wanted to sue over one of the headlines – "The Hitman and Her!" I got on great with her by the way, a great girl.

Thanks Tony, I really appreciate your time. Is there anything else you'd like to add?

Well, I enjoyed my time at Hillsborough, and I really appreciated working with Len. If we'd been a bit luckier, we'd have got the club up before Jack Charlton did! Good luck with the book, I'd love to have a read when it's out.

THE FANS' PERSPECTIVE

"It is a strange paradox that while the grief of football fans (and it is real grief) is private – we each have an individual relationship with our clubs, and I think that we are secretly convinced that none of the other fans understands quite why we have been harder hit than anyone else – we are forced to mourn in public, surrounded by people whose hurt is expressed in forms different from our own." (Nick Hornby, Fever Pitch.)

In many ways this section *is* the book. Football fans are the beating heart of the game. Or put another way - without the fans there is no game. The experiences of the supporters during a time when the team were struggling are worth remembering and remembering well. That the team struggled is obvious, but that does not mean that the fans were always miserable. This section shows how following the team is more than results.

Family, away days, tall tales, camaraderie, exciting games, terrible games, crowd trouble, friendships - all form part of the rich tapestry of what it was to be an Owls' fan at the time. This chapter aims to do justice to the experiences and memories of the fans who stuck by the team at its "Lowest Ebb". Nick Hornby's point is a good one; each fan experienced the period in their own way. This section of the book aims to cover that range of experiences.

To investigate the views of the supporters I adopted what the social research people might call a "mixed methods approach". In simpler terms, I created a survey using a popular online tool and distributed it to as many supporters of the era as I could. To help with this, I enlisted the help of various supporters' groups and fanzines. I also put messages out on the various Sheffield Wednesday Facebook groups, and online message boards, along with setting up a Twitter feed.

Finally, I also spoke directly to many fans – some of whom I knew before this process began – and others who contacted me, or who

I contacted, as the project developed. Nearly 100 fans completed the initial survey and the total number of fans who have contributed in one way or another is over 200. I am grateful to them all for their thoughts and support. Some fans have been quoted directly while others I have kept anonymous, or paraphrased their words.

The initial survey asked where the fans were living in 1973. Around 60 per cent lived in Sheffield, another 20 per cent elsewhere in South Yorkshire, and 15 per cent in wider Yorkshire. Just over five per cent lived elsewhere in the UK. I went on to ask how often the fans attended games (home and away). The fans surveyed were generally dedicated to the cause, with over 80 per cent of them attending 11 home games or more a season, and many attending plenty of away games on top. They were predominantly living in Sheffield and South Yorkshire, though others did travel from further afield. It is not possible to make any academic generalisations from the group, or from the research (I'm not a clever enough researcher to concoct some infallible scheme) but there is a wide range of opinion here from a good number of fans. The chapter covers several different areas relating to supporters' experiences, beginning with those who followed the team in an organised fashion.

Supporters' Clubs

The official Supporters' Club had been an important part of the fans' experience for decades. Formed in 1929 and based at Hillsborough, the club sold merchandise, organised coach travel to away fixtures, held an annual dinner-dance (at the Embassy Suites, Mansfield Road, Intake – tickets £1.80 in 1973!), arranged the club's player of the season vote (around 1,000 supporters voted each season by handing their slip into the Supporters' Club office), and in 1975 arranged a six-a-side soccer tournament at the Middlewood Road training ground.

In a nod to how the 1970s were different to today, the club also helped organise the annual Miss Sheffield Wednesday competition (to give it the official title: The Sheffield Wednesday Supporters' Club Personality Girl of the Year). This was won in

1975 by Lorraine Downing (from Chapeltown), Yvonne Fletcher in 1974 and Jacqueline Carl in 1973. The secretary of the Supporters' Club for much of the 1970s was Keith Nettleship, the treasurer Sylvia Bellamy and Fred Stones the chairman.

The chairman was presented with a "Chain of Office" where his name (and it always was he) was added to the names of previous holders of the position. In addition to this, branches of the Supporters' Club were developed in Darnall, Killamarsh, Penistone, Chapeltown, Stocksbridge and elsewhere – each organising their own social activities and match day travel.

The central Supporters' Club had a regular slot in the matchday programme – advertising the most current events and often commenting on what was happening on and off the field with the club. The club had an office at Hillsborough which was open between 7pm and 8pm from Monday to Friday, where membership could be registered, and tickets bought for away travel during those times: "Any other enquiries will be answered to the best of our ability." Mr Nettleship's (Dronfield) address and phone number were published in the programme for anyone who found those hours not to their convenience.

In 1975 a plea was published for fans to use a new number, as the new owner of the Dronfield address was a little tired of receiving calls at all hours asking for details of the latest coach journeys! In December 1975, the club finally had a telephone installed in their Hillsborough office. The Supporters' Club also published an annual yearbook publicising their activities, recapping the previous season, and looking forward to the next. The Supporters' Club sponsored the matchball on occasion, and placed regular "rallying cries" in the programme suggesting, for example, that fans "rally round and cheer them on as much as possible".

Although membership lists are lost to the mists of time, one Supporters' Club committee member told me that around 2,000 fans were members, including the 800 or so who were part of the auxiliary branches. Not all fans were members, but many of the more dedicated supporters were.

The Supporters' Club had a degree of power and influence. The 1974-75 yearbook had a message from Supporters' Club chairman Fred Stones, who said that he, "along with many thousands of Sheffield Wednesday supporters have faith in our manager Mr Burtenshaw and our old friend and coach Gerry Young to put Sheffield Wednesday F.C. in the top flight again." This followed the 1973-74 message where Stones stated: "I sincerely hope that is going to be a memorable one for my friend Mr Derek Dooley and the players as they achieve FIRST DIVISION FOOTBALL" (His capitals).

Steve Burtenshaw's message read: "I want to thank you once again for your loyal support to the club in our efforts to pull away from the threat of relegation last season... Now (the aim is) to join the elite of the First Division as soon as possible." Keith Nettleship added: "I am sure that our new team manager will bring success to this great club of ours." This followed a similar desire for "FIRST DIVISION FOOTBALL AT HILLSBOROUGH" the previous year. We of course know how the season turned out, but the quality of the production of the yearbook, the featuring of the manager, along with images of key players, along with one of Matt Sheppard and new Sheffield Wednesday board members, gives an idea of how influential the Supporters' Club were.

I would not like to say that to be a "true" Owl at the time you needed to be a member. Keith Nettleship did go close to that, though, stating: "It is in these sorts of times, when the football club is not doing so well, that the True Blues stand out from the rest of the so-called Wednesdayites." The club was certainly influential and well organised.

In some ways, the Supporters' Club might be considered the "corporate" element of the fan base – they had direct links with the club and its management. That link was stretched to its limit with relegation in 1975. Fred Stones was quoted as saying in the aftermath: "I put the blame on Mr Sheppard and no-one else. Last April he said that Wednesday would never be in the same position again, but they have got worse." He continued: "I am deeply sorry for the many supporters I represent, the thousands who have travelled to every ground Wednesday have been to. I think they have been let down."

Mr Stones continued as chairman of the Supporters' Club,

adding: "I stay while they want me. I've been watching Wednesday too long. It's too late to stop now." He remained until 1977, when replaced by Mr W. (Bill) Heap. The link between the club and the Supporters' Club declined in the later 1970s and 1980s as the club took on arranging its own transport to games and developed a more corporate approach to merchandising.

Some of the day-to-day organisation took place at branch level. Adrian Hurst, who was chairman of the Chapeltown branch of the Supporters' Club for much of the 1970s, described their activities to me:

"We had between 100 and 150 members in Chapeltown and as you say, we did coach trips to away games and a football tournament. In some of the more local matches we ran our own coach and for the long-distance trips used to share a bus with Stocksbridge or Penistone branches. We used a company called Dragon Coaches from Stocksbridge for our away games as they were always the cheapest – even if they were somewhat dilapidated and used to chug along at around 50mph on the motorways! I remember that they used to charge us £50 for London and similar distance trips – it costs almost that much for a single person nowadays!

For a short period of time we also ran trips to home games, but it wasn't popular because the local bus service used to run directly to the ground from Chapeltown at about a quarter of the price that we had to charge. We used to meet most weeks during the winter in the upstairs room of the 'Coach and Horses' pub on Station Road, where members could book for forthcoming away games while enjoying a couple of beers. At the time I was chairman, Raymond Appleyard was secretary (I don't know what happened to him) and Nigel Taylor was treasurer (he is still an active supporter and I see him occasionally).

We used to have an issue with the main branch because we had to pay them 50 per cent of the subscriptions raised – and we didn't feel that they did anything in return. I remember that we had an end of season disco in the Newton Hall in Chapeltown and players/team manager were invited to attend. We did a 'play-

er of the year' presentation at this time, and I do remember that Steve Burtenshaw once attended."

Swallownest branch helped fundraise directly for the club, providing a new roller for the Hillsborough pitch in 1976 and having their picture taken with Len Ashurst and others as reward. As Adrian tells us, though, there was a certain degree of rivalry and mistrust between some in the branches and the main group based at Hillsborough. One fan suggested the group became "very political at one point" and another believed that the "main branch was not too fond of some of us upstart branches".

This rivalry led to some supporters setting up unofficial groups, organising travel and coaches independently; leading in turn to further political issues about how well such unofficial groups represented the club. The official Supporters' Club banned alcohol on its coaches after 1975, for example, but there are stories of some of the unofficial coaches being a little freer and easier about what they allowed on board, and where they stopped for refreshments pre-match. There was a happy end to this story for one fan, at least, who admitted they "always had a great time on those trips. In fact, I met my husband on one of them!"

In addition to the official Supporters' Club, other fans travelled across land and sea to watch the Owls. Two good examples of these unofficial groups are the Limavady Owls from Northern Ireland and the London Owls, from, erm, London. Jake McAffrey, founder member of the Limavady Owls, said: "The mid-1970s were about the time The Limavady Owls were born. Mr Hugh Green hailed from Grenoside, near Hillsborough and was a teacher at Limavady High School. He was an avid Wednesdayite and the kids all adored his gentleness and calm method of teaching. However, they noticed he was always sad and grumpy every Monday morning and wondered why.

"One brave boy found it in him to ask 'Sir' what was wrong. When Hugh confided in the group that his sadness was caused by another defeat for his beloved Owls, the kids got together and wrote a letter to the club begging them to try harder to help rid 'Sir' of his malaise. The club wrote back and assured the kids that all the players had read their letter and would try to turn things around. From this, a Supporters' Club was formed in Northern Ireland, one in which I was lucky and honoured to be part of. We would make an annual pilgrimage to Sheffield and were treated wonderfully by the club. At its height, we would have brought over 80 kids to Hillsborough and wanted for nothing. Happy memories from a dark period!"

The London Owls formed unofficially in the early 1970s, before becoming a more organised group in 1974. Vernon Grant, an early member of the group, explained to me how the London Owls enjoyed their regular trips to Hillsborough: "Every home game was an away game for us. Standing on an open Kop, in all weathers, watching the likes of Prendergast, Sunley and Joicey scoring for the Owls. We always caught the 10am train from St Pancras for home games and the train just after 6pm back home to London. Some weeks the buffet car was open, and we often found ourselves travelling up to or back from games with opposing London teams (in the days when football teams travelled by train). Malcolm Allison buying all the drinks for us after we had beaten Crystal Palace was a memorable train journey, for example! When we arrived for home games, we always went to the Howard Hotel opposite the Midland station before getting the bus to the ground and going to the chippy for pre-match 'snap.'"

Another member said: "We actually officially formed the London Owls in 1974 – during those darkest of days – and before that there were a group of us who followed the team through thin and thinner. At the same time, some great memories of trips and friendships formed that remain today."

The second quote comes from Colin Grant, who wrote to the club in 1975 describing the activities of the group in some detail:

"Dear Sir,
We London Wednesday fans noticed in the programme recently (vs Wrexham) the piece about a lack of news from Supporters' Club branches, so here's a brief resume of our activities.
We formed three years ago and ran several successful coach trips to games, but as results took a turn for the worse so did

the turnout! However, about ten of us (six every week) travel to each game, usually by train and sometimes by car. Even the British Rail ban on cheap tickets couldn't deter us from going to the Wrexham game – we hired a car! A turn of fortunes (and couldn't we do with it!) would probably see a returning interest from stray-away Londoners, but our regulars stick to the task. Three went by train for the Darlington cup-tie - £9.95 return – and didn't get back until the early hours. We can also still boast one ever present for the season. Thought this might be of interest. Cheers! Colin Grant (for London Wednesdayites)"

The London Owls went from strength to strength as the Owls' fortunes improved in the years after our period. The group still exist today, and travel in numbers to home and away games. As the 1970s progressed, the group developed and expanded – even producing their own newspaper for a period.

"As I recall, we contacted the club at the time to let them know we had formed a Supporters' Club for fans in London and South East and they were pleased to hear the news," Colin Grant told me in 2019. *"So, I guess you'd call it an independent club with approval of Wednesday. During the time you are particularly interested in, there were a handful of us (up to about 10) who made the trips every week, home and away ... usually by train but occasionally by car share.*

Plus, a minibus/coach for 'big games' ... Palace FA Cup second replay in 1973, Chelsea cup tie in following round, Man United 4-4 game at Hillsborough and that vital last game of season win over Southend in 1976. However, for most of the time it was us handful of diehards making the trips - week in, week out, with little to cheer. That meant that on the rare occasions we won - such as the 5-1 win at Notts County in 1974 - we would celebrate like we had won the cup. But then again, we always had a great day out whatever the result!

It was a situation where a group of blokes dotted all over London and the south east, who didn't see each other during the week, all turned up at St Pancras, Kings Cross, Euston or wherever every Saturday to set off to see the lads - and probably wit-

ness another defeat. We all had one thing in common - Sheffield Wednesday - and we all got on so well."

The club's matchday programme responded to Colin's 1975 letter with the short comment: "As we say... we've got the best supporters in the land!". Many clubs would make similar claims, I am sure. There is something in the dedication of the Owls' supporters at the time that merits recognition though. This was a team that had been in a downwards spiral for many years and was heading for its "Lowest Ebb". Despite this, a large and loyal group of supporters stuck by the team throughout, with many of them travelling large distances. The organisation of the official and unofficial supporters' groups allowed fans to travel and to follow the team with like-minded people. This chapter goes on to describe the match-going experience of fans both within and outside of the groups.

Memorable Games
In my fans' survey I asked supporters to describe memorable games of the period. I suggested that they might include information about the key players, goals scored, tactics or incidents in the games. Some of the first few responses I received were as follows:

"None!"
"Very few!"
"Absolutely none that were memorable!"
"We were lucky to get a corner in those days; we were that poor."

I began to wonder if I had asked the right question, or indeed picked the correct topic to research! However, the answers soon started coming in with much more detail and with many more stories. Fans began to tell me about games in the period that the Owls had won convincingly. One such game was the 3-0 home win against York City on November 9, 1974. Goals were scored by Ronnie Ferguson (on debut), McMordie and Potts. As we know, this was a rare victory that season and was a game which Vernon Grant remembers clearly: "Sadly I missed most of the match as I was arrested entering the Kop turnstiles after the police searched my Mitre bag and found a cassette player, cassettes and a glass with BR (British Rail) stamped on it.

"When the buffet attendant on the train up to matches told us there would be no buffet on the return trip, it was agreed we could take a glass as long as we left it on the train when we got back. The police gave me a hard time and even accused me of stealing the Mike Oldfield Tubular Bells cassette from a record shop. I showed them the receipt I still had from the record shop, but no joy."

The proverbial "Murphy's Law" at play right there! One fan who did see that game remembers the quality of the play: "You should have been stood on the Kop right behind it! (McMordie's goal) It was a belter! Eric Potts' goal as I recall it was a diving header after a long sweeping move similar to the first goal. That was our best victory of the season and all three goals were crackers."

A third fan recalls: "We won 3-0 and there was a streaker!" The streaker, it turned out, was a middle-aged man with some health issues. Perhaps therefore it's pushing the point too far to compare him to the club at the time. The win and the play that day though was impressive, and it is easy to see why that game may have been remembered above other much more mediocre performances of the era.

Two games against Notts County are remembered for similar reasons. These were both away games. The first a convincing 5-1 victory in March 1974, the second a pulsating 3-3 draw one week after the York game in November that year. The 5-1 win was achieved with goals from Prendergast (2), Joicey (2) and Potts. As one fan put it to me it was "totally unexpected", and London Owl Colin Grant expanded on that theme. "We went into the game with two wins in previous 20 league matches I think and down in 20th place in the old Division Two. Prendo and Joicey got two apiece, one of Prendo's an absolute cracker from edge of box, and another from Eric Potts. After weeks of rubbish we couldn't believe what we were seeing and had just a little celebration drink or two on the way home!" A third fan also could not believe what they had seen: "Notts County 1-5 Wednesday. It just never happened!"

The 3-3 draw the following season was another dramatic game. The Owls goals were scored by McMordie (2) and Potts. Steve Archer remembered the game this way: "Notts County away. Went from 1-0 up to losing 3-1 in less than three mins. Courtesy of an Ian Scanlon hat-trick. Game ended 3-3, think Potts scored the equaliser." Another supporter had the events slightly differently: "We had a great draw 3-3 after being losing 3-1 with a late goal from Eric McMordie who scored two! A great game!"

Memory is a funny thing, but it was in fact McMordie who scored the equaliser, Potts scoring the second with a spectacular 30-yard shot. The hat-trick of Ian Scanlon's was scored in two and a half minutes (the fastest ever for Notts County). Owls' fans, though, had seen the team score six goals in two games; so it is easy to understand again why these dramatic away games stuck in the memory of those who were there.

A defeat to Aston Villa is remembered by many fans. The result was 4-0 in April 1975, with the Owls long relegated. Villa needed the points to help ensure their promotion back to Division One, and brought a huge contingent of fans in the 23,605 attendance. As one fan, "Chris", put it to me: "I clearly remember Villa at home, a night match which we lost 4-0 and I remember players like Brian Little and Ray Graydon for them and what seemed like huge following all over the ground." Another fan told me that the game was marred by hooliganism as Villa fans tried to "take" the Kop and that the game "made my parents think it was too early for me to go the match without their presence".

A third supporter remembered the "phenomenal number of Villa fans at the game."

The previous season's game also saw a large crowd of over 22,000 at Hillsborough, to witness a 4-2 defeat for the Owls. "The Kop that day was shared by Yorkies and Brummies alike," supporter David Bentley remembered of that game. "Tommy Craig on a powering run down the middle. 'Shoot Craig' was the cry. He went around one, then another defender. 'Shoot Craig' the Kop cried in unison. He went around a third, 'Shoot Craig' was the cry for a third time.... He shot, an unbelievably powerful drive - shamefully over the top of the crossbar and high into the Kop. 'Somebody shoot Craig,' said a lone voice from the masses on the East Bank. Story of our life... sad but 100 per cent fact."

An amusing story that illustrates well the gallows humour that kept fans going through some of this period. The Villa games also show how matches with large crowds stick in the memory - even if in this case much of that crowd was from Birmingham.

Other games are memorable simply for being truly awful for the Owls' supporter. One example of this was the trip to Middlesbrough in April 1974. At this stage, the Owls were desperate for points to avoid relegation to Division Three. Middlesbrough on the other hand were already champions, under the management of future Owls' boss, Jack Charlton.

Any thought that that Teesside team might take it easy on the Owls were soon put to rest as the home team raced into a 3-0 half-time lead. One fan, did tell me that this was a little unfair as "we could have led 3-0 very early on - there was a disallowed goal and Joicey I believe hit the woodwork twice."

True or not, the game went downhill from there on for Wednesday. Danny Cameron took up the story with me: "(Graeme) Souness had the freedom of the midfield and he killed us. I've always contended that had I marked Souness the game would have been a closer contest. Tactically, we got it wrong, but I don't recall us being poor in possession. The 8-0 scoreline was difficult to take and I for one kept my head down around Sheffield the following week." So, 8-0 it was come full time in a game that the Owls needed to take something from.

Defeat set up the showdown with Southend that finished the season and prolonged the fans' agony over whether their team would be relegated. To add insult to injury on that day, several fans recalled tales of suffering at the hands of Middlesbrough hooligans after the game.

"We got absolutely hammered plus I got set upon by three Boro fans in the aftermath," said one Owl, while John Stabler recalls leaving the ground at 6pm and still running into "a mob of Boro waiting outside".

One tale of woe is my favourite though as one fan talked me through his trip to the North East. "We lost 8-0, my wife's treat while we were on honeymoon in Scarborough, stood in the home end. Big Jack and the Boro team were presented with the Second Division trophy before the game, a real party atmosphere (for some!)" A very difficult game and result. But a game that stands out in the memory of the fans who travelled to it – if only for the wrong reasons.

Football fans are an interesting bunch, though, and some Owls' fans remember other games for more obscure reasons than those given above. Martin Clarke remembers vividly a 1-0 win at Bolton in September 1975, with Wednesday leading and a Bolton cross in the dying seconds. "As the ball was on its way into the net," he recalled, "the ref blew for full time. We all looked at one another, wondering 'have we won or drawn?' We won!" The low attendance made Wednesday's 1-0 win over Colchester in March 1976 memorable for another Wednesdayite, Philip Baynes. "It was bitterly cold… I'm sure there was a brief blizzard at some point. I can remember Phil Henson running through to slot home the winner, in front of 6,905 – our lowest-ever league attendance in modern times."

A fellow Owl remembers the game for more simple reasons. "The biggest cheer of the day came with the announcement that the Blades were getting hammered 5-0!" Other fans talked through memories of attending games with their families and friends and the enjoyment of watching games with like-minded people. Richard Coates shared his memories of (finally) celebrating a goal in April 1975 - the first home Owls goal since the previous December: "We were a sparse crowd – we created a 'hole' on the Kop and barged each other about a bit - splitting into Foxhill and Parson Cross groups and singing 'We took the hole' … just having a laugh." Other fans enjoyed the atmosphere of evening games and yet more enjoyed the excitement of cup matches.

Memorable games so far then have been memorable because of the quality of the football, the result, the comeback from defeat, and for the opposition and the support. Less obviously: the weather, key incidents (lucky escapes), low attendances, memories of family and friends, the excitement of floodlit games and those in the cup - and the pleasure taken in the struggles of Sheffield United - all helped the fans in my survey remember matches. To return to the theme of the book, this period saw the club reach its "Lowest Ebb". However, this does not mean that there were not memorable matches for the fans. These memories were sometimes about the quality of the football. There is a plethora of other reasons why fans remember certain matches. This period provided plenty of those other reasons along with the occasional excellent performance.

Experiences of Hooliganism
In many ways, this is the most difficult section of the book to write. It is difficult to define what is meant by hooliganism, though many people will have their own ideas. It is also important to remember that the 1970s were different to today. The same, but different. Thousands of people attended football each week (just like today), but stadia were unsegregated, with large standing areas and usually with a pay on the day option (different). Hooliganism was also experienced and reacted to differently by different people. Some people were horrified and appalled by it, others found the tribalism and danger exciting. Some people were put off attending matches by it; for others it made no difference at all.

Fans who attended away games had a different experience to those who attended home games only. It is also important to remember that Owls' followers did take part in football hooliganism, at times instigating it. Here, I aim to illustrate the experience of the "ordinary" fan. To do that, I'll let those fans talk through the experience of big games, more typical home matches, away days, and broader reflections about the nature of hooliganism at the time. For this section the recollections of supporters are kept anonymous.

Type "football hooliganism 1970s" into a favoured search engine and it doesn't take long to find lurid accounts of the various "firms" of the period. There are plenty of videos available online showing film footage from the time, and many of those who took part have shared their accounts in books, newspapers and films. There are lots of compelling stories about the violence that happened at and around football matches in the 1970s. In many ways though, that is what we have – stories. It is much more difficult to find specific evidence about the extent of football related violence.

One reason for this is a problem of definition. The term "hooliganism" can be traced back at least as far as the 19th century. Football related hooliganism came to popular attention in the 1960s – attracting the nickname of the "English Disease" in the media. Although there was other violence at the time that attracted attention (Mods and Rockers) and outbreaks of disorder relating to spectators of other sports, *football* hooliganism had entered the popular consciousness by the end of the 1960s.

"Hooliganism" is not a crime. Indeed, some behaviours that may be considered as related to football hooliganism are not criminal at all (like drunkenness) whereas others are criminal but maybe seen as more anti-social (say, urinating on property). Other behaviours are clearly criminal (vandalism, assault).

Sometimes the behaviour may have taken place at the ground, on other occasions elsewhere (railway stations, pubs).

The behaviour may have been organised (two crews arranging a fight), other times it may have been spontaneous. Sometimes property is damaged, sometimes any violence may be against the person. A full definition is therefore difficult to reach. Sociologist Eric Dunning attempted to do so in the European Journal on Criminal Policy and Research:

"(Those who use) the term are liable to use 'football hooliganism' in a 'cover-all' sense which includes: forms of verbal as well as physical violence; the throwing of missiles at players, match and club officials and other fans; the vandalising of club and private property; fist fights, fights involving kicking, and fights involv-

ing weapons such as knives and even guns. It is also important to realise that such behaviour takes place, not only at or in the immediate vicinity of football grounds, but also involves fights between groups of males who share a claimed allegiance to opposing football clubs and which take place on days other than as well as on match days and in contexts, e.g. pubs, clubs, railway and bus stations, which are sometimes far removed from football stadia... As one can see, 'football hooliganism' is a complex and many-sided phenomenon."

Whatever the definition, the problem was widespread and seemingly rising. Some of the hooliganism was organised through "crews" such as Birmingham City's (Zulus, Zulu's Warriors, Zulu's Army, The Zulu), Derby County's Derby Lunatic Fringe, Chelsea's Headhunters and so on. Some of the hooliganism was less organised with young men congregating and defending "their" end of a ground, for example. A popular pursuit among supporters at away games was in trying to "take" the home end – i.e. the space where the home fans would normally stand. Home fans would attempt to defend their preferred area. Hooliganism would also take place way from the ground with home fans defending "their" pubs and attacking the coaches of visiting supporters. Sheffield Wednesday were heading for their "Lowest Ebb" during our period. This did not mean that the club and its supporters were immune from the problems of hooliganism. In his book, Richard Crooks details several unpleasant experiences at away games, at train stations and on supporters' coaches, for example. Owls' fans themselves were not immune from criticism for their actions, with the club's own programme admitting "words cannot express the disgust this club felt after reading about the behaviour (*of supporters*)." A few weeks earlier fans were urged to "cut the aggro", with a piece in the programme asking, "Why do we have to see this kind of behaviour...?"

The Supporters' Club acted by insisting on membership cards on coaches, barring alcohol and banning supporters who caused issues. The tale of four such supporters is recounted in another 1976 programme, again encouraging Owls' fans to behave themselves. The situation among the Owls hooligan contingent – known as the East Bank Republican Army (EBRA) - is recounted by Paul Allen in his book *Flying with the Owls Crime Squad,* which details the "terrace culture that seemed to leave a trail of destruction wherever it went." In his book *I Hate Football*, John Firth describes the fighting: "Sometimes it could be ferocious and yes, sometimes people would get hurt, but generally it was just a few fisticuffs… but, like it or not, violence at the football… was always present."

OWLS FANS SLAMMED FOR CHAOS AFTER CUP DEFEAT

OWLS FAN JAILED AFTER JUDGE BLASTS "ANIMALS"

OWLS FANS ON RAMPAGE AFTER "LOCAL DERBY" CLASH

Sheffield Star headlines 1975-76.

The largest crowd for any game involving Sheffield Wednesday during our period was the 35,000-plus that saw the game with Manchester United in December 1974. The game itself is described elsewhere in the book but it has become notorious for the hooliganism that took place. United had been relegated the previous season, and some of their fans were determined to make their mark on Division Two.

One fan told me about his experience of hooliganism before and after the game: "My wife and I attended the match and sat in the North Stand. In those days the tribalism that exists today was nowhere to be found at that time. We were sat with Man U fans and when we went 3-1 up my wife and I, of course, were cheering the Owls on at the top of our voices. A Man U fan, three rows in front of us, threatened my wife, so I told him he would have to go through me first, at which point he sat back down.

"That evening we went to the Penny Black in Pond Street and just sat down when the abusive Man U fan, at the match, came over and apologised and bought my wife and I a drink. We all sat together and had a good chat about football, although at that time Wednesday didn't play any football to speak of. Because fans sat and stood together, you did get quite a lot of banter between opposing supporters and there was the occasional punch-up but nothing on the scale it happens today."

A second fan who attended the game felt that the hooliganism was worse: "That match was scary... I was in that area on t'Kop when Jim Holton (Manchester United player) broke his leg ....it kicked off reyt ...police horses on t'pitch ....I ended up at other side of Kop near to North Stand .....and it still kept kicking off all through t'match." There certainly were plenty of incidents at that game, which was described to me by another supporter as a "hugely enjoyable 4-4 draw. At least it would have been if it wasn't for ducking under flying bottles and escaping from the masses of thugs predominantly wearing red who were determined to create havoc, both on the Kop and in the streets both before and after the game."

For those interested, the disorder has been immortalised on a YouTube clip entitled: "Football Hooligans - Sheffield Wed v Man Utd – 1974." Perhaps the other biggest games of our period were the aforementioned ones against Aston Villa but, as the Owls dropped down the divisions, the teams that brought large followings with them to Hillsborough became few and far between.

The experience of home games other than the big games may well have been very different. One fan explained to me how he felt hooliganism affected home games: "Once relegated to the old Division Three, Hillsborough became something of a 'no-go' area for visiting supporters. Wednesday's away following built up a feared reputation, and it was rare to see visiting fans. Those that were brave enough were surrounded by police, who in turn became surrounded by us. The Leppings Lane had a hard-core group of home fans that lay in wait for any visiting fan and even in the North Stand, there were groups of seasoned hooligans.

I recall well a family of Mansfield fans, a young boy with his mother and father sitting in the north for the game against the Stags, in 1976, I think. They suffered constant abuse after the first goal went to Mansfield, and when the inevitable happened

- Mansfield scoring again - it was ugly. They were spat at, had scores of cups of hot Bovril and tea hurled at them, and were ushered out by a small contingent of police." Another fan remembered "Millwall fans getting on the Kop early and chasing us round the Kop until the Wednesday hooligans (who were in the Ozzie Owl club) got word, and mayhem ensued!" This "ownership" of Hillsborough was clearly important to many.

The experience of hooliganism varied for those going to away games. One fan recalled the tale of a trip to Millwall: "The coach driver refused to drop us off at the ground due to Millwall's reputation, so he dropped us off in central London instead. We had to get the Tube to the ground. After the game we were chased to the Underground station by loads of skinheads. I've never been so scared – I thought they were going to push us on to the tracks. Luckily at the 11th hour police came on to the platform and got on the Tube with us."

Other fans give further descriptions of what away days could be like: "There wasn't really any segregation back then and generally it was standing only. I lost count of the number of times we got chased on the terraces, I recall my friend one time went flying and I had to drag up to get to safety. I had a couple of bad experiences at Cardiff. Their fans were just allowed access to our coaches and threw bricks at the windows. One time the brick went through the window I was next to, just missing a child's head who was sat next to me." Another fan recounted similar experiences: "Going to away days from the late 1960s and throughout the 1970s was like going to the Wild West. I got involved at so many grounds; you either stood up to the yobs from the other side or you went under."

A further view of away days demonstrated how Owls' fans liked to "take over" some of the smaller grounds: "We were very big fish in the old Division Three - especially with the numbers we took away from home. Remember it was mainly terracing, and not all ticket, so we surprised most away grounds with the numbers that turned up. Trying to take the home team's Kop became the main part of the day for our hoolies. If the coppers brought them round the pitch to put them on the away end, they were by and large cheered like war heroes." The trouble also took place away from the grounds. At Hull City in 1975 the local press reported "Skinhead Football Fans in Hull Riot", detailing how Sheffield Wednesday supporters spread a "trail of destruction" along Anlaby Road in the city.

The report outlines how Owls followers broke windows, shouted insults and tried to overturn a car. One Hull City supporter recalled how Wednesday fans arrived in the city on the night before the game (something he felt was unheard of at that time), pulled the emergency cord on the train into Hull, trespassed on the line and made liberal use of aerosol paint in and around the stadium. Eighty fans were ejected from the ground and fines totalling £255 were issued by magistrates afterwards. It is possible to see a pattern here, therefore; linking the desire to keep "ownership" of Hillsborough, and to "take over" opposition grounds and areas. Fans who were not interested in hooliganism could therefore sometimes be caught in the middle of a battle over territory.

It is difficult to estimate the extent of hooliganism. The concept is difficult to define, and much of what happened went unrecorded or unpunished. One fan explains the period this way however: "In terms of hooliganism, it was everywhere in those days, even with the small clubs. Everyone had nutters; bigger clubs just tended to have more of them. Most of the time it was handbags, shouting and pointing, then one side would charge. When that happened, you had one of three outcomes. One would be that the fans being charged turned and ran. The other would be that the team being charged would stand their ground, which often resulted in the aggressive fans backing down.

The third (and rare) outcome would be a general melee and they could get nasty. Also given what happened later at Bradford, we were utterly and completely stupid and would go to certain grounds (Preston sticks in the mind, but also I believe Walsall, Port Vale, one or two others) and where they had wooden terracing, build a bonfire and then bounce up and down whilst singing 'Preston's ground is burning down!' It was the absolute height of stupidity. Coaches frequently had their windows put out and had to run red lights to get away from aggressive home fans and occasionally after a defeat, trains would be trashed too."

Hooliganism, it seems, could take many forms and this account supports my view that things were different in the 1970s. As the fan says, hooliganism was everywhere and, like it or not, it was part of watching Wednesday at the time. Another fan described his experiences this way: "In the 1973-76 era hooliganism was rife with weekly battles going on up and down the country, near football grounds but also in town centres, on trains and at motorway service stations. Indeed, many service stations refused to accept supporters' coaches. In our case I think that the problem got far worse in our Division Three days as we visited such places as Southend, Chesterfield, Chester and Grimsby - places that simply couldn't cope with such a massive influx of visiting supporters.

"I remember going to Oxford and enjoying a few drinks in a pub before the game. When it was time to leave, several fans went out of their way to destroy the place - then wondered why, when we went again the following season, every pub was closed with police outside!"

Wednesday followers were certainly not innocent of starting trouble, a further example was a notorious away day at Chesterfield. The Sheffield Star gave a blow by blow account of the damage caused by Owls' followers in September 1975, detailing "the toll of damage, injury and destruction" that had been caused. In total, 22 people were treated for minor injuries and two policemen ended up in hospital.

There were 11 arrests made after exit doors at Chesterfield's Saltergate ground were broken; windows at the railway station were smashed and toilets were spray-painted. A total of 17 windows at a local taxi firm were broken. The Supporters' Club promised to ban anyone found to have been involved and the club condemned that trouble, and other instances of it. It did not stop it.

One reason for this may have been that some supporters simply enjoyed the experience. "I was a teenager during the 1970s and to be honest, the majority of young males between the age of 14 to mid to late 20s were hooligans," one said, "including myself and all my mates. It was the way things were back then, a kind of rite of passage, and almost every young man was daft enough to follow suit.

"There were literally thousands of us, and it was the same everywhere. Even the smaller clubs had two or three hundred or more. I suppose like gangs today, you felt that you were part of something - an army of sorts - and it was exciting, sometimes dangerous and there was that sense of camaraderie between you all." Another fan made a similar point: "Those days were great. You got chased and attacked away from home and did the same to them at Hillsborough."

A fellow Owl did not consider himself a hooligan but stated: "The hooliganism was ridiculous, but the camaraderie and humour were what kept us going through those dark times." It is interesting that both these fans use the word "camaraderie" to describe their experiences. It helps provide an understanding of why young men might take part in such activities.

It is difficult to tell whether the hooliganism at the time affected whether people attended games. For most fans who I spoke to or who completed my survey, it did not stop or restrict their attendance. As one fan put it: "You had to take it in your stride back in the day as trouble happened all the time. We became streetwise very quickly." Another fan simply said: "Never put me off; never would". There were occasional replies hinting that others stopped going.

One fan told me how his grandad had spent his life dedicated to watching the Owls, before hooliganism stopped him in his tracks in the 1970s and he never went again. Others remember the period being difficult for women and kids, as rival fans were attacked simply for wearing opposing colours. With typical Sheffield humour, one fan put declining attendances in the 1970s down to that fact that "Wednesday were crap beyond description."

The voices of the fans here illustrate the difficulty of defining and explaining hooliganism during the period. Perhaps it is enough for our purposes to accept that it existed, to describe its varying forms, and to understand that the experience of hooliganism varied.

Away Days

Away days helped form some of the most positive memories of Owls' fans who remember our period. Responses to my survey included the following comments:

"Away games...We always took an amazing following... It was like we wore our ineptitude like some badge of pride... and only WE were allowed to rip the p*ss!"
"Teams used to love us visiting as they invariably recorded their record attendance. We used to sing 'We're sh*t, and we know we are!'"
"Away days were great, and you just went without expecting them to give you a result to cheer about!"

It was these comments and more that pushed me to consider further the away day experience. In this section, fans will recall certain games, and I will also consider more broadly why it was that fans enjoyed the experience of away days so much. Of course, the term away days is important. The game was only part of the day. Fans travelled to and from the game in several ways and enjoyed days and nights out in differing towns and cities. The travel to the games was part of the experience that fans often enjoyed. As fan John Hill put it about a trip to Sunderland: "I'll never forget going up the A1 with what felt like hundreds of coaches."

Travelling by rail could be just as enjoyable as supporter Stephen Willsher explained: "I always travelled by train in those days, good days out - a few beers had too!" As a third fan, Ian Wharton, put it to me: "I mainly went away on the coach, sometimes by car and occasionally by train, always enjoyed it!" The Supporters' Club coaches sometimes helped fans make a day of it by returning late from certain games. For example, Supporters' Club coaches to away matches in London often used to return from the capital at midnight, not straight after the game. On occasions there were also late return trips from Blackpool, Preston and Bolton to allow the fans to go to Blackpool for a night out after the games.

One irony for some fans was that the coach company who transported fans to away games from Pond Street in the city centre, and who advertised in the programme, were called S.U.T. – Sheffield United Tours! One fan summarised the whole experience: "We tried out many beers from around the country... we enjoyed mixing with the home fans at away games, had some good laughs in pubs and sometimes on the terrace or in the stand." None of these memories mention the game. Travel, alcohol and good company explain the fond memories of these fans at least.

Other fans enjoyed the feeling of being part of a large group of supporters. As supporter Steve Archer put it to me: "I remember the look of amazement on the faces of the opposition fans when the Wednesday fans appeared in droves on the terraces of far flung places like Gillingham!" Another fan put it simply: "We always took thousands, often taking over entire towns!"

This large-scale support for the Owls was a regular occurrence during our period and as the Owls dropped into Division Three it also became more obvious, as the club's fixtures were in some of the smaller stadia of that league. One example of that phenomenon was the Owls' trip to Southend on August 16th, 1975. This was Wednesday's first game of the season, and first-ever game at Division Three level. It was also a summer Saturday at a club based by the seaside. All these factors combined encouraged a bumper number of Owls' fans to attend the game. The attendance for the game was 6,775.

One Owls' fan estimated that of that crowd, 5,000 supporters were from Sheffield, and 'Stevie', quoted in *Flying With the Owls Crime Squad,* remembered "a mass of Wednesday on the seafront... a carnival atmosphere." The game went much less positively for the Owls and one fan described the standard of football as a "culture shock". Wednesday did take a 1-0 lead into half time with a goal from Mick Prendergast, but two second half goals from Southend saw the Owls slump to a 2-1 defeat.

After the match there were outbreaks of hooliganism from some of the Owls contingent and the 'carnival atmosphere' that Stevie remembered from earlier in the day turned increasingly violent as more drink was consumed. Despite the ensuing trouble, and the journey home in the early hours, Stevie still remembered "a brilliant day... one of the best." Despite, it seems, the performance of the team.

Some fans did still follow their club in the hope of witnessing a good Owls display though, even if their results away from home were disappointing at best. Indeed, after December 1974, the Owls did not win another away game until after the seasons covered in this book - an astonishing sequence of 36 games.

This did not necessarily put off fans from attending – perhaps because no-one wanted to miss Wednesday's next away goal, or maybe even victory. One fan recounted to me his memory of a lengthy trip to Shrewsbury: "I had this notion that if I went to a game we'd somehow play better and get a result.

So, that morning, I decided that I simply had to get to the game from London. I managed to get a half day at work, got on the train and changed at Wolverhampton (I think). Arrived in Shrewsbury about 6pm and managed to find a pub nearby. This, of course, was the old Gay Meadow ground which was just the other side of the river and I'd worked out on a map how to get there.

"Of course, back then the floodlight pylons gave grounds away and I got to the ground about half an hour before kick-off. Gay Meadow was next to a school and you entered in one corner right by the school wall and could walk round virtually the whole ground. Found the small group of Wednesday fans in the opposite corner including some guys from the place in Sheffield I'd just left. P*ssed it down all evening, as I recall, but we got a 0-0. Terrible, terrible game but the result was all important and just avoiding defeat was like a victory!"

The dedication to the cause is what was of key importance to that fan and many others. As supporter Leon Rodziewicz said to me: "So it was for much of the 1970s, you just knew that what could go wrong would go wrong and it did. So, the attitude had to be that good times are just around the corner. Well I tell you what, we must all have been around Brands Hatch about 50 times before we finally turned that particular corner!"

The fans kept going in hope rather than expectation, and the wait for an away win was a long one. One fan went to the trouble of working out some statistics: "I was at Southampton with about 2,500 Owls on Dec 28, 1974 as Eric Potts slid in to pinch a 1-0 away win. That was it for the rest of the season, though we did manage a further goal at Fulham in a 2-1 defeat. Won none, drawn one (0-0), lost seven. Goals for, one. Goals against 14. The following season, 1975-76: Won none, drawn 10, lost 13. Goals for, 14. Goals against, 34." It certainly took some dedication to follow the Owls in this period.

One further away game deserves mention. On Friday January 31, 1975 the Owls travelled to York City. Wednesday were already bottom of the table and into the period of the season that would see them only score two more goals. The Sheffield Star had launched its "Save our Owls" campaign, encouraging fans to support and encourage Wednesday, and many thousands travelled to York that evening. One fan takes up the story of what happened when the Wednesday supporters arrived during what he described as the "Save our Owls thingy". "An unbelievable following," he said.

"We were met at York railway station by a couple of coppers and a dog and I'll always remember the walk to Bootham. One 60-year-old copper, a small Alsatian, and God knows how many Owls just off the train. The copper was brilliant... laughing and joking and takin' the p*ss... he didn't get an ounce of trouble over what I recall as a bloody long walk...over a mile or so I reckon...took ages." Another fan took up the story and result: "We played York away on a Friday night and there were SOO posters and patches by the thousands.

"We took 3,000 up that night and got behind the lads – who, as usual, put in an inept performance and lost 3-0.". The stickers certainly showed some longevity. "I stuck a load of Save our

Owls stickers to my sheepskin coat which was the fashion at that time," one Owl remembers. "Unfortunately, they were so sticky it was a real pain to get them off and I more or less ruined the coat in the process!"

Urban legend says that Save our Owls stickers can still be seen on the lamp posts of York. The journey back to Sheffield saw more instances of 'hooliganism' as, despite the presence of transport police, train carriage fittings were damaged and the stop-cord was repeatedly pulled. These incidents saw the train delayed by 99 minutes, finally arriving back into Sheffield long after midnight. A frustrating end to a frustrating evening.

Away days are still a favourite memory of many of the fans of the period; and clearly not because of Wednesday's performances. The Owls went long periods without scoring away from home, notching only one further goal in their trips away from Hillsborough in 1974-75 after an Eric Potts winner at Southampton in December, for example, never mind winning a game. The love for away trips is better explained on the one hand by the memories of travelling to new places and enjoying the hospitality of different towns and cities. On the other it can be explained by a certain masochistic determination to "see it through" and the pleasure gained in being part of what nowadays might ironically be called a "massive" support. It may indeed be a mixture of all these factors. In the words of one fan: *They were brilliant memories!*

The Match Day Experience

Although attendances dropped dramatically during this period, it is still the home game experience that was the standard one for most fans. The stadium and the experience of watching the game is covered elsewhere. Here we consider what else fans got up to on matchdays; from travel to the game, to the local shops, to the Ozzie Owl Club.

The Ozzie Owl Club has somewhat legendary status among some of the fans of the era. The "Ozzie Owl Social Club" was opened on May 3, 1968 in the South Stand car park and quickly became a popular haunt for Wednesday fans. The opening ceremony was attended by Diana Dors and opening night acts included the comedian Bert Lyall and vocalists/instrumentalists Dave and Judy. By 1973 the Social Club was converted into the "Ozzie Nite Owl" and advertised in the programme as "the ideal place for meeting soccer friends on matchdays and every day of the week".

Also advertised was the "Owl Restaurant" which was described as "ideal for your private party, annual dinner, social evening or dinner and dance... fully licensed refreshment bars provide and excellent service, before, during and after the game."

Fans tended to know the "Nite Owl" as simply the Ozzie Owl Club, with one fan remembering a "marvellous brown wooden-cladded 'building' that appeared to be on stilts!" Supporters also shared plenty of stories about the venue and the events within. One fan told me about what would happen pre-match: "The Ozzie Owl club was near the main road at the end of the car park. There was a yard of ale contest which same bloke won every time, downing it in a few seconds. Then there was the comedian and the stripper (yes it really is true!)" Another fan continued: "It just wouldn't be appropriate today I suppose. I used to go in for a drink every home game and the place was packed. Can't remember the bloke's name with the yard of ale but he just stood with his back arched and it went down in seconds. Some good local comedians graced the stage, which if I recall correctly was in the bottom right hand corner. Happy days - certainly not for the football, but so what!"

One supporter remembers one of the comedians having a catchphrase of 'kinnel – "obviously a shortened version of, well, the obvious I suppose!" - and the yard of ale drinker was apparently known as Jibber Johnson – and did indeed win every week. Some suspected he must have had the technique nailed, as fans remember either having a go and dropping much of the Mansfield Bitter over themselves or laughing as others spilled it all over the place.

The club was popular and usually full pre-match, even in the days of low attendances, and fans had to be in there by 1pm on matchday to guarantee a decent seat for the compere, comedian, strippers and the yard of ale competition. One fan chuckled as he recalled the only time he saw the club empty in minutes – "when someone walked in and said 'Millwall fans are on the Kop!'"

The Ozzie Owl Club also provided food while the Owl Restaurant advertised "excellent cuisine". But to further evidence my theory that the 1970s were the same but different to today, one fan who described himself as a "regular at the restaurant" remembers food that was as "predictable as Tony Toms running on the pitch with his bucket and sponge."

Much of what went on in the Ozzie Owl Club would not be seen as acceptable today and drinking competitions, strippers and scampi in a basket, in their varying ways, date the club to the 1970s. It is though somewhere that many fans remember with great fondness and it another example of how, at the team's "Lowest Ebb", supporters still enjoyed themselves and why many remember the time affectionately.

Another favourite spot, more suitable for fans of all ages, was Quinn's sweet shop. This establishment was based in a row of terraced houses, immediately next to the entrance to the ground for the North and West Stands. One fan, Paul Whitaker told me: "It was one of those shops where they used to keep the sweets in jars and measure them out on scales - my Dad used to take me in there before games."

Another supporter, Nigel Short, remembered his Grandad, who worked on the players' entrance, would send him to Quinn's for some Kopp Kops, offering his grandson a quarter of midget gems for his trouble. "Sometimes I'd get sherbet lemons that went really sharp if you sucked them. You couldn't help but pull a face when you made it through to the sherbet! Just thinking about them now and my cheek is twitching!" Matchday has never just been about the game and these nostalgic memories of family, and of tastes and flavours and Quinn's sweet shop, illustrate that point perfectly.

There were as many different matchday experiences as there were fans. Supporters, after all, were of different ages, genders, and travelled from different places. There are, though, some themes that can be identified. One is travel to games. Some fans travelled with the Supporters' Club: "I travelled in on the Mosborough supporters club coach from the George & Dragon pub", recalls Pete Goodison, " I met Len Ashurst and Mick Prendergast at this pub the once. Mick had a full-length pot on his leg which he was happy for us to sign!"

Others took public transport, on organised travel to home games by the bus companies – often after games, there would be two double-decker buses waiting on Catch Bar Lane waiting to take fans home again.

The buses arrived early – one fan remembers getting the football special bus from Concord Park and getting in the ground for 1.45pm, killing time by reading the programme and the Football League magazine it contained – and could get very busy, especially on the return trip. So, fans would rush to get to them. "Near the end of the game we positioned ourselves at the very top of the Kop to run for the bus on the final whistle," John Cashman remembered. "Chaos - then trying to get on the buses lined up on Parkside Road. Then into town to wait for the Green 'Un at the kiosk at the bus station." The fare for the football special was 4d (1.5p) in 1970, which had increased with the decade's rampant inflation to 5p (new currency) by the middle of the decade.

Not everyone took public transport to games, but even travelling by car did not always mean that there was not a rush at the end of the game. "I sat in the upper tier of the West Stand with my Grandad and we usually parked off Middlewood Road across from the park," Sean Fenelon remembers.

"We always left early to 'miss the rush' so often missed crucial goals!" Not everyone took any transport at all and one fan's matchday consisted of drinking Trophy Bitter in the Five Arches pub, from the age of 14, and "blowing out of my arse on the way back up after the game, usually in the rain. Back to Phoenix at Brinsworth… and repeat!"

The memories of travelling to and from the games, and of the experiences with friends and family are ones which many fans remember with great clarity. Watching football is a social experience, and the memories of travel help explain the fondness that some fans have for the period.

The Experience of Female Fans

Many of the fans who contributed to this book have been kept anonymous. Most of those fans are male as are many of those who are named. Female fans, and particularly young female fans, had some experiences that were different from those of the men. The experience of female fans is one that has not been explored as fully as it might have been in academic literature. As Dr Caroline Dunn puts it in her doctoral dissertation: "Women's experience as football fans has largely been excluded or marginalised from the mainstream academic literature... in much research, any fans who do not conform to the 'traditional' fan identity... have been dismissed as 'inauthentic', or simply gone unrecognised." This section is my attempt to give a voice to female Owls fans of the period.

One female fan remembers the Ozzie Owl Club strippers. "I've told people about this before, but I think they think I'm joking. I remember going in the Ozzie Owl Club before matches – there was no discrimination about girls and women being allowed in – and I can't have been all that old, although I must have been over 18. There was also a Yard of Ale competition every match – and I never took part in that either! I don't remember being either intimated or embarrassed about the strippers – I don't think I took much notice of them and I never got any harassment from the guys.

"I think you're right about the world being pretty much a sexist and racist place in those days, so the strippers were the norm. I don't think Hillsborough was any better or worse than anywhere else. I do remember the Miss SWFC Personality Girl competitions, although I'm not sure how much 'personality' came into it! There weren't the overt displays of body parts that could have gone with such a competition as I recall, but a bit of leg on show. I don't think all the applicants were necessarily Owls' fans either – could have been wannabes hoping for a stepping-stone to something, maybe?"

Another female fan, Ellen Rhead, who began watching Wednesday when she was eight and is now approaching 65 told me: "I have always been around the grounds, home and away, along with two younger sisters a bit later on. There was and still is some sexist chanting (Get your t*ts out for the lads, that kind of thing, but not so much these days). Funnily enough, though, after a while, I think the guys looked on the regular girls/women as part of their group and were protective of us when there was any chance of hooliganism which was around at that time.

I was a 'skinhead' girl in the mid 70's and I was quite boyish (although you would never have confused me with a boy) with a longer version of the haircut and we wore the same clothes as the guys – Ben Sherman shirts, Stay-Press trousers, Harrington Jackets, Trevira Coats and brogue shoes. I thought I was the bee's knees! A bit later on, we added silk scarves round our wrists and tartan turnups on the Stay-Press (ala Bay City Rollers) – not so cool!"

"Times have changed," she added. "I think girls and women nowadays would stand up for themselves more than we did and wouldn't put up with the sexism and racism – which of course, nowadays I wouldn't either – and men have changed too. It WAS a different world back then."

Another female Owls' fan, Pamela Sawyer, remembers travelling with a female friend to an away game and being subjected to sexist comments as they made their way down the aisle of a Supporters' Club coach. "When travelling with male friends I was treated as 'one of the lads' to some extent," she added, "although they did seem to think that having me there kept them out of trouble (not sure if this was because they were on their best behaviour or because they were less likely to be set upon with me there)!"

One "superfan", Leslie Davies, discussed how she came to watch the Owls when she was interviewed in the club programme in 1973. "I chose to watch the Owls because the club has great style," she said. "The atmosphere at Hillsborough is absolutely marvellous, the staff are friendly, and the facilities are second to none." Davies went on to explain how she persuaded her husband to follow the Owls as a result of her enthusiasm!

Perhaps the most startling thing about following Wednesday in the 1970s is that at many grounds there were no female toilets, which illustrates the differences in the 1970s most clearly to me. The sexism of the period was no more prevalent at Hillsborough than anywhere else in society and strippers, personality girls, lack of facilities, sexist chanting and what would now be seen as sexist advertising were emblematic of the times.

There was one small bonus for female fans of Wednesday in the 1970s, though; in 1973-74, an adult season ticket in the centre of the North or South Stand was £16 for a man, and £15 for a "lady". It didn't make that much difference, though, as one female fan estimated crowds at the time to be "97 per cent male, on the Kop at least". This is not an academic book, by any means. It seems to me though that experiences of female fans are "authentic", and I hope therefore not ignored.

Songs and Chants

A request for fans to send any interesting chants to a researcher at Hull University featured in the programme in 1973. I asked Owls' fans from the era what songs and chants they remembered. I was sent a wide selection, reproduced below as they were written by the supporters.

When Michael Prendergast scores a goal, hurrah, hurrah,
When Michael Prendergast scores a goal, hurrah, hurrah,
When Michael Prendergast scores a goal
You can shove your Currie up your hole
'Cos we'll all go mad when Prendergast scores a goal.

Bertie Mee said to Bill Shankly, have you heard of the North Bank Highbury? He said no, I don't think so, but I've heard of the East Bank Aggro!

Do wa, do wa, we do wa day, do wa do wa we day oh!
We whistle and we sang till the East Bank rang and we'll win the Cup and the League

Ay ay ay ay, East Bank Republican Army, we're barmy, we'll fear no foe, wherever we go, Cos we are the E.B.R.A...

Our Lowest Ebb?

Mrs Hall's Toffee rolls are the best, Mrs Hall's Toffee rolls are the greatest,
She takes strawberry milk from the breast,
And her husband does the rest...
Na na na, Na na na, Na na na...

All we are saying is give us a goal
(To the "tune" of John Lennon's "Give peace a chance")

From the green, green grass of Hillsborough to the isle of Sicily, we will fight, fight, fight for Wednesday 'Till we win the Football League, to hell with Liverpool to hell with Man City. We will fight, fight, fight for Wednesday till we win the Football League.

We are mad, we're insane. No one takes the Leppings Lane. Na na, na na, na na (Repeat)

And it's hi ho Sheffield Wednesday
Everywhere we go there's aggro
I see your boots are shining
We'll come and make a fuss
Come and start with us

Sammmmeee, Sammmmee, I'd walk a million miles for one of your smiles, ohhhhhh Saaaaaa....aaaaamyyyyyyyy.....

O this year we're going to win the league – Hey Sheffield Wednes-day
The best team that you've ever seen – Hey Sheffield Wednesday
The people come from miles around to – See Sheffield Wednes-day
And how many goals they will score,
Sheffield Wednesday, they'll score four....

La, la, la, la, la, la, hey Sheffield Wednesday etc
(To the tune of Viva Espana)

Some of the themes from elsewhere in the book are obvious in the songs and chants. The territorial need to "keep" Hillsborough for Owls supporters; references to "aggro" and to hooliganism along with the dry humour of simply asking for a goal! Neither I, nor the fan who sent me the "Mrs Hall's…" song, have an idea of what it meant – and neither did other supporters who remembered it. The "Sammy" chant was initially aimed at Owls player Sam Ellis in the late 1960s, encouraged by his blushing response.

By the mid-70s, the chant was aimed at one fan, Sammy Cousins, who would often be taking part in what might best be described as various antics during the game. Sammy is famed for regularly being hoisted at head height above the crowd on someone's shoulders – waving his silk scarf above his head for example! The final song was published in the programme, I am not sure how often it was sung at matches! The songs and chants clearly reflect the era, and many are remembered (if not sung anymore) by fans to this day.

Miscellaneous Memories and Tall Tales

As we have seen, some fans at least remember this period with fondness and nostalgia. Some supporters remember their away days, others some of the players and matches, and others their match going experiences with friends and family. This section includes some of the wackier tales I was told. It's the place for the kind of stories that would be recounted back in pubs, clubs and living rooms in the days, weeks and years afterwards. I have anonymised some of the stories – to protect the innocent as they say!

The first comes from one of our London Owls. "One day the train pulled into Sheffield station for the return journey after a Bank Holiday Monday game. The train was already mobbed and loads of passengers trying to get on. Then we noticed the old-style buffet carriage had stickers on them saying 'reserved for Sheffield Wednesday'. We got on and went to the buffet expecting to see the team… only to find out that the regular buffet steward had reserved three tables for us as his most loyal customers. One of the few results we had all season!" A fair reward after all the train journeys up and down the country, I would suggest.

The next story comes from just after our period, as it related to the share issues of late 1976. That said, it made me smile, and demonstrates the dedication of some fans to the team, so it stays in. This supporter told me that he "made the national papers by selling the car in order to stock up on the share issue that was made by Wednesday. I placed the advert in The Star and to give it gravitas, they sent up a photographer... The cheeky sods sold it on to all the tabloids. To be fair a three-month old Mark III two litre was a bit steep for me... I finished up with £250 in shares and a clapped-out Hillman Hunter!"

On Boxing Day, 1976, Wednesday were at Bury and a pub close to Gigg Lane, the Rose and Crown, was full, so the door was closed. That didn't stop Owls' fans getting in after someone inside opened a window, and supporters crawled through.

"At that game a fan nicked about 30 boxes of Birds Eye fish fingers from a corner shop near the ground," one supporter re-members, "and spent the whole game lobbing them at coppers!"

The game was an uneventful 0-0 draw, Wednesday holding on after striker Roger Wylde was sent off. That fan at least made his own entertainment, as his fellow fans were forced to do at Walsall in 1975 when the game was abandoned after 25 minutes due to a waterlogged pitch.

One fan remembers "1,200 Owls' fans heading back to their coaches across a park, where a local game is in progress. Sudden-ly, we've nicked the ball and it's five-hundred-a-side, Wednesday v Wednesday. Then someone booted the ball into the river. An-other game abandoned!"

Unfortunately, some stories from the time have unpleasant undertones of racism and hooliganism, and Owls fans were not always the innocent party. One supporter, Nigel Drake, remem-bers drinking before a game at The Victoria pub, full of Wednes-dayites, when a black man walked in. "Some fool sang 'The mon-key wants a banana'," he said. "The pub exploded in the scariest imaginable bar fight with bar stools and bottles used as weapons. I was at the bar with two friends. Two of us left our drinks and dived for the door, but the third stayed behind. Once outside we waited in horror; listening to the shrieks, crashes and bangs, and watching every window get put through as some poor bugger's business was trashed.

"We were sure our friend was at least very badly injured. But no. He calmly stepped out of the smoking ruins, finished his beer just outside the door and carefully placed his glass on the door-step before casually strolling over to re-join us!"

An example of making the best out of a very difficult situation, I think.

As previously mentioned, Wednesday played York away on the first night of the 'Save our Owls' campaign. "Me and my mate went early to York by train and after we had downed a few pints, we proceeded to stick Save our Owls stickers all over York city centre," Owls fan Chris Hardy recalls. "We stuck a few on a shop door and an old lady confronted us. We both thought a telling off was coming but to our surprise, she commended us. The old girl thought we were trying to save the endangered barn owl!" An image I love!

The next story, I will leave as short and sweet as how it was told to me. "Southend away in 1976 - all the hotels and camp sites were full as the Owls brought thousands for the Bank Holiday game. I therefore slept in a graveyard on the Friday night with a few mates!"

As we know, away days were a struggle for the Owls in terms of the results. The next tale is from outside of our era (just) after a period where the Owls had not won away from home for a season and a half. Some Owls' fans went to game after game, determined eventually to witness a Wednesday victory. John Hill takes up the story:

"Reading, September 1976. Me and my mates set off knowing we had not won away in over a year. There were two cars and we decided to have a couple of beers in Towcester. When leaving Towcester, the lads in the other car needed to fill up with petrol so we stopped at the petrol station with them to travel on together.
The lads in the other car also needed to use the toilets but we were fine and waited in our car ready to lead the way to Reading.

So, they filled up, came out of the toilets and off we went in our old Cortina followed by their even older Anglia.

After driving about 20 miles we realised that the Anglia was no longer in sight but as this used to happen a lot in those days, we weren't too worried - thinking that we would meet up at the first pub in Reading.

We carried on and saw the signs for Reading – 20 miles. The next thing we knew a police car with its blue lights flashing pulled us over. Our driver never had a drink when driving so we were not worried. The policeman though had different ideas, smiling, but saying that we did not indicate. The policemen leant in the window taking the keys out of the ignition. 'We are taking you back to Towcester,' he said. We obviously protested, asking what for. "'Criminal damage,' he told us.

Apparently the lads in the other car had been fooling around in the petrol station toilets and had broken something. We told him we had not got out of our car but to no avail. When we got back to the Towcester police station the other lads were there and we asked what they had done. 'Not much,' they said. So, there we were ten of us in three cells being taken out separately, giving statements and asking how long we were going to be detained, hoping to still get to the match. The police had other ideas.

After an afternoon of slow interviews and being told by the police that Wednesday had lost, they finally released us. We were not happy with the lads in the other car and set off back home stopping at motorway services to fill up and grab a bite.

We had filled up and were walking into the eating area when we saw Hughie Dowd and realised the Wednesday team bus was in. 'How did we get on Hughie?' we asked. 'Won 1-0,' he told us. 'Where have you boys been?'.

We made up a story about having broken down, feeling a little embarrassed about it. When we got back home to Conisborough, the other lads told us that one of them who could not take his drink had pulled a toilet off the wall. He admitted it and had to go back down to court. We never saw him at another game after that! So that is the story of how we missed the first away win for the Owls since December 1974!"

The London Owls were certainly dedicated. The next tale is of one of their group, "John", who was a TV repair man for one of the big companies at a time when most people rented their sets. He had to work every other Saturday but got around the prospect of missing the Owls games by getting his Saturday call sheet on the Friday.

He would then call his customers early that evening and arrange to carry out the repairs that night! I am told that this worked a treat nearly every time - jobs all done, customers delighted at receiving such service and John first at the train station on a Saturday morning to join the rest of the London Owls for what was often another Wednesday defeat! He did though find it very stressful if Wednesday did take the lead, often leaving such games early and walking the streets around the ground instead.

Our final tales come from the family of W.M. (Martin) Lee, who was an outspoken and committed Wednesdayite. In the 1970s and 80s he frequently wrote letters that were printed in the Green 'Un, often challenging the status quo at the time.

Later he became a prolific writer in many of the club fanzines during the 1990s and 2000s, writing columns such as W. Martin Lee's 'School of Charm'. He went to his first game in 1968 and his final game in 2018 (a few months before his death). During his 50 years as a fanatical Wednesdayite, he witnessed over 1,000 games and got himself into some bizarre situations.

Back in the dark days of the 1970s, he would often hitchhike to games from his base in Worcestershire. He wrote about this in a fanzine article called 'I nearly died for The Wednesday'. He was hitchhiking back from an Owls match in London as what he described as "a scrawny 16-year-old" and was offered a ride by a burly man who drove him through Oxford and the Cotswolds. After some polite chit-chat, the man opened his glove compartment to reveal an array of graphic male pornographic images.

Martin answered his question "So, you aren't interested in these then?" with a firm no and the mood instantly changed, the driver becoming quite angry. After some moments of incredibly awkward trepidation the driver slammed on the brakes (on an isolated country road) and ordered Martin to get out of the car.

He duly obliged and jumped into a nearby field, the car sped off and then slammed on its brakes again a little way down the road. After what seemed like an age, it finally drove off.

After walking in the dark fields for a few miles, wondering if every passing car was the would-be rapist/killer returning, Martin eventually went back to the road and hitchhiked home! A near miss indeed, and all in the name of Sheffield Wednesday!

In the mid-1970s he 'romanced' and 'educated' his first wife Rose, by taking her to watch the Owls in the early stages of their relationship. "Wednesday were in the Third Division when Martin first started taking me to Hillsborough," Rose recalled. "I remember in the second half of games; my feet would get so cold I couldn't feel them. I would get very bored, so I used to count the stewards in their yellow coats. It always seemed like Wednesday were losing.

Most of the time we sat in the North Stand, and occasionally the top tier of the Leppings Lane end. I remember some away games from around that time; being squashed at Sincil Bank, and wooden stands that smelt rotten at places like Reading and Bradford. The pies seemed to be filled with cat food and the Bovril was so hot it burned your mouth." Strangely, these experiences didn't put her off too much and the couple went on to have two boys, Chris and Phil, who are both Wednesdayites to this day.

Often oblivious of the dangers of going with the home fans, Martin would put himself (and later his sons!) in hazardous circumstances at away games. He was physically throttled by an aggressive Blackpool fan for celebrating a Wednesday goal, and was punched in the face at Cardiff for the same crime. The tales of Martin's experiences following the Owls reminded me again of how football fandom is only partly related to the success or otherwise of the team.

Conclusions
This chapter began with a quote from Nick Hornby explaining how football supporters experience the game individually within the larger group experience. This chapter has aimed to give voice to the differing experiences of fans, both in groups, and as in-

dividuals. It cannot cover the entire experience. I hope that the book will provoke further memories and discussions – as one aim of the project is to "rescue" the period. The fans who stuck by the team in these years are certainly due some recognition for their patience, stoicism and, where needed, gallows humour.

Snippets

The research for this book threw up some interesting "odds and sods". As they don't fit anywhere else directly, here they are!

• The 1975-76 season was the last in English football where goal average was used to decide positions in the table when points were equal. Goal difference replaced goal average from 1976 onwards. The period involved two points being awarded for a win, and one for a draw. Three points for a win was not introduced in England until 1981.

• In 1973-74 the three-up and three-down system of promotion and relegation was introduced (as opposed to two-up and two-down).

• In 1973-74, Wednesday sported a new logo on their shirts. The new Owl symbol was designed by 19-year-old Robert (Bob) Walker. Bob was one of 90 art students at Granville College of Further Education who were invited by the club to give the logo a facelift. He won the competition and was made guest of honour at the first home game of the season. The Lord Mayor of Sheffield attended the ceremony, though made it clear that he supported both Sheffield football clubs.

• From 1971 onwards, Owls' fans could buy match tickets from a concession next to the food hall in Cockaynes, a department store in Sheffield city centre. In 1972, the Owls advertised upcoming fixtures on the side of Sheffield's "corporation" buses.

• The Owls were not awarded a single penalty throughout the 1975-76 season.

• At least two first team players took on other jobs to supplement their wages. Eric Potts' home telephone number was published in the programme with details of his painting and decorating skills.

- In 1973-74 future Owls' manager Jack Charlton was named "manager of the year" after leading Middlesbrough to the Second Division Championship. He was assisted by ex-Owls' player Ian McFarlane.
- Outside Hillsborough at almost every home game throughout the period stood men holding placards. One read: "The Wages of Sin is Death" (sic). Another read: "Seek the Lord".
- Swindon's programme of September 1975 referred to the Owls as "The Wednesday", a name the club had not gone by since officially changing to Sheffield Wednesday in 1929.
- Two Owls players of the period were involved in interesting substitutions for other teams. In 1974, Denis Law scored a goal for Manchester City against his previous club, Manchester United. Law felt that the goal may have been enough to relegate United. He didn't celebrate the goal and was soon substituted (seemingly distraught) and replaced by Phil Henson. In 1975, Danny Cameron was involved in a substitution for Preston North End's reserve team. He was replaced by World Cup winner Nobby Stiles with 30 minutes remaining, for what would prove to be Stiles' last game as a professional footballer.
- There was just a one match combined programme produced for the games against Millwall on March 29 1975, and Southampton two days later. The reason given by the club was 'production, printing and delivery schedules, tighter than usual because of the Easter holiday period'.
- In 1973 and 1974 some match programmes were single sheets due to production issues caused by the three-day working week. The FA Cup third round replay at Coventry was an example of this – a game which kicked off at 1.30pm on a Tuesday.
- Also, during the power crisis that led to the three-day week, the office and ground staff at Hillsborough finished work at 4:30pm rather than 5pm, altering their breaks to cater for this. Evening training was also cancelled.
- Owls defender A. Thompson is known as both Alan and Allan across the programmes of the period. For clarity, I refer to him as Allan throughout the book.
- The Owls played in the largest away defeat and largest away

victory in Division Two in 1973-4; the 8-0 defeat at Middlesbrough and 5-1 win at Notts County helping them gain that obscure record.

• John Holsgrove was a talented guitarist. As far back as 1971 he was pictured in front of the Kop having a kickabout with popular group of the time – the Barron Knights.

• In the summer of 1975, the club had arranged for the famous American stunt motorcyclist Evil Knievel to appear at Hillsborough, an event that would have brought much-needed revenue into the club. Unfortunately, he was forced to cancel the performance after injuring himself in a preceding display at Wembley.

• Thousands of Wednesday fans made their way to Hillsborough to see the Owls beat Southend and ensure survival in Division Three in April 1976. Also in Sheffield that night, playing at the City Hall, was rock star Rick Wakeman. He recognised that some of the audience were missing the match and gave updates on the score. One fan remembers hearing him announce simply, at full time: "Wednesday are stopping up!"

MEMORABILIA

Football fans are hoarders. Well, at least some of us are. This section celebrates the memorabilia that Owls' fans have kept since the dark days of the mid-1970s. It is for all those people who have a box of programmes in the loft or shed. For those who have kept shirts, pennants, stickers and autograph books. It is also for those who have not. For those who sold them, or who threw them out in a house move. Or for those who have the worst tale of all – their Mum threw their memorabilia out when they left home!

It's also for those who were not around at the time, to give a flavour of what Owls' fans could buy to show their support of the team, and what some people have kept ever since. This section will recount the stories of those who kept the material and drag it out from those dusty boxes back into the light where they truly belong.

The club offered a good selection of memorabilia at the time. There was also material available from the Supporters' Club and from various vendors around the ground and the city. In 1974-75, the list of items available at the Owls' shop was vast and covered the usual ties, scarves and pennants with items like combs, wallets, teddy bears, jewellery and beakers.

Silk scarves were very popular among fans at the time. They were reasonably priced and available in a selection of colours and styles. One such scarf has remained in the possession of Owls' fan Dave Thompson since the early 1970s.

Dave moved to New Zealand in 1996 and recounted the story of the scarf to me from the other side of the world. "I can't remember the precise year I purchased the scarf, but it would have perhaps been around 1972?" he told me. "Around that time, I used to go to Hillsborough with my father and his best mate, Uncle Tom. Uncle Tom wasn't my real uncle, but he lived in Walkley and sometimes we all used to walk down the steep hills to get to the ground from his house. For a while we used to stand in the

North-West corner/terrace and to get there we'd go in through the gates on Leppings Lane then up the ramp to the standing area as it was then. Partway up the ramp, but not very far up was a kiosk (perhaps more a table with a back-display stand) that sold scarves and badges and the like, and my silk scarf was purchased from that kiosk. I'm sure I can remember looking at the prices for the scarf on one occasion previously and not having enough money, I had to move on. But I'd saved up enough by the time of the next home game.

"School dinners cost 12p in those days and I may have skipped a few to afford the difference I needed for the scarf! I'd forgotten how much I paid for the scarf but the 60p on your price list sounds somehow familiar. As 11 or 12-year-olds, we used to tie our scarves on to one of our wrists, so we could look tough! Some of the older kids would have three or four scarves on their wrists from other teams, claiming to have 'won' them, but I never saw any fights."

Dave went on to tell me how the scarf had survived so long. "I once tried to iron the scarf but not knowing anything how to do this, I had to stop when the white ink started to melt and stick to the iron. A few of the white tassels have fallen out over the years but mostly it's intact. The colour though has not faded but if anything has changed to more of a bluish purple, far darker than the original royal blue colour it once was. Today it sits on my tie rack along with two other blue and white scarves; one a Wednesday scarf from just a few years ago and the other from Napier City Rovers, the local team I 'support' here in New Zealand."

Dave now follows the Owls from afar – and has made the long trek back to watch the Owls on several occasions since his move. "The last time I came back I took my son, who was 15 at the time, to his first game on the Kop, 2016 vs Cardiff… perhaps the most boring game I'd seen since the 1970s!"

Silk scarves were certainly popular. Another fan told me of the fashion of wearing a woollen scarf around the neck and a silk scarf around the wrist – "a lot of us did that" while another remembered wearing a scarf around the wrist was "the height of fashion". Wherever they were worn – or however they were acquired – they were certainly very popular, though perhaps not really designed for longevity. One fan recalled flying one out of the side of the car window on trip over the Pennines to Oldham. Suffice to say, the scarf didn't survive the journey!

Dave's story made it clear to me how much the collection of memorabilia is tied up with memory and nostalgia. Dave remembers with remarkable clarity the experience of going to the game, and what it was like as a young fan. The scarf is of obvious importance to him. Another fan, Philip Bradish, has kept his autograph book from the period. Philip also remembers how he collected the autographs. "I was only around nine or 10," he told me. "I used to wait outside the players' entrance at the back of the South Stand, and players always turned up between half one and two o'clock.

"I was lucky and got loads from that era. Most of the players were happy to stop and sign something for us kids." One page includes the signatures of Allan Thompson, Mick Prendergast and Tommy Craig. Philip went on to tell me how he tried to add Pele's autograph before his visit with Santos in 1972: "For the Pele one there were loads of fans around the players' entrance, so it was impossible to get near. I had to wag school for the game because it was played in the afternoon during week because of power cuts." Both Dave and Philip's stories are nostalgic, and show how childhood memories remain powerful later in life.

Other fans have kept larger items of memorabilia. One fan, Mick Jeffries, showed me his collection. I was particularly interested in a large cushion, which the Supporters' Club hired out to fans in the North Stand. "I stuffed it up my jumper one day on a whim," he said. "I used to be a development club agent and once a year, around Christmas, you got a ticket for the North Stand. But the rest of the time I could be found in my usual spot at the back of the Kop under the scoreboard."

The cushions had been hired out to fans for many years, at least since the mid-1960s. They were occasionally thrown on to the pitch by fans frustrated by the team's performance, annoyed by the club's ownership or management (see the last days of Sir Andrew Stephen's chairmanship), or even upset by the actions of the match officials. As one fan put it to me: "It wasn't always against the team or the management. I remember one game (against Luton I think) where the ref had a shocker and the flask and blanket brigade went into full on soft furnishing punishing frenzy." Another fan remembered that game's reaction differently: "I was there. We were winning 2-0. Their equaliser prompted a rain of cushions from the North Stand."

A third fan told me that his "abiding memory is the cushions raining down on to the pitch to express displeasure at another woeful performance." The cushion throwing was a semi-regular event, but by 1976 the club clamped down on it. A message in the programme read: "The hire of cushions has been terminated due to incidents where several were thrown on to the pitch. This type of behaviour could lead to the club being disciplined by the FA. The hire of the cushions was operated by the Supporters' Club who have decided to forgo the revenue rather than risk a repetition."

This has led to the cushions becoming something of a collector's item in recent years, with the price of a 1970s cushion on eBay or elsewhere reaching somewhere between £40 and £50 on the rare occasions they go on sale. I think that Mick, or anyone else who has one, should therefore look after it and perhaps keep it as an heirloom!

Vernon Grant, as we see elsewhere in the book, was a founder member of the London Owls' supporters club. He went on to have a successful career in television production, before retiring to Spain. It was from there that he sent me the images of tickets he had kept from all those years ago. The tickets themselves are interesting. Without the barcodes, or credit card sized season tickets of today, they reflect again how football was the same but different in the 1970s.

The tickets are individual to each club and reflect the time and place they came from. Vernon, in common with many football supporters, has kept a box of such memorabilia over the years. Mostly programmes, but with some pictures and other bits and pieces. He struggled to explain why – but when showing the material to me, said: "Look what you've started!"

He then produced material about the London Owls that again had been kept for over 40 years, along with pictures of the Owls from his time working in the newspaper industry. Mick and Vernon's stories are almost opposite in how they have kept their memorabilia. Vernon's in a box in the loft (proverbially), Mick's out on display at home.

Paul Whitaker, who many Owls' supporters who follow social media will also know as Dunsby Owl, has a large collection of Owls memorabilia which he generously shares via several Facebook groups, his Twitter feed @DunsbyOwl, and on various forums. Paul contacted me to share his memories of the time, and some of his collection. His collection is different again to any of those mentioned so far.

Paul is meticulous in his record keeping and on an almost daily basis shares "on this day" material about the history of the Owls via those social media platforms. He shared with me a copy of his share certificate – issued after the "Lowest Ebb" but still in 1976 along with a copy of a full set of player pictures that he had stuck into a scrapbook as a boy and kept ever since. The share certificate (worth £10) was bought for Paul by his father and therefore holds some value to him in that regard. The scrapbook is more evidence of how powerful childhood memories can be.

Micheal Roe sent me a copy of his "Save our Owls" poster, complete with two stickers that he had kept since the campaign of 1974. As we know, the campaign was not a resounding success so when, in 1974, Micheal asked his newsagent if he could have a copy of the poster and stickers, she was happy to say yes. The newsagent was his local one at the Netherside Shops in Shiregreen, Sheffield. In the process of my research for this book, I have looked long and hard for any surviving examples of these posters and stickers. Micheal's is the only example I have found. It was kept until recently in a box with programmes from the time. Micheal thinks that he will now frame it!

Adrian Hurst has been an Owls fan all his life. Now living in South Wales, he still attends games regularly, both home and away. In the 1970s he helped organise the Chapeltown branch of the official Supporters' Club and attended almost every game. He shared with me his programme collection and a tankard from the Supporters' Club. In a similar way to tickets, programmes clearly reflect the time and place in which they were sold. They provoke memories and remind their owners of their feelings at the time.

Owls' programmes during the period were a perfunctory affair. For each of the three seasons covered by this book, the programme was 16 pages long, and cost 10 pence. This was at a time of rampant inflation though the initial 10 pence must have seemed relatively expensive when compared to (say) a West Bromwich Albion programme at six pence, or a Millwall one at seven pence in 1973-74.

Opposition programmes did increase in price across the period, so that by 1975-76 10 to 12 pence was the norm. The 1973-74 Owls programmes did come with a "player picture" inside – effectively a postcard with an image of one of the team, a copy of their autograph and a few simple facts about them.

In the final of our three seasons, the Owls experimented with changing the colour of the programme from the standard blue. Programmes were printed with green, orange and purple colours – but as the club said: "The colour we won't be using is RED (obviously); the nearest we come to that terrible colour is purple… Your opinions…. Would be greatly appreciated and if you think it's a load of rubbish, we'll forget it." I'm unsure whether fans thought the idea was rubbish or not, but the programme did return to its usual colour before the end of the season. The programmes were not a huge money-spinner for Wednesday, with profit from their sale falling from £6,301 in 1973 to a low of £3,715 in 1975. Some of this of course relates to the falling crowds of the period.

The programmes alter in style and appearance over our three-year period. Those for 1973-74 are produced in a portrait format. The front cover was in a standard format, but with a changing central picture each time (almost always of the featured player that issue). They included a series of action photographs of recent games, and some reasonably detailed articles.

Derek Dooley kept his spot in the programme during the months before his sacking and wrote a page of honest sounding feedback about the situation of the team at the time of each game. There was also a "profile" section written by local sports journalist and author Keith Farnsworth, a two-page spread about the opposition, and a player picture (postcard style) in each issue.

There were also results and statistics for recent games for the first team, reserves and youth team. As the 1974-75 season started, the programme moved to a generic front cover (showing Peter Rodrigues in action) and was produced in a landscape format. "The Owl" as the magazine was now called no longer featured the manager's thoughts solely – instead they were included (usually) in a feature called "Voice of Hillsborough". There were still two pages of information about the opposition and pictures of recent games. The profile section was replaced by a shorter "Focus On" feature (featuring highlights like Brian Joicey – "Miscellaneous dislikes: Dirty ashtrays and people being late for appointments").

The results page was expanded in size but not in detail. The programme feels more cheaply produced and although priced the same as the previous season (10p) this does not cater for the rampant inflation at the time. Programmes from 1975-76 remained titled "The Owl", and again were produced in portrait style. They had an action shot on the front cover (usually a player) and 'The Voice of Hillsborough' had added the "the"!

Matchday pictures were now titled "Owls Action" and individual interviews or "focus on" a player had disappeared. The programme was still priced at 10p but felt flimsier than in previous seasons. Perhaps this lack of quality allowed the club to make more money from the programmes, however, as their profits on sales did rise slightly that season.

Programmes from away games provoke memories of those games for those who were there. They also provide an interesting perspective of the Owls at the time. Many opponents commented in one way or another on the Owls' position in the leagues. Millwall described Wednesday as "distinguished visitors with an illustrious past" while West Brom suggested the Owls were "one of those teams who you feel do not belong in Division Two".

Tommy Docherty, as Manchester United manager, said:

"Nothing that Sheffield Wednesday could produce today would surprise me!" It's interesting also to see how the same players are described differently by different teams. Joicey, for example, was "high on the list of dangermen" according to West Brom, "a more than useful goal-getter" to Millwall and "a leading goals-corer" to Orient. Of course, the programmes for away games are written with the home supporters in mind, but their views of the Owls and the players are interesting in providing different views.

Despite the lack of quality and detail of the home programmes at least, many people, such as Adrian, have kept large collections of them. My own family kept a large box full of programmes and other memorabilia in the loft. I have a feeling that is where many such collections are. The programmes themselves are worth only pennies – I was able to fill in gaps in my collection for less than a pound a programme during my research for the book. I conclude therefore that fans keep them for nostalgic reasons and for the fond memories that they (sometimes) provoke.

The Supporters' Club, which is discussed in detail elsewhere in the book, produced memorabilia of various kinds for sale through their site at Hillsborough and through their various branches. Adrian has a tankard in his collection. The club had also produced badges for decades through the world-renowned badge-makers "Fattorini and Sons" of the Jewellery Quarter in Birmingham. By the 1970s the badges were still produced, but seemingly in a more generic (maybe cheaper) fashion. Certainly, sometime in the late 1960s/early 1970s the badges moved from being branded as Fattorini and Sons with a clutch back, to being unbranded with a pin back.

The logo remained the same. One sits in my family's collection and, to the best of my knowledge, dates from the mid-1970s.

Dave Thompson, who we met earlier with his silk scarf in New Zealand, contacted me again a few weeks after our initial discussions to tell me that he had found his collection of Wednesday player cards, that he felt were from the 1973-74 season. A quick glance at the pictures showed that it was indeed that squad. The pictures were produced by the *Sheffield Star* newspaper who provided a free wallchart to attach them to.

The wallcharts were available at Hillsborough or at local news-agents. There were 16 photographs in total – so Dave has the full set! Fans were to collect "Soccerpix" vouchers that were published in The *Star* each day. Two pictures were then available each week, meaning a full set would take eight weeks to complete. Dave couldn't recall how the pictures were then made available to him – possibly by post, or possibly by collection from The *Star's* offices. Whichever way it took a degree of organisation to ensure that all were collected, and I'm impressed that they've survived all these years and a trip to the other side of the world!

Pamela Sawyer contacted me in the autumn of 2019 having seen some of my material for the book on the Internet. She told me that as a teenager in the mid-1970s she had kept a scrapbook of her experiences watching the Owls and asked me if it would be of use to me. I was very interested and agreed to meet Pamela to have a chat about what she had kept and her experiences watching the team. The scrapbook is a fascinating treasure trove of material. Pamela had written immaculate records of games she had attended with details of players, attendance, goalscorers, substitutions and details of the kits of both teams.

The kit detail even included the different coloured socks of each team's goalkeeper! Along with Pamela's own notes, there are newspaper clippings from local and national papers detailing the games and other events surrounding the team. I was hugely impressed at Pamela's efforts in compiling this. She did tell me, self-effacingly, that she had maintained such efforts for a while, before just tucking in cuttings into the back of the book! Pamela had good memories of supporting the Owls in the 1970s. She did feel, looking back, a little surprised that her parents let her travel to away games though – relaying stories of being chased down a canal towpath at Lincoln, and of Owls' fans outnumbering those of Darlington and pushing several of their fans into a ditch after a game.

Included with the book was a silk scarf and Pamela wasn't entirely sure of when it dated from, though she did clearly remember wearing such a scarf wrapped around her wrist in the popular style of the time. She has followed the Owls ever since, for many years travelling to games from the Midlands. "It's in the blood," she told me. She had never felt able to throw her scrapbook away, keeping it during several house moves over the years. She agreed with me that there is a certain fondness for the mid-1970s which the book represents. I was touched by Pamela agreeing to lend me the book, and for the conversation and memories which she shared with me.

David Herbert played for the Owls 19 times across the 1974-75 and 1975-76 seasons, scoring four goals. Sadly, David died in 2002 after a battle with cancer, leaving his wife and two children. The Herbert family contacted me via Twitter in spring 2019. They "liked" a few of the pictures that I'd posted and sent me a few of their own. David's wife and son both communicated with me and asked if I'd like to look over their collection of material about David, sport, and the Owls more generally. I arranged to visit Jayne Herbert at her home in Dronfield, where she shared with me a wealth of material.

It is difficult to do justice to the amount, and interest, of the material that Jayne held, or to the warm welcome I was given. It was very clear that David's family are hugely proud of his achievements.

The material started with David's youngest days, as his parents had collated a scrapbook of achievements from his time as a schoolboy. There were two further folders stuffed full of clippings, photographs, letters, cards, telegrams and other material following David's career. Early material included a newspaper clipping celebrating David scoring over 100 goals for his youth team, Hackenthorpe Juniors, and a congratulatory letter from the Owls hoping that he would soon replicate these feats for Sheffield Wednesday!

There were also references to successes in athletics and further success with the Sheffield Boys team. Later folders included details of David's successes in the Northern Intermediate team at Hillsborough, followed by the reserves (Central League) and finally the first team. I was fascinated to see copies of David's various contracts for the club. His first professional contract (for six months) in 1974 was signed by Eric Woodhouse Taylor on behalf of the club and saw David Ronald Herbert agree to "play in an efficient manner and to the best of his ability for the club." He was also to "do everything necessary to get and keep himself in the best possible condition" and was not to "engage in any business or live in any place which the Directors (or Committee) of the club may deem unsuitable". In return for this he was paid £20 a week. In addition to this Jayne showed me a copy of the club's bonus scheme for 1975-76.

This was somewhat complicated, but had the team found themselves in the top two (wishful thinking maybe) the players would have earned an extra £30 per point gained, and in the unlikely event of a Division Three club reaching the League Cup final, the players would have earned an extra £500 each.

There were plenty of other opportunities to earn bonuses depending on the time of season, points gained, and appearances made. David's basic pay also went up to £30 a week for the 1975-76 season, which Jayne told me was more than she earned in a month at the time – so it felt good money to a young couple in their late teens.

The collection also included plenty of material about David's career after leaving Hillsborough, including a short spell at Chesterfield and then goals galore for several years at Buxton. There was also further material about Sheffield Wednesday more generally, including pictures of Hillsborough at the time, and season tickets held by David and his son Matthew in the 1990s. I was also interested to see the detailed, handwritten, report on a yellow card that David received playing in a Central League game at Coventry in April 1975.

There were plenty of examples of the human side of a footballer's life also. David made his debut at West Bromwich Albion in March 1975. Included in the folders of material were telegrams from friends and family, delivered to the Hawthorns dressing room with varying messages of good luck.

Also included from earlier in David's career were "get well soon" cards and messages following a knee ligament injury. Sheffield Wednesday offered a message of support on that occasion. The Owls sent several letters to David in his younger years, including invites to training and holiday camp. The letters were always professional yet personable and supportive. Jayne told me that David had grown up as (whisper it) a Sheffield United fan but found the support and atmosphere at Hillsborough more to his liking and therefore signed for the Owls. The deal may well have been completed after the Blades invited David to Bramall Lane but, as it was matchday, tried to charge him admission!

The family attended as many games as they could in which David played and had an extensive collection of programmes from those games. These included the brief four-page documents that were produced for reserve team games, along with home programmes and those from several away games. One of these games was away at Crystal Palace in September 1975 (a programme costing a huge 15p). This game featured on that night's *Match of the Day* – a real rarity for the Owls in those days.

A link to those highlights is available today on YouTube. I had shared the link recently on Twitter. Jayne told me that ironically, she and David were going out that evening and that, in the pre video days, he had never seen the footage – and that neither had she until this year. That conversation turned into a wider conversation about family, Sheffield Wednesday, sport and life. We chatted about how this project had provoked further discussions with her friends and family, with her brother reminding Jayne of the Save our Owls campaign and the later share issue. We talked a little about other sports, with Sheffield Steelers ice hockey being a favourite of David and Jayne's son. Jayne very kindly lent me a few items from the collection, and then it was time for me to leave.

The items that Jayne and the Herbert family hold is a treasure trove of fascinating material. Its historical relevance to the writing of this book has been huge. The collection reminded me (if I needed reminding) of the human aspect of the game. David Herbert was obviously popular and well regarded. It seemed to me important to remember the person as well as the footballer. One of the aims of the book is to "reclaim" the period for posterity. The Herbert family story reminded me why this is worth doing.

My research for this section of the book has shown me that

people keep different memorabilia for differing reasons. There are collectors (programmes, tickets), those who keep items for nostalgia's sake (autographs, card collections), those who keep things as they remind them of family (share issue), those who keep material for display (Save our Owls poster, cushions) and those who keep things as they were directly involved. I am very grateful to everyone who has shared items from the time for use in the book. I have found the various materials fascinating to look over, and equally as interesting to understand some of the reasons why people have kept them.

CONCLUSIONS

The book began by quoting other Owls' historians describing the mid-1970s in exclusively negative terms. I am of course doing something of a disservice to those writers by choosing those short quotes from far longer and more detailed works. This book does not aim to gloss over the difficulties of the period. It bears repeating that the seasons from 1973 to 1976 saw one relegation and two last-day escapes. The 1973-74 season saw the Owls fall to two eight-goal defeats, sack a manager on Christmas Eve and suffer from a "notorious virus". In 1974-75 Wednesday scored two league goals after Christmas and won only five league fixtures.

The 1975-76 season saw the Owls finish in their lowest-ever league position and break the record for lowest post-war crowd. Those descriptions of the "the darkest hour" and of a time where "Wednesday spiralled ever downward" in a period "long on gloom" are certainly based on a realistic reading of the evidence. The title for the book includes a question mark – *Our Lowest Ebb?* The question mark is there for several reasons beyond the facts and statistics.

My research has shown that there are fans who remember the period with a degree of fondness. Some supporters remember trips to away games, others some of the players and matches, and others their match-going experiences with friends and family. It took a degree of resilience to follow the Owls then, demonstrated by those who travelled in numbers to away games throughout the period, even during the long months without a win. This book is in a way a tribute to those fans, and I hope has offered them a voice to share their experiences. Those experiences are worth remembering for those who were there, and worth reflecting on for those who have begun following the team in more recent times.

It was no doubt a thoroughly miserable time for many, and I do not aim to downplay that. Supporting a team is not always about the results, however, and some supporters remember the period well despite the performances on the pitch. The amount and extent of memorabilia that survives from the period is further evidence of how some fans remember the period with nostalgia at least.

Each player I spoke to was warm in their memories of their time at Hillsborough. For those who played at youth and reserve level it may have been the pinnacle of their footballing career. For those who played for the first team at Hillsborough, it still provoked positive memories. For those players it was not a low ebb. Hillsborough Stadium remained a world-class facility during the period. There remained a clear pride in the stadium and its architecture from many fans.

The cantilever structure of the North Stand is something that many who attended games comment on favourably. The use of the stadium for FA Cup semi-finals and international games show the high regard in which the stadium was held by the game's authorities. Not a facility that was at its lowest point.

The games and players I mention are laid out in detail in the book. The project was sparked by a simple tweet of a picture of Mick Prendergast. It provoked a very positive reaction. He, and many other players, deserve remembering well for their efforts. The 4-4 draw with Manchester United in late 1974 and the 10 goals in two games salvo of March that year are just two reminders that there were also thrilling games and excellent team performances during our period. Derek Dooley's team was one that had previously finished mid-table and included some talented players, with some playing at international level.

Steve Burtenshaw endeavoured to ensure that his teams played good football. Flickeringly they did just that. Len Ashurst took a more utilitarian approach, doing what needed to be done to win games. Each manager's team, however briefly, had their moments of success.

I argue that the seeds of later recovery were sown in this period. The green shoots of recovery became clearer as the period reached its end in 1976. Firstly, the club's finances were still in a parlous state at this stage, but the difficult decisions made by

Matt Sheppard and then Bert McGee had put a base in place for later improvements. The share issue and increased help from the development fund that followed in the later 1970s saw the club's finances improve rapidly in the years that followed. It is unlikely that this would have been possible without the decisions made in our period.

Secondly, the club had followed a policy of developing young players for several years. Len Ashurst's turn in the manager's chair saw the end of several promising young players who had come through in the previous seasons. He did, though, oversee the development and success of David Cusack, Rodger Wylde and, to some extent, Peter Fox. The work of Steve Burtenshaw in developing the Middlewood Rovers team also bore fruit in the years afterwards, with a steady stream of players making their way into the first team.

Finally, Ashurst and Tony Toms inherited an unbalanced squad who were used to losing games. Their focus on fitness and hard work, together with what was inevitably a brutal restructuring of the playing squad at the end of the 1975-76 season, saw the Owls break that losing habit. Bert McGee certainly felt that Ashurst's efforts were a vital part of the club's return from the dark times.

Tony Toms remained at the club as part of Jack Charlton's staff, as did several players that Ashurst had brought to the club or played in his teams. Ashurst's changes to the club were not without casualties and his methods did not endear him to everyone. On balance, though, he turned the Owls from a team that was used to losing – albeit playing good football at times – to one that was prepared to fight and to battle. He was unable to complete the recovery, but he left a team and club that Charlton was able to develop into a promotion-winning one.

I started the book by wondering how those who followed the team in its darkest times coped. I have discovered that even in darkness, there were glimpses of light. The question mark in the title is a justified one. By the end of 1975-76 the green shoots of recovery were beginning to sprout. As much of the book is about the memories of the fans, I'll end with one final quote to illustrate the themes of the book: "Great memories. I remember the camaraderie above all… the fans stuck together and, despite how poor we were at times, I still recall some of the players with a good degree of fondness."

Despite attending my first Owls game several years after the events of this book, I have also grown fond of this era. I salute the management, players and fans who saw the period through and eventually reaped the rewards of the 1980s and 1990s. I believe that the period should be remembered and remembered well. It is my hope that this book does just that.

Postscript

August 25, 1984 saw Sheffield Wednesday face Nottingham Forest at Hillsborough. A crowd of 31,925 packed into the stadium and saw the Owls win 3-1, with goals from Mel Sterland, Imre Varadi and John Pearson. The game was the Owls' first in Division One since their relegation in 1970. Only eight years had passed since the team had reached its *"Lowest Ebb"*, and the club were successfully back at the highest level. The Owls were promoted to Division Two under the management of Jack Charlton in 1979-80. Rodger Wylde and Jimmy Mullen were important players in that season's promotion push. Tony Toms remained as part of the club's backroom set-up.

By the time of the Owls' promotion to Division One in 1983-84, there were no players remaining in the first team from the 1973-76 period. There were, though, several players in the squad who had made their way through the Middlewood Rovers set-up, including Mark Smith, Sterland and Charlie Williamson. To stretch an earlier metaphor, the club were now harvesting the fruit from the trees that grew from the green shoots of the mid-1970s. Finances, attendances, and performances on the field had all improved from the dark times. Fans who stuck it out could look forward to a long period of relative success for Sheffield Wednesday.

ACKNOWLEDGEMENTS

This is my first book. I am hugely grateful to many people for their help and support. This cannot be a complete list and is in no particular order. First, to my wife Shelana – for putting up with me spending hour after hour at the computer. And even when not there, having my head somewhere in the 1970s. Despite having very little interest in either the 1970s or Sheffield Wednesday, she also read and offered welcome guidance on various sections of the book as it was written. To my two children Joe and Sam who, so far at least, are Owls' fans also.

To Mum and Dad, for helping make me an Owl. Rest in Peace Dad, I'm sorry you never had chance to read the finished book.

I am grateful to the following for spreading the word early on that I was looking for opinions of the fans: Wednesdayite, London Owls, West Midlands Owls, SWSWSWs, The New Barrack Tavern and Owlstalk. Without the message being out there so widely, I would never have heard from so many supporters.

War of the Monster Trucks, Steve and Paul, for taking a real interest and publishing the first article on the topic. It provoked a very positive response. Thank you.

The former players' associations at Coventry City (Jim Brown), Sunderland (Philip Crossley-Lowes), Glentoran (Ian) and Preston North End (Graeme Atkinson) for helping put me in touch with some of the people I have spoken to and interviewed.

Lots of fans have helped along the way. Thanks to the following for going over and above:

Adrian Hurst, for detailed memories and pictures of his time with Chapeltown Owls; Paul Whitaker: for encyclopaedic knowledge, and generosity with his memorabilia; Andrew Fox: for helping me structure the fans survey; Vernon Grant: for advice and for detailed information about the London Owls; Colin Grant: for detailed information and material about the London Owls. Jake McCaffrey: for the story and details of the Limavady Owls; Lee

Hicklin: for reserve and youth team facts and figures; Pamela Saw-yer: for access to her scrapbook and memories; Dave Thompson: for photos and memories from the other side of the world; Rich-ard Crooks: for encouragement and helpful thoughts and ideas; Nigel Short: for interest, encouragement and information about the Supporters Club; Andrew Cooper: for encouragement and for answering my questions about Eric Taylor and other matters. Chris Lee: for encouragement and tales of his father.

Richard Letts: for assistance with filling in the gaps in my pro-gramme collection, and for encouragement.

To Sheffield Wednesday Football Club. In particular to Trevor Braithwait for his support and encouragement. To Peter Law, club historian and archivist, for the materials provided and again for support and encouragement. To Steve Ellis, club photographer, for his generosity, time and support.

To the staff at Sheffield Local Studies Library for their expert help and assistance in locating much of the source material for my research.

To Alex Miller at the Sheffield Star for his interest in the period and support.

To Alan Biggs, for his memories, support and encouragement.

To everyone who I have interviewed or who has provided thoughts. Including: David Cusack, Ken Knighton, Eddie Prud-ham, Danny Cameron, David Sunley, Neil Ramsbottom, Phil Henson, Francis Smith, Len Ashurst, Willie Henderson, Kev Lan-caster, David Barker, Steve Woodhead, Tony Toms and Chris Turner. Danny Cameron and Eddie Prudham deserve thanks for hunting through their scrapbooks and files and provid-ing me with plenty of photographs and further information.

To all those who provided me with memorabilia to share. In par-ticular the Herbert family for welcoming me and sharing their memories of David Herbert (R.I.P.)

A huge number of people have provided help, support and memories through social media. My thanks are due to all of the following and more: Shawn Shelton, Jim Hope, Tim Archbould, Ron Clayton, Andrew Thorpe, Nigel Dean, Graham Denton, David Harpham, Irma Kennedy, Mark Hope, Michael Cryans, Stewart Merrill, Steven Kay, David Bonser, Nigel Lowes, David Snowden, Robert Bonser, Ken Blackburn, Charlie Grummitt, Sean Fenelon, Paul Prendergast, Chris Hardy, Andrew Clayton, Mark Ford, Tosh Warwick, Pete Hurn, Steve Phelps and Spencer Vignes.

Thank you to all the fans who have provided me memories in varying ways. Again, my thanks are due to all the following and the many others who contributed anonymously: John Hill, Ian Wharton, Stephen Willsher, Steve Archer, Richard Coates, Pete Goodison, Mark Goodison, John Cashman, Ellen Rhead, Bob Hull, Pete Gelder, Philip Baynes, Philip Gascoyne, Nick Turner, Phillip Mitchell, Nigel Drake, David Harpham, David Hebblethwaite, Philip Bradish, David Bentley, John Stabler and Martin Clarke.

To Vertical Editions and Danny Hall for believing in the project and providing the support and guidance I've needed to get it off the ground.

FINAL LEAGUE TABLES

Division Two - 1973/74

		P	W	D	L	Gav	Pts
1	Middlesbrough	42	27	11	4	2.567	65
2	Luton Town	42	19	12	11	1.255	50
3	Carlisle United	42	20	9	13	1.271	49
4	Orient	42	15	18	9	1.31	48
5	Blackpool	42	17	13	12	1.425	47
6	Sunderland	42	19	9	14	1.318	47
7	Nottm' Forest	42	15	15	12	1.326	45
8	West Brom	42	14	16	12	1.067	44
9	Hull City	42	13	13	12	0.979	43
10	Notts County	42	15	15	14	0.917	43
11	Bolton	42	15	8	15	1.1	42
12	Millwall	42	14	14	14	1.00	42
13	Fulham	42	16	17	16	0.907	42
14	Aston Villa	42	13	15	14	1.067	41
15	Portsmouth	42	14	12	16	0.726	40
16	Bristol City	42	14	10	18	0.87	38
17	Cardiff City	42	10	16	16	0.79	36
18	Oxford Utd	42	10	16	16	0.761	36
19	**Sheff Weds**	**42**	**12**	**11**	**19**	**0.81**	**35**
20	Crystal Palace	42	11	12	19	0.768	34
21	Preston NE	42	9	13	19	0.645	31
22	Swindon Town	42	7	11	24	0.5	25

Preston North End deducted 1 pt.

Division Two - 1974/75

		P	W	D	L	Gav	Pts
1	Manchester United	42	34	9	7	2.2	61
2	Aston Villa	42	25	8	9	2.469	58
3	Norwich City	42	20	13	9	1.568	53
4	Sunderland	42	19	13	10	1.857	51
5	Bristol City	42	21	8	13	1.424	50
6	West Bromwich Albion	42	18	9	15	1.286	45
7	Blackpool	42	14	17	11	1.152	45
8	Hull City	42	15	14	13	0.755	44
9	Fulham	42	13	16	13	1.128	42
10	Bolton Wanderers	42	15	12	15	1.098	42
11	Oxford United	42	15	12	15	0.804	42
12	Orient	42	11	20	11	0.718	42
13	Southampton	42	15	11	16	0.981	41
14	Notts County	42	12	16	14	0.831	40
15	York City	42	14	10	18	0.927	38
16	Nottingham Forest	42	12	14	16	0.782	38
17	Portsmouth	42	12	13	17	0.815	37
18	Oldham Athletic	42	10	15	17	0.833	35
19	Bristol Rovers	42	12	11	19	0.656	35
20	Millwall	42	10	12	20	0.786	32
21	Cardiff City	42	9	14	19	0.581	32
22	**Sheffield Wednesday**	**42**	**5**	**11**	**26**	**0.453**	**21**

Gav = Goal Average

Division Three - 1975/76

		P	W	D	L	Gav	Pts
1	Hereford United	46	26	11	9	1.564	63
2	Cardiff City	46	22	13	11	1.438	57
3	Millwall	46	20	16	10	1.256	56
4	Brighton & Hove Albion	46	22	9	15	1.472	53
5	Crystal Palace	46	18	17	11	1.326	53
6	Wrexham	46	20	12	14	1.2	52
7	Walsall	46	18	14	14	1.213	50
8	Preston North End	46	19	10	17	1.088	48
9	Shrewsbury Town	46	19	10	17	1.034	48
10	Peterborough United	46	15	18	13	1.00	48
11	Mansfield Town	46	16	15	15	1.115	47
12	Port Vale	46	15	16	15	1.019	46
13	Bury	46	14	16	16	1.109	44
14	Gillingham	46	17	9	20	1.00	43
15	Chesterfield	46	12	19	15	0.853	43
16	Rotherham United	46	15	12	19	0.831	42
17	Chester	46	15	12	19	0.694	42
18	Grimsby Town	46	15	10	21	0.838	40
19	Swindon Town	46	16	8	22	0.827	40
20	**Sheffield Wednesday**	**46**	**12**	**16**	**18**	**0.814**	**40**
21	Aldershot	46	13	13	20	0.787	39
22	Colchester United	46	12	14	20	0.631	38
23	Southend United	46	12	13	21	0.867	37
24	Halifax Town	46	11	13	22	0.672	35

ROLL CALL

Players who made first-team apppearances during our period

Name	Apps	Gls	Name	Apps	Gls
Derek Bell	5	1	Ken Knighton	79(5)	4
Bobby Brown	17(4)	3	Fred McIver	39(3)	0
Danny Cameron	38	1	Eric McMordie	9	6
Dave Clements	1	0	Jimmy Mullen	85(5)	2
Roy Coyle	23(3)	2	Ian Nimmo	13(7)	6
Jim Craig	3(1)	0	Neil O'Donnell	32	1
Tommy Craig	63	9	Eric Potts	136(1)	20
Dave Cusack	40	0	Mick Prendergast	74(3)	24
Hugh Dowd	44(2)	0	Andy Proudlove	12(5)	1
Peter Eustace	28(4)	1	Eddie Prudham	11(6)	2
Peter Feely	10(2)	1	Jimmy Quinn	52	1
Bobby Ferguson	5	0	Neil Ramsbottom	22	0
Ronnie Ferguson	10(1)	1	Peter Rodrigues	65	1
Peter Fox	50	0	Bernard Shaw	109(4)	4
Colin Harvey	48	2	John Sissons	6	0
Willie Henderson	18(4)	1	Peter Springett	66	0
Phil Henson	47(3)	8	Dave Sunley	62(5)	9
David Herbert	13(6)	5	Allan Thompson	90	4
John Holsgrove	37(1)	2	Richard Walden	8	0
Gary Hull	6(2)	0	Barry Watling	1	0
Brian Joicey	75(4)	17	Roger Wylde	27(8)	1
Michael Kent	5(1)	0	**(Sub appearances in brackets)**		

BIBLIOGRAPHY

Sheffield Wednesday/Sheffield Football

Allen	Paul (with Douglas Naylor)	Flying With the Owls Crime Squad	John Blake (2008)
Cooper	Andrew	Eric Taylor: A Biography	A. Cooper Publications (2011)
Cronshaw	Anthony	Tales from the East Bank	ALD Design and Print (2002)
Crooks	Richard	Wednesday vs United: The Sheffield Derby	Pitch Publishing (2018)
Dickinson	Jason	One Hundred Years at Hillsborough	Hallamshire Press (1999)
Dickinson	Jason	Sheffield Wednesday: A Pictorial History	Amberley Publishing (2014)
Dickinson	Jason	Sheffield Wednesday Miscellany	Pitch Publishing (2010)
Dickinson	Jason	Sheffield Wednesday On This Day	Pitch Publishing (2009)
Dickinson	Jason	Sheffield Wednesday The Official History	Amberley Publishing (2017)
Dickinson	Jason	WAWAW Fans' Memories Through the Generations	Amberley Publishing (2017)
Dickinson	Jason (with John Brodie)	Sheffield Wednesday: The Complete Record	DB Publishing (2011)
Dickinson	Jason (with John Brodie)	The Wednesday Boys: A Definitive Who's Who of Sheffield Wednesday Football Club 1880-2005	Pickard Communication (2005)
Ellis	Steve	Hillsborough: A 21-Year Photographic History	Hallamshire Press (1997)
Farnsworth	Keith	Sheffield Football: A History Volume II, 1961-1995	Hallamshire Press (1995)
Farnsworth	Keith	Sheffield Wednesday: A Complete Record 1897-1987	Breedon Books (1987)
Farnsworth	Keith	The Blades & The Owls: A Pictorial History of the Sheffield Derby Matches	Breedon Books (1995)

Farnsworth	Keith	Wednesday!	Sheffield City Libraries (1982)
Farnsworth	Keith (ed)	Wednesday Every Day of the Week	Breedon Books (1998)
Firth	John	I Hate Football: A Fan's Memoir	Peak Publish (2009)
Gordon	Daniel	A Quarter of Wednesday: A New History of Sheffield Wednesday 1970-1995	Wednesday Publishing (1995)
Hayes	Dean	The Hillsborough Encyclopedia: An A-Z of Sheffield Wednesday FC	Mainstream Publishing (1997)
Holmes	Howard	Owls Trivia	Unicorn Press (1989)
Liversidge	Michael (with Gary Mackender)	Sheffield Wednesday: Illustrating the Greats	Pickard Communication (2004)
Sparling	Richard A.	The Romance of the Wednesday 1867-1926	Original Edition (1926)
Matthews	Tony	The Men Who Made Sheffield Wednesday Football Club	Tempus Publishing (2007)
Waring	Peter	Sheffield Wednesday Head to Head	Breedon Books (2004)
Whitworth	Tom	Owls: Sheffield Wednesday Through the Modern Era	Pitch Publishing (2016)
Whitworth	Tom (with Chris Olewicz)	Sheffield Wednesday 20 Legends	Vertical Editions (2012)
Young	Percy M.	Football in Sheffield	Dark Peak Publishing (1981) Third Edition

Autobiographies

Ashurst	Len	Left Back in Time	Know the Score (2004)
Atkinson	Ron	Big Ron: A Different Ball Game	Andre Deutsch (1998)
Dooley	Derek (with Keith Farnsworth)	Dooley!	Hallamshire Press (2000)
Dunphy	Eamon	Only a Game?	Penguin Books (1987)
Keith	John	Colin Harvey's Everton Secrets	Trinity Mirror (2005)
Leslie	Colin	Six Foot Two Eyes of Blue: The Authorised Biography of Jim Holton	Empire Publications (2019)

Our Lowest Ebb?

Megson	Don (with Chris Olewicz)	Don Megson A Life in Football	Vertical Editions (2014)
Palmer	Carlton (with Steven Jacobi)	It Is What It Is	Vertical Editions (2017)
Regis	Cyrille	My Story	Carlton Publishing (2010)
Sawyer	Rob	Harry Catterick: The Untold Story of a Football Great	deCoubertin Books (2014)
Swan	Peter (with Nick Johnson)	Setting the Record Straight	Stadia (2006)
Turnbull	Eddie (with Martin Hannan)	Having a Ball	Mainstream Publishing (2006)
Tynan	Tommy (with Richard Cowdery)	Tommy: A Life at the Soccer Factory	Bud Books (1990)

General Football

Crooks	Richard	Grandad What was Football Like in the 1970s?	Pitch Publishing (2017)
Inglis	Simon	The Football Grounds of England and Wales	Willow Books (1983)

General Histories

Beckett	Andy	When the Lights Went Out: What Really Happened to Britain in the Seventies	Faber and Faber (2009)
Sandbrook	Dominic	State of Emergency: The Way We Were, Britain 1970-1974	Penguin Books (2010)
Sandbrook	Dominic	Seasons in the Sun: The Battle for Britain, 1974-1979	Penguin Books (2012)
Turner	Alwyn W.	Crisis What Crisis? Britain in the 1970s	Aurum Press (2008)

Articles

Dunn	Caroline (Dr)	The experience of female football fans in England: A qualitative study.	Doctoral, Sheffield Hallam University (2012)

| Warwick | Tosh (Dr) | Northernness, Sheffield and the 1966 World Cup: The "Steel City" on Display | International Journal of Regional and Local History, 12:2, 92-106 |

Miscellaneous

Newspapers	The Star (Sheffield)	1973-76
	The Green 'Un (Sheffield)	
	The Telegraph (Sheffield)	
	Post and Mail (Birmingham)	
	Daily and Sunday Mirror	
	Daily and Sunday People	
	News of the World	
Programmes	Sheffield Wednesday matchday programmes for all home matches	1973-76
	Matchday programmes as referred to in the text for a large number of away games	1973-76
	Programmes for testimonials, friendlies, FA Cup semi-finals and County Cup games	1970-1979
Other	Supporters Club Yearbooks	1973-76
	Sheffield Wednesday Club Yearbook	1974
	Club Accounts	1974,1975 and 1976

Websites

www.adrianbullock.com	Statistics
www.owlstalk.co.uk	Fan Site
www.soccer-history.co.uk	Football History
www.warofthemonstertrucks.com	Fanzine
www.sheffield.gov.uk/archives	List of material about SWFC history